Advances and Techniques in Restoration Therapy

Advances and Techniques in Restoration Therapy focuses on the practical elements of the Restoration Therapy Model to help mental health professionals working with individuals, couples, and families, to restore broken identities and senses of safety, and to move toward action that is functional and healing. Richly illustrated with case examples from experienced clinicians, this volume brings new insights and a range of established and emerging therapeutic techniques to the framework and Restoration Therapy community. This is an innovative and much-needed step-by-step manual, which will provide marriage and family therapists and counselors with practical ways of applying key interventions to varied situations of pain, to help clients find functional, healing solutions with integrity.

Terry D. Hargrave, PhD, LMFT, is the Evelyn and Frank Freed Professor of Marriage and Family Therapy at Fuller Seminary in Pasadena, California. Dr. Hargrave is nationally recognized for his pioneering work with intergenerational families and for co-founding the field of Restoration Therapy. He has authored over 30 professional articles and 14 books, including *Restoration Therapy: Understanding and Guiding Healing in Marriage and Family Therapy* (co-authored with Franz Pfitzer). His work has been featured on *ABC News 20/20, Good Morning America,* and *CBS Early Morning,* as well as in several national magazines and newspapers.

Nicole E. Zasowski, MSMFT, LMFT, is a licensed marriage and family therapist in the state of Connecticut, where she maintains a private practice. She is also a contributor to several publications, speaks regularly at local seminars, and recently co-authored *Families and Forgiveness: Healing Wounds in the Intergenerational Family (2nd Edition)* with Dr. Terry Hargrave.

Miyoung Yoon Hammer, PhD, LMFT, is Associate Professor of Marriage and Family Therapy and Chair of the Marriage and Family Department at Fuller Theological Seminary in Pasadena, California. As a medical family therapist, Dr. Hammer has been especially interested in applying the concepts and techniques of the Restoration Therapy Model in her work with individuals, couples, and families affected by illness or disability, and minority populations.

"Is there another book that is so inspiring, practical, humane, and creative, all at the same time? Systemic therapy has been begging for a model that uncovers love, safety, and the virtuous truth within every person! Hargrave and colleagues have surprises on every page. Interventions for children, Asian-Americans, and those with personality disorders illustrate the versatility of restoration therapy. These thoughtful questions and transcripts demonstrate how mindfulness cycles liberate our families from pain and conflict."

—**Suzanne Midori Hanna, PhD, LMFT,** senior scholar at the Hiebert Institute, instructor at Capella University and Touro University Worldwide, and author of *The Practice of Family Therapy: Key Elements Across Models, 5ᵗʰ Edition*

"This excellent new edition uses facts from neuroscience to explain how humans process and then relive their individual pain cycle. From there, the book provides therapists with a guide to helping clients move into the peace cycle, using diagrams, cases and dialogue to learn and perfect their skill. Beginners and seasoned therapists that desire a model that resonates with family therapy will find the book easy to follow and the work rewarding to practice."

—**Linda Metcalf, PhD, LMFT, LPC,** director of graduate counseling programs at Texas Wesleyan University

"If you are not yet familiar with the new kid on the block, restoration therapy, you are in for a treat. Hargrave and colleagues have created a contemporary model based on the wisdom of attachment theory and contextual therapy. This sequel goes deeper into the theory with the bonus of practical interventions to move a client to truth and healing. I highly recommend this work to enhance your inner work as well as that of your clients."

—**Jackie L. Halstead, PhD, LMFT,** CEO of the Selah Center for Spiritual Formation

Advances and Techniques in Restoration Therapy

Terry D. Hargrave, Nicole E. Zasowski, and Miyoung Yoon Hammer

Routledge
Taylor & Francis Group

NEW YORK AND LONDON

First published 2019
by Routledge
52 Vanderbilt Avenue, New York, NY 10017

and by Routledge
2 Park Square, Milton Park, Abingdon, Oxon, OX14 4RN

Routledge is an imprint of the Taylor & Francis Group, an informa business

© 2019 Terry D. Hargrave, Nicole E. Zasowski, and Miyoung Yoon Hammer

Library of Congress Cataloging-in-Publication Data
A catalog record for this title has been requested

ISBN: 978-1-138-54108-5 (hbk)
ISBN: 978-1-138-54109-2 (pbk)
ISBN: 978-1-351-01201-0 (ebk)

Typeset in Bembo
by Newgen Publishing UK

For my students who have taught me well.

Terry D. Hargrave, PhD, LMFT

To the Restoration Therapy community. I love learning and growing with you.

Nicole E. Zasowski, MSMFT, LMFT

To my parents, Won Kil and Choon Ja, who struggled, sacrificed, and loved so much so that Tim and I could live a good life in America. To my husband and love, Jeffrey, and our children, Asher, Sophia, and Isaac, you inspire me and help me believe that anything is possible. My cup is full.

Miyoung Yoon Hammer, PhD, LMFT

Contents

Preface

Restoration Therapy (RT) is a therapeutic model containing an inherent paradox. In one sense, it is one of the newer approaches in the work of marriage and family therapy that looks at the implications of love and trust-worthiness and works to restore as much of that love and trustworthiness as is possible and feasible to the individual and his or her relationships. In other words, in one sense, *everything is new about the Restoration Therapy Model.* In another sense, there is *nothing at all new about Restoration Therapy.* RT actually utilizes well-known theories and techniques along with the latest research. Of course, Restoration Therapy has particular "twists" of these theories and techniques to fit the organization of the model, but the reality is that a seasoned therapist reading about RT for the first time will have some familiarity with almost everything we say and believe. Restoration Therapy is a unique blend of the best of what we know from attachment theory, the work and benefits of emotional regulation, and the practice of brain research and mindfulness in order to utilize a new approach that is both organized and efficient in bringing people to the point of change. In terms of techniques, we utilize and adapt tried and true practices in marriage and family therapy in order to yield best practices that not only work in the short term but are capable of producing long-term change. Although there is much in Restoration Therapy that is theoretically novel, most of what is new in the model comes from the organization, objectives and goals, clarity, simplicity and understandability of the process of RT for the client. When people new to Restoration Therapy come and study with us a while, we inevitably get a comment from them regarding how simple yet how profoundly deep the model is in practice. As you read this book on *Advances and Techniques in Restoration Therapy,* you will likely experience the paradoxes yourself: Everything is new about the approach and at the same time, nothing is new; the approach is extraordinarily simple, yet at the same time profoundly deep; the approach is insight and experientially focused while at the same time is driven by skills and behavioral mindfulness. We feel these paradoxes ourselves and feel like they give testimony to the soundness of the model.

Although the approach of Restoration Therapy has been "cooking" for several decades, it has only been the last 12 years that we identified it as a new working model. In 2008, we started training therapists to practice the approach in the marital intensive model of therapy. The first articles on the approach were published in 2009 and the first comprehensive book on Restoration Therapy was published in 2011. In that year, we also began teaching an academic class in marriage and family therapy specifically on the Restoration Model and supervising students in their practicums and internships in the approach. Needless to say, we have learned much about the evolution of the model in the last seven years and it was clear that it was time to do a latest iteration of Restoration Therapy by articulating the advances in our thinking and the adaptations of our techniques. The book is the product of what we have learned in this intense practice in the last seven years.

It has never been the goal of Restoration Therapy to have a huge impact. We are, relatively speaking, a "postage stamp size" of a theory in terms of the number of practitioners. Honestly, we tend to like it that way as we have always seen ourselves as working more with the "ones" than the "hundreds" or even "thousands." But the RT community has steadily grown over the more than a decade of practice. We have made hundreds of presentations to local, regional, and national conferences articulating the model. We have practitioners in 30 states and 15 countries. We now have a conference every other year called the RT Summit where we have had our third event. We are growing in terms of numbers and reputation because, very simply, the approach works in helping clients change. Whether the reader is interested in becoming an exclusive restoration therapist or just one who wants to utilize the approach in an already successful practice, we believe you will find that RT helps the client organize in an efficient way and move to not only address long standing issues, but reform his or her behavioral practices in a mindful way.

A few helpful notes about the book itself. In Part 1, The Restoration Therapy Model, we realize that many are new to the Restoration Therapy Model and wanted to do a primer to help new readers catch the flow of the theory. In Chapter 1, Understanding the Patterns of Pain, we unfold the basics of the theory and the importance of love and trustworthiness in the formation of identity and sense of safety. Further, we include an overview of the four objectives or goals of the model. Finally, we help the reader understand the task of accessing the narrative of the client in order to access what we call the pain cycle. In Chapter 2, Finding Truth and the Peace Cycle, we seek to give the reader a perspective on understanding how to help the client with the arduous task of emotionally regulating the pain of injured identity and sense of safety by use of a powerful "truth" the client claims for him or herself. This further sets the stage to draw another cognitive map that is both loving and trustworthy and is called the peace cycle. Finally, this chapter contains a short overview of the mindfulness practice used in RT called the four steps.

In Part 2, Advances, Techniques, and Interventions, our focus is the heart of this book: Mainly to give the reader detailed information on what we have learned about the approach to make it better, more efficient, and more effective. In Chapter 3, Organization, Sequence, and Structure, the reader will learn how to ask questions and access information in the RT framework according to identity and safety. As well, information on sequencing the information in an efficient way is given in order to produce a structure that is capable of producing the cognitive maps for the client called the pain and peace cycles. As with all the chapters, special care is given to include in depth case examples and narratives in order for the reader to learn more effectively how we actually practice. In Chapter 4, we discuss in detail Interventions to Identify Truth and Expand Emotional Regulation. Very little attention was given to the technique of helping clients with the emotionally regulating truth in the first RT book and given the importance of the process, it was far too brief. Here, we expand to help the reader understand in detail how emotional regulation takes place and how it is accomplished in therapy. In Chapter 5, The Truth About Safety, the reader will get more detail about another neglected area in Restoration Therapy. We have noticed through the years that therapists tend to give much attention to the pain clients feel in their identities, but very little to the pain related to safety violations. This chapter corrects and balances that information.

In Chapter 6, we are excited to expand on the concepts of Practice, Self-Control, and Mindfulness. Perhaps more than any other area, neuropsychology and mindfulness advances have given us new tools in understanding the brain and how to work best to produce change. The reader is given a cadre of techniques and ideas in this chapter to expand the practice, habituation, and mindfulness to the point where clients can actually get additional leverage in making the changes they desire.

In Part 3, Considerations in Restoration Therapy, we give the reader an overview and examples of how Restoration Therapy is utilized with different populations and in special situations. This information is contained in Chapter 7, Using Restoration Therapy with Special Populations and Situations. Finally in Chapter 8, Questions and Answers Regarding Restoration Therapy, we give the reader common questions and answers that usually come up during trainings and supervisions of the RT approach.

No work in any model of therapy takes place in a vacuum. We are blessed and grateful to the many students and practitioners who have done the hard work of learning RT not only for the sakes of their clients, but also their own sakes as they have applied the principles and changes to themselves.

We continue to be indebted to therapists and owners who practice in the marriage intensive format utilizing Restoration Therapy exclusively at The Hideaway Experience. Finally, we are thankful to the many clients who have endeavored to travel this therapeutic road with us. It is always an act of courage to enter therapy and do the work of change in ourselves and in our relationships. Our clients are heroes in this endeavor of courage and we learn from them every day.

But most of all, to our spouses and families, we express our deepest love and affection for you all. You are the people that help us restore identity and safety to our own brokenness and make life fulfilling and meaningful.

Part 1

The Restoration Therapy Model

1 Understanding the Patterns of Pain

The Restoration Therapy (RT) Model was first developed in the 1990s by Terry Hargrave and evolved out of his work with understanding and developing new techniques for contextual family therapy (Boszormenyi-Nagy & Krasner, 1986). Through identification of reactions to pain involving both love and trustworthiness (Hargrave, 1994), assessment and understanding reactivity (Hargrave, 2000; Hargrave & Pfitzer, 2003), and eventually the use of a therapeutic process called Restoration Therapy (Hargrave, 2010; Hargrave & Pfitzer, 2011), it has since been the theoretical foundation for diverse clinical practices including marriage intensives, therapy support groups, psychoeducation groups for couples, psychoeducation groups for individuals, and conventional therapeutic practice for individuals, couples, and families. With the various applications of the Restoration Therapy Model has come the energy of a growing community of clinicians and researchers who continue to explore new ways to apply the model with an ever-broadening scope of clinical populations. Members of the RT community have been energized by the results they have found in their clinical work and, for many, this model has been transformative in their personal lives. In fact, we believe that an important part of being a good therapist is knowing ourselves in our own pain and possessing an awareness of our intrapersonal and interpersonal patterns that grow out of that pain. We, too, are in need of tools to remain regulated so that we can stay focused on the task of facilitating transformation and healing with our clients.

In writing this advances and techniques book, our goal is to highlight some of the concepts and interventions that deepen our therapeutic work as well as expand the possibilities of the model's application. It is important, however, to build on the work that has evolved by first going back to the roots of the theory. This will enable those familiar with the model to remind themselves of how the model works, facilitating organization and focus as well as assisting those who are new to Restoration Therapy to learn the basic concepts of the approach so they are well enough versed to be able to capture the content of the advances and further developed techniques. This first chapter will give an overview of the theory and the four objectives in the approach, move to understanding an in depth discussion of the work involved in the first objective where the primary task is to identify the client's emotional pain. Finally, we will illustrate the first objective of identifying pain by using a clinical case example to walk through the conceptual and practical steps that are involved in the beginning phase of the model.

The Restoration Therapy Model: An Overview

As a family therapy model, Restoration Therapy is grounded in family systems theory and gives credence to the significance of understanding the client's presenting issue within the context of the client's larger social systems, particularly their family system. Family systems theory posits that there is mutual influence between the individual and the larger system, whether it be the family or the broader community in which the individual is embedded; we shape and are shaped by the people and experiences around us (Hanna, 2014). Therefore, when working with clients, we situate their story and their presenting issue within the social contexts of their past and their present. For this reason, we are substantial believers in *attachment theory* (Bowlby, 1988) and appreciate the dynamic impact early bonding and attachment experiences—usually from the family of origin—have on the developing individual. We do, however, clarify this attachment framework within the context of the relational actions of *love* and *trustworthiness*. We believe that in early attachments, how an individual is loved teaches him or her everything he or she knows about his or her *identity*. But just as important in the relational and attachment development is the concept of trustworthiness in relationships. Trustworthiness is essential in relationships because it teaches the individual the concept of *safety* in relating, both in the balance of what the individual justly receives in the relationship, and also in the ability of the individual to justly give back to the relationship. Identity and safety are the key elements in understanding primary emotions with clients (Hargrave & Pfitzer, 2011).

Because we explore our clients' historical narratives as well as help them identify patterns and connect experiences to their psychological and relational states, they generally must possess the ability to delve into their stories, achieve insight about the root of their difficulties, and seek a pathway toward restoration not only in their basic and primary emotions dealing with identity and senses of safety, but also in the actions and coping mechanisms of their reactivity. Although we might rely upon client narrative to identify the root of clients' pain, the heart of the work happens in the current, here-and-now context. The current context refers to the client's current life circumstances, but also includes what is happening in the session. In other words, the root of the client's pain with regard to identity and sense of safety is well intact as the individual grows and develops. He or she will continue to play out similar or same pain patterns not only with regards to the past, but also in current relationships and even in the therapeutic relationship. Pain associated with identity and safety issues that originated in the past with clients is, in reality, the same identity and safety issues that will play out in current relationships and experiences (Hargrave & Pfitzer, 2011). In fact, restoration therapists balance the tasks of listening to the story that is being told with observing the process and remaining responsive to what needs to be addressed in the room. Furthermore, restoration therapists pay particular attention to the intrapersonal *and* interpersonal patterns that have been formed in these social contexts. We believe that life develops and is lived out in patterned ways. The way humans develop their cognitive processes, attribute emotional significance, and carry out behaviors are all patterned. Addressing these patterns and the underlying primary emotions that drive them will lead to long-term, sustained, second-order change. Thus, identifying patterns becomes an important first step to understanding our clients' internal dynamics and the way they shape interpersonal interactions.

The Four Objectives of Restoration Therapy

In Restoration Therapy, the therapist learns that there are four objectives or goals in the therapeutic process. The first objective of the therapist is to identify and understand the pain cycle of the client(s). In the second objective or goal in RT, the therapist endeavors to help the client understand and identify an emotionally regulating "truth" message that is directly aimed at the painful primary emotion in the pain cycle. While we believe in attachment theory as a means of understanding the client narrative with regard to the past, we also believe that insight into the past alone is insufficient to produce healing and change. Therefore, we also believe very much in the process of *emotional regulation,* that is, helping the client exert control with regard to these painful emotions that give rise to patterned and destructive actions of coping (Baumeister & Tierney, 2011). While we believe the process of emotional *co-regulation* (Johnson, 2004) is eminently appropriate in the work of parenting a child through his or her development, we very much prefer the concept of emotional *self-regulation* when it comes to this adult therapeutic process of identifying the emotional truth. The third objective or goal in the therapeutic process of Restoration Therapy is to assist the client in identifying and understanding the peace cycle. Although this is an extension of learning and identifying the emotionally regulating truth in the previous objective, it also is inclusive of working with the resulting choices of actions of the client that naturally flow from a regulated state. Finally, the fourth objective and goal of Restoration Therapy is to assist the client with practicing movement from an emotionally dysregulated state in the pain cycle to an emotionally self-regulated state in the peace cycle. We recognize that this process of emotional regulation takes place in and greatly benefits from the practice of *mindfulness*. In Restoration Therapy, therefore, we have specific mindfulness practices that assist the client in the work of the resolution of pain, the change of unloving and untrustworthy behaviors, and the experiential practice of intimacy in relationships.

Objective One: The Pain Cycle

More specifically, in the first objective of the Restoration Model, therapists focus on identifying clients' intrapersonal patterns that relate to their pain and understanding the impact this has on their relationships. In other words, we detail the narrative of damaged identity and safety the client feels from their past attachment relationships and then delineate the specific actions the client employs in a reactive or coping behavior. We refer to this as the client's *pain cycle*, a cognitive map that represents the connection between primary emotions and reactive responses; in essence, the way clients cope with their primary emotional pain. The pain cycle is the starting point for what becomes the client's narrative of how past imperfections and disturbances in the display of love and trustworthiness have shaped a distorted identity and sense of safety about him or herself and the world around him or her. Illuminating and gaining an organized and understandable awareness about this narrative of pain and the impact it has on his or her identity and, consequently, his or her relationships, is one of the primary treatment goals in this first objective or goal of RT therapy. This first objective of Restoration Therapy will be the primary focus of this chapter, while the remaining three objectives are covered in Chapter 2.

Objective Two: Identifying Truth

The focus during the second objective is identifying client truths and laying the groundwork for developing alternative narratives to his or her pain cycle primary emotions. Truths are the primary emotions that result from messages that promote positive self-construal and are a direct (and often opposite) response to the pain the client has experienced in his or her identity and sense of safety. In this work dealing with the second objective, the therapist works with the client to restore a narrative that affirms his or her core identity of assets, talents, and strengths. When the client is able to recognize and affirm his or her positive qualities, he or she is better positioned to live out of these truths and have an emotionally regulated, non-reactive presence. Further, the therapist works with the client to identify regulating truths such as empowerment, virtue, and connection in dealing with emotional dysregulation that comes from lack of safety. The work during this second objective or goal represents the first step in making an intentional move away from reflexive patterns of reactivity and turning instead toward intentionality and emotional regulation where the individual can then be freer in choosing loving and trustworthy behaviors.

Objective Three: The Peace Cycle

One of the real benefits of Restoration Therapy is the clarity with which clients can see and understand their complex internal processes and how those processes play out in relationships. In Restoration Therapy, therapists actually draw cognitive maps of the pain cycle and here, in the work of the third objective, the cognitive map of the peace cycle. These two cognitive maps of the pain and peace of the client help organize and clarify his or her internal processes, facilitating greater clarity about the aims and objectives of emotional regulation. As we are fond of saying in the process of Restoration Therapy, "People are good at heart. They are only bad when they are bad." When they are emotionally dysregulated people are "bad" or act as the worst versions of themselves. On the other hand, the peace cycle includes regulating the emotions and truths that were worked out in the previous objective. When truths are identified, a new pattern of actions and behaviors based on these truths is constructed. In very many real ways, this peace cycle reflects the "good" or best version of the client. He or she is assured of a clear identity and sound sense of safety and therefore has the freedom and feeling of peace to be able to choose actions that are loving and trustworthy of others. Instead of connecting to pain that yields reactivity, the client connects with truth to non-reactive responsiveness and agency (Hargrave & Pfitzer, 2011).

Objective Four: Practice of the Four Steps

In the first three objectives of the Restoration Therapy Model, the client has gained insight about the deep-rooted patterns of his or her pain and reactivity and has learned an alternative pattern to live out his or her truths with non-reactive agency responses that promote peace, love, and trustworthiness in interactions. The pain cycle is not eliminated, but the peace cycle provides a choice and a new possible way of living for the client. In the fourth objective, the client learns to implement the practice of recognizing his or her pain cycle *when it is happening* to him or her, *to regulate the painful primary emotions* with self-regulating truths, and then *to choose his or her peace cycle actions* over and against the pain cycle. This practice piece of the work

```
The Mindful Process of the Four Steps

Step One:  Say what you feel.
Step Two:  Say what you normally do.
Step Three:  Say the truth.
Step Four:  Say what you will do differently.
```

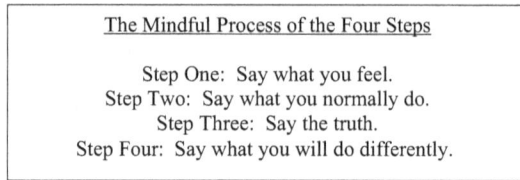

Figure 1.1 The Four Steps Used in Restoration Therapy

in the fourth objective is primarily governed by the Restoration Therapy mindful practice learning tool called *the four steps* seen in Figure 1.1.

The four steps are a mindfulness based intervention that helps move the client toward emotional regulation when his or her pain has been activated. The four steps together are a narration of the pain cycle and the peace cycle. Steps One and Two are an iteration of the pain cycle. In Step One, clients identify and acknowledge their pain by saying what they feel. Step Two is a statement about how they usually cope or react to their pain by saying what they normally do. Steps Three and Four are a description of the process of moving into the peace cycle. In Step Three, clients say their emotionally regulating truths. Finally, in Step Four, clients identify actions that align with their emotional regulation by identifying what they will do differently (Hargrave & Hargrave, 2015). Repetition and practice are vital during this fourth objective of the therapeutic work to deepen the alternative pattern and maintain therapeutic gains.

An important point to keep in mind is that the four steps do not solve presenting problems because it is a tool that operates at the level of process, not content. In other words, clients use the four steps to bring mindful awareness of their internal experience and to regulate their emotions (process) so that they can be more effective in dealing with the issue at hand (content) without being swept away with reactivity. Additionally, the four steps can serve as a beneficial disruption to the downward cycle of client pain as well as the unhealthy sequence of interactions that develop out of emotional dysregulation and reactivity (Hargrave & Pfitzer, 2011).

Identifying and Understanding the Pain

Alongside the task of joining with our clients, identifying and understanding pain is the first objective in laying the foundation for the therapeutic work. We conceptualize pain as being insidious, like a furnace that dwells in the deepest cavity of our beings. It is always at a low-grade burn, nourished by the steady stream of messages we receive from the people and the world around us about being unloved and unsafe. We might receive counter messages, but it often seems that these messages of pain are the ones that both stoke the flame of our pain and reverberate and take hold more often than the other messages. Why is this so? Two reasons stand out in neuroscience.

First, the brain has a strong preference for what it already knows (Hanna, 2014). The brain is a creature of habit. In order to illustrate this reality, the average person has a vocabulary ranging from 15,000–20,000 words and most people actually use only between 750 and 1,000 different words each day. We know and understand many more words, but we do not use them very much at all. But even more humbling is the fact in any given day, 80 percent of the language we use is limited to between 120 and 150 words (Atkins, 2013). Most of the words we utilize are words we use over and over again. Some of these, of course, are grammatical words, but the point is clear: The brain has a tendency to gravitate to words and thoughts it already knows well. The brain is used to the very powerful and formative processes in the development of identity and sense of safety. The insidious feelings that have been present from the beginning and the subsequent reactive and coping behaviors have been felt and practiced literally thousands of times. It is quite normal for these painful messages to be the ones that take hold even in the face of contradictory new messages.

But there is another reason that these painful messages concerning identity and safety continue to haunt and dysregulate people. All other things being equal, the brain will choose to dwell on the negative instead of the positive (Hanna, 2014). There may be an evolutionary reason for this as we have learned behavior to be on the lookout for predatory threats to our well-being (Siegel, 2007). As Hanson (2014) states, negative experiences tend to stick in the brain like Velcro while positive experiences are handled more like Teflon. The brain is actually twice as likely to hold on to negative messages than positive ones and this is not only true for people who experience trauma. This characteristic of neuroscience is true for all people. Whether a client has dramatic disturbances in his or her identity and sense of safety or slight imperfection in the same, recurring pain stokes the flame of these negative messages in our brains.

We begin with pain because every behavior that engenders personal and relational difficulties is rooted in pain. Whether we escape using alcohol, pornography, or other substances that alter our ability to remain present and engage meaningfully with ourselves as well as others in our lives, or we control by being critical and demanding, pain drives those behaviors. So often therapists address the behaviors because those are what can be seen and has the most obvious and immediate consequences. But in fact, behaviors are the harbingers of pain and we as therapists are more effective when we go for the pain in the primary emotions, the driver and the source of behavioral problems.

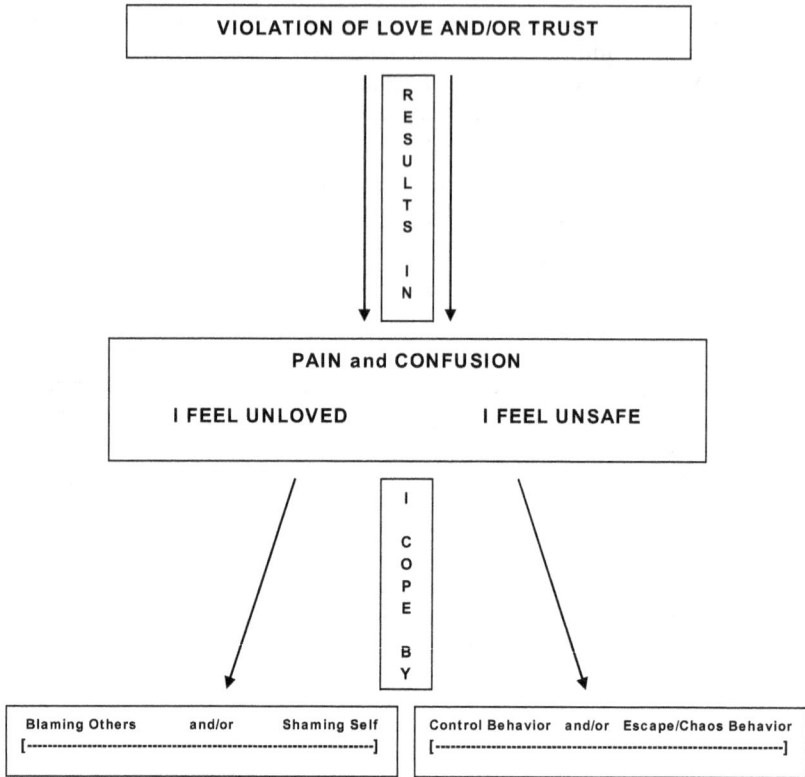

Figure 1.2 Illustration of Pain Chart and Reactivity

As mentioned before, an abiding assumption of the Restoration Therapy Model is that pain results from violations of love and trustworthiness—the two twin pillars or fundamental building blocks of our well-being, identity, and sense of safety. As seen in Figure 1.2, violations of love and trustworthiness produce a sense of pain in the individual and disturbances of identity and safety ensue. In turn, these disturbances and stresses of pain then promote a *fight or flight* reactivity in the individual that results in the four coping strategies of *blame, shame, control, and escape/chaos.* Blame and Control behaviors typically represent *fight* reactivity on the part of the individual while Shame and Escape/Chaos behaviors typically represent *flight* reactivity from the individual. It is important to realize the individual may utilize both fight and flight reactive strategies to cope with pain.

As the individual experiences violations of love and trustworthiness from original caregivers, peers, mentors, teachers, coaches, or even violations from traumatic and unexpected events in the world such as crimes and natural disasters, he or she is impacted in his or her sense of identity and safety. It is helpful to summarize some of the essential information here concerning identity and safety.

Identity

What we mean by identity is the core beliefs and perceptions we have about ourselves based on the messages we receive from our external environment, most often from our primary caregivers, about being loved. However, others do play an important role in shaping our sense of being loved. Others may include our peers, siblings, important teachers, or mentors and spouses. Love is a powerful force that can transform and heal and is the primary vehicle through which messages sent to us from our primary caregivers are transmitted, forming our identities during the early stages of life particularly, but also throughout our development. We often point to three types of love and what they do for the developing individual (Hargrave & Pfitzer, 2003). Each type of love has a unique expression and nuance and can be experienced with greater strength in some relationships than in others.

The first type of love is an *altruistic love*. Altruistic love is the aspect of love that is characterized by sacrificial and unconditional giving. This love communicates the essential profundity of our worth and value—that someone would sacrifice his or her own well-being for my sake tells me that I am worthy of his or her sacrifice. *Romantic love*, on the other hand, is the facet of love that is passionate and adoring. Erotic or romantic love is most often associated with the libidinal love that is exclusive to romantic and sexual relationships. While that kind of amorous love is derived from this particular aspect of love, it is not to be so narrowly applied. A parent, for example, can have passionate love for his or her child, a kind of exhilaration and excitement about the child's fascinating interests or accomplishments. We often see this in the pride a parent might have in his or her child when they have received an award or accomplished a great task. The kind of excited, passionate love that is elicited in that moment sends the message that the person is *unique* and *special* and is distinctively different from the altruistic aspect of love that sends a different kind of message of worth and value.

And finally, the third type of love is *companionate love*. Companionate love, unlike the sacrificial and passionate parts of love, is defined as the companioning or partnering part of love. This companionate love causes us to desire friendship and companionship with the beloved because we are interested in the gifts, talents, thoughts, and processes of the individual. It is from this kind of love that the message of belonging and being connected is derived. Unlike the other aspects of love that express sacrifice or passion, companionate love expresses shoulder-to-shoulder companionship or the desire to have the other person with you on the journey. Together, altruistic, romantic, and companionate love make love complete and form the identity of the beloved by teaching that he or she is worthy, unique, and belongs. It is possible for someone to experience only some types of love and he or she can benefit greatly from only that portion. However, for love to be fully expressed and for the inputs into one's identity to be holistically felt, all three aspects of love must be experienced and known (Hargrave & Pfitzer, 2011).

To be clear, in this discussion of identity we are not referring to demographic categories that describe our physical attributes, social affiliations, or life experiences. Although these categories shape and inform our developing identities, we are referring to identity that is transcendent of culture, gender, health, and social affiliation. We are describing the fundamental claim that all humans have the need to be loved, known, belong, and have a sense of worth and the messages that communicate these truths are originally, primarily, and most vitally derived from love. We believe there are objective truths about identity and safety that transcend generations, cultures, gender, socioeconomic status, education, and any other demographic variable that provides nuance and differences among people. The first truth is that all people are meant to flourish and grow. This flourishing is possible when the following truths are a reality: All people are meant to be loved; all people have worth and value; all people are meant to be known; all people are meant to belong.

Safety

Love is essential and this fact is well established in our society. But just as important in terms of relationships is the concept of *trustworthiness*. Trustworthiness teaches the individual that he or she is safe in relationships for the purpose of engagement for the intimacy, mutual care, and support that they can bring (Hargrave & Zasowski, 2016). Relationships are the mechanism that brings us the behaviors, actions, and engagements of the family. Essentially, relationships are the way messages and actions are carried from one member of the family to another. But these messages are not only about love. Trustworthiness tells us about *the way* or *process* by which these messages are carried.

In order for the relationship process to be trustworthy, first it must be *predictable*. Predictability or reliability essentially means that from one time of interaction to the next, we can count with some degree of reliability on individuals we have relationships with to act and behave the same way from one time period to the next. Without this element of reliability, individuals will pick up the erratic behavior of the relational partner and will likely learn to avoid the relationship altogether (Hargrave & Pfitzer, 2011).

We also expect relationships to be *fair* or just. Boszormenyi-Nagy and Krasner (1986) believed that relationships were governed by an innate drive of justice or balance. In all relationships, we realize that there are things we are obligated to do for the good of the relationship and, as a result of our giving, we are entitled to take merited benefits from our relational partners. In this way, we learn that we are competent to give and entitled to receive in a balanced and fair way. If the relationship is unfair, we will likely retaliate with threats and manipulation to get our entitlement or give up and withdraw from the relationship (Hargrave & Pfitzer, 2003). In the vertical parent-child relationship the balance inherently cannot be mutual with a 50/50 contribution to the relationship. Parents have the responsibility to give to their children without the same expectation of taking from them as they would in a horizontal peer relationship such as a spouse, partner, sibling, or friend. In the vertical relationship, the balance is struck with the long view of time. Children grow up to become adults who then offer care and love to the next generation without the expectation of mutual give and take as did their parents. These adult children also have the opportunity to give without taking from their elderly parents who are now in need of care and not able to give back in return of their earned entitlement—what is owed to them for what they have given (Hargrave & Pfitzer, 2003).

The final element of relationships is *openness* and essentially being trustworthy in relationships. The reason is that it provides the individual with the information and knowledge that there are no secrets that negate predictability or justice. If people are open and honest in relationships and transparent to one another, the relational process is a "what you see is what you get" interaction. If the relationship is not open, it drives relational partners away from mutual giving as individuals are driven by a need for protection (Hargrave & Zasowski, 2016).

As described earlier in this chapter, we are relational beings inherently in need of and desirous of connection to others not as a matter of indulgence, but rather as a matter of survival and the chance to thrive. In our early years of life, we are dependent upon our primary caregivers for these connections and we need psychological and social nourishment from them in order to form the basis of our identity. Moreover, the process of interactions must be predictable, based in balance or justice, and open in order to achieve a sense of safety. This nourishment and process is derived from love and trustworthiness and comes in a variety of forms, most of which are embodied: The way we are physically engaged through touch and physical nourishment as well as actions and messages about being cared for, valued, and loved in consistent, fair, and open ways. The words that are spoken to us and the tone that is used can send messages of belonging and being loved and that we are safe with our caregivers. When we are gazed upon and congruently mirrored in our affect, we receive messages that we are known, we belong, and that we are safe and secure.

These are examples of ways that our identity begins to form based on our initial experiences of being loved and consequently being known, having a sense of belonging, and believing we have worth. Additionally, our interactions over time give us a secure picture that relationships are reliable, balanced, fair, and honest. We can have a sense of security and trustworthiness and develop a sense that we are safe. These experiences are interpersonal but also have biological implications. Not only are we receiving messages that go to the heart, but our brains light up and trigger the release of endorphins and hormones that increase our physical, emotional, and mental euphoria (Siegel, 2007). Over time, the association between the inputs we receive and the physiological response solidifies in our brains that these are positive messages that contribute to our healthy growth and development.

As we grow and develop, the scope of influence on our identity expands as siblings, teachers, mentors, peers, and others begin to play significant roles in our lives. It is in the context of these relationships that we seek connection and learn about attachment, that we receive messages about our identity, regardless of how healthy or dysfunctional those relationships may be. Furthermore, the messages that can have an imprint on our identities are transmitted from society and the culture around us via the media, practiced traditions, and the mores expressed in our social contexts. We would also assert that factors such as temperament and extraordinary circumstances such as illness or disability will contribute to the messages we receive and how we internalize those messages. Whether our identity is formed by messages received from people with whom we are in close relationship or from the words and images translated through the screen, the impact transcends time and space and can have enduring consequences well into adulthood (Hargrave & Hargrave, 2015).

Violations of Love (Identity) and Trustworthiness (Safety)

Violations occur when our identity or safety has been compromised or diminished through words, actions, or events. Often times these violations occur within the context of the relationship where the caregiver or others on whom individuals depend are imperfect, as human beings, and therefore do not always love or act in trustworthy ways (Hargrave & Pfitzer, 2011). These violations may have occurred long ago during childhood or they could have occurred recently, perhaps involving the relationship system that is being treated. The violation can occur in a one-time incident such as a natural disaster or an injurious comment from a parent or the violation can occur repeatedly such as having an abusive parent or a berating coach. Regardless of when the violation occurs or the frequency of the violation, the consequences have an enduring impact because our core identities and our fundamental need to feel safe in our world have been harmed. In an attempt to survive the resulting pain, the person employs coping behaviors that are effective for getting him or her through the violation, but by nature are behavioral actions that are unloving and untrustworthy. That pathway from pain to coping becomes ingrained over time as it is reinforced with repetition. Eventually a cognitive map of this pathway is formed (Yoon Hammer & Hargrave, 2016) so that anytime the person's pain is triggered, regardless of context or situation, he or she reflexively reacts to that pain as if it were the first time.

These messages may be overt and conscious, but are often received at a subconscious level. The messengers are not always aware of the messages they are transmitting and often times it is because they are sending messages from their own pain resulting in tragic unloving, or untrustworthy actions (Hargrave & Pfitzer, 2003). This dynamic of intergenerational transmission is not new in the family therapy world. One of the trademarks of family systems theory is the significance that is placed on the family-of-origin. Exploring the client's family-of-origin to understand how the client's current presenting issue stems from relational patterns and notable events in his or her family-of-origin is a common move for many family therapists.

It is important to understand that while coping behaviors may be transmitted intergenerationally such as alcoholism, abuse, or neglect, the meaning of the pain does not necessarily get transmitted. For example, we have a parent who copes with pain resulting from violations of lack of safety by escaping with alcohol. The violation of safety occurred when the parent experienced an incident of sexual assault during college, but never addressed the psychological impact of that event and has continued to experience the pain of living in an unsafe world. Years later, the child of that same parent might learn this coping behavior of escaping with alcohol and begin to utilize the same coping mechanism or drinking behavior. From the outside, it would appear that we're seeing the common intergenerational pattern of alcoholism in the family system. But if we explore below the behavior we often find that although the parent and adult child both demonstrate similar coping behaviors of escaping, the pain messages originate from a different source. For the parent, it is that the world is unsafe, and for the adult child the message is that they are alone and do not have worth. Growing up with a parent who was emotionally and, at times, physically absent due to the alcoholism, the message the child received was that he or she is alone and does not have worth. The adult child experienced repeated violations of identity as a result of the parent's dysfunctional coping behaviors of his or her own pain.

Table 1.1 Clinical Descriptions of the Feelings of Being Unloved and Unsafe

Descriptors clients use when identity violations have been experienced	*Descriptors clients use when safety violations have been experienced*
Unloved, Unworthy, Insignificant, Alone, Worthless, Devalued, Defective, Rejected, Unaccepted, Unwanted, Judged, Unappreciated, Hopeless	Unsafe, Insecure, Unsure, Used, Unfair, Guilty, Helpless, Powerless, Out of Control, Controlled, Vulnerable, Disconnected, Unknown, Abandoned, Inadequate, Failure, Invalidated, Unable to Measure Up

Clients describe the pain they feel from violations in various ways. Globally speaking, all pain can be boiled down to the feeling of being Unloved (reflective of identity) or Unsafe (reflective of safety). These descriptors are not a variety of primary emotions, but rather descriptions of pain clients feel that are versions of the feelings of being unloved and unsafe. It is important to note here that clients may feel a violation of love or a violation of trust-worthiness or, in many cases, a violation of both. The client descriptions we hear often in therapy are found in Table 1.1.

We hold a holistic perspective of pain, understanding that pain is often born in relational contexts, endures within the individual's psychological and neurological landscapes, and can be expressed through the body with somatic complaints and medically unexplained symptoms. Whether or not a violation of identity or safety occurs in the relationship context, the repercussions of the violation show up in relationships.

Humans are incredibly resilient and have the innate ability to survive the most destructive and dangerous circumstances. Throughout history and even today, we hear stories about survival from natural disasters and human-made catastrophes such as concentration camps, genocide, and war. Though the loss of life and dignity is always much more than anyone can bear, there are those stories that emerge from the ashes that remind us that hope for survival is real and that the drive to defeat that which threatens life can be strong enough to win. There is not always a clear answer as to why it is that some are able to survive while others perish, but what is irrefutably true is that humans have the capacity to survive.

Coping and Reactivity

As described above in defining what we mean by violations, we noted that this drive to survive enables people to cope with emotional and psychological pain. This coping has a social and a biological component, what is referred to as "adaptive biosocial processes" (Hanna, 2014) which is the interplay

Table 1.2 Clinical Descriptions of Behaviors Relating to Blame, Shame, Control, and Escape/Chaos

Blame	Shame	Control	Escape/Chaos
Blames others	Negative	Perfectionistic	Irresponsible
Angry	Hopeless	Defensive	Disconnected
Sarcastic	Shaming of Self	Judging	Addicted
Arrogant	Inconsolable	Isolated	Avoidant
Fault-finding	Self-critical	Critical	Numbed Out
Harsh	Depressed/ Unhappy	Controlling	Out of Control
Threatening	Egocentric	Closed	Provocative
Grudge Holding	Catastrophizes	Invulnerable	Unreliable
Retaliatory	Manipulative	Demanding	Secretive
Threatening	Whiney	Suspicious	Impulsive
Impatient	Needy	Nagging	Selfish
Withdraws to Punish	Withdraws to Pout	Withdraws to Defend	Withdraws to Escape

between social interactions and the brain's registry of meaning. For example, when a child expresses his or her need to a parent, the parent's response to the child either establishes or reinforces an association between the affect related to the need and the message that is sent via the parent's response. The association between the need and the response then becomes the basis for the child to create meaning—meaning about the parent, meaning about him or herself, and meaning about his or her relationship with that parent—at an intuitive level.

In the Restoration Therapy Model, we focus particularly on the meaning that the child creates about him or herself. With clients, we describe it as "the messages that are received" and we connect those messages to the way they cope with those messages, particularly the ones that are part of their pain. We identify four categories of coping or reactive behaviors, namely: blame, shame, control, and escape/chaos as seen in Table 1.2. Each of these coping behaviors can result from both identity and safety violations, but we often see that those who cope with identity violations tend to blame others or shame themselves and those who have experienced safety violations tend to cope by controlling others and their overall environment or by escaping by detaching, numbing, or distracting themselves. Again, some people can experience a safety violation and cope by shaming or blaming and other people can experience an identity violation and cope by controlling or escaping. Crossover among categories is possible and because identity and safety violations can occur simultaneously, this is the case more often than not. In each category, there are words that describe the type of behavior that we commonly see in clinical settings among clients

Three Hallmarks of the Restoration Therapy Model

There are three hallmarks of the Restoration Therapy Model that we want to highlight. These hallmarks illuminate what we believe to be some of the more significant aspects of the model. The three hallmarks are: 1) The theory of change that places the locus of change on primary emotions, as opposed to secondary emotions or behavior; 2) The focus on self-regulation and healthy relationships, as opposed to co-regulation when working with couples; and 3) The importance of repetition and practice to address change at the neurobiological level.

Theory of Change

Our assumption about change is that the primary locus of change is in primary emotions. Behavior is the tangible manifestation of our emotions that allows us to express ourselves and be known. However, making alterations to our behavior without first understanding the root of those behaviors will result in short-lived change that does not transcend time or circumstance. We seek second-order change that has sustained results with long-term implications. A helpful analogy is a tree. A tree's branches and leaves are an expression of the health of the roots deep under the soil. The branches and leaves are what we can see and provide evidence of how healthy or unhealthy the unseen roots beneath the soil, in fact, are. Although trimming and pruning can yield results, if the roots are shallow and unable to absorb nutrients in the soil, the tree cannot survive. In fact, in instances where the soil is damaged or toxic (ecological context), the tree must be uprooted and moved because the life or death of the tree is dependent upon what occurs at the root level. By tending to the roots (primary emotion), a natural outcome will be a transformation and growth in the branches, its leaves, and any fruit that is born (behavior). Therefore, if a couple came in for therapy to address their communication skills, we have the choice of either addressing their communication behaviors and helping to modify *how* they communicate or we can help them understand *why* they communicate as they do and, consequently, get stuck. What is occurring at the emotional level that causes them to hinder productive interactions by disengaging or attacking, for example? By addressing the why, we are able to get to the root of the problem and, thus, generate sustainable change. This work of delving deep into the roots is more challenging, but will yield meaningful, sustainable change and greater client satisfaction in the long term.

Therefore, in pursuit of second-order change, there are three moves we make with our clients. First, we help them develop a consciousness of their primary emotions and the pain that results in reactive coping behaviors. Second, we continue to work at the root level of their primary emotions and help clients identify an alternative narrative to the pain based on a healthy and grounded understanding of themselves or what we refer to as their truths. Third, we invoke the use of agency and a commitment to choosing the alternative narrative based on their truths, over the narrative of their pain. Here, the fact that pain does not desist is important for clients to understand. Often times clients believe that if they have changed they will no longer experience pain. This is impossible. If we were to anthropomorphize pain we would say that it hovers and awaits moments of vulnerability to pounce on our innermost being. In our theory of change, we posit that the change is not in the existence of pain, but rather it is in the client's ability to respond to pain in a grounded and self-regulated way based on their truths and then they are able to behave in ways that promote connection to self and to other and result in healthy relationship interactions.

Self-Regulation and Healthy Relationships

Humans have an inherent need for relationships (Buber, 1958). It is within relationships that we have the opportunity to fulfill our basic needs of connecting with, belonging to, and, consequently, being authentically known. Our ability to thrive psychologically, physiologically, spiritually, and socially depends on the health of our relationships and the inverse is true— that when we are deprived of such basic relational needs, we fail to thrive. Thus, if relationships and the experience of being connected to another person are fundamental to survival and even more so to thriving (Hanna, 2014), then we can surmise that it is undoubtedly the case that others carry some responsibility for our emotional well-being. While some would agree with this statement, we would disagree and say that in adult relationships— not associated with parents and children—although others have an *impact* on our emotional well-being, they don't have a *responsibility* for our emotional well-being. This distinction is not mere semantics. We recognize that as relational beings, we affect each other. For better or for worse, we are shaped by our experiences and by the people with whom we are in relationship.

However, it is our responsibility to regulate our own emotions as a matter of both fairness and freedom. The reason why this is a matter of fairness is because when we understand that we hold the jurisdiction of our own actions then we are less likely to place blame on others and more likely recognize the impact of our dysregulation and put our corrective efforts in their proper place. We believe that parents have a responsibility to emotionally regulate children as is explained in the intergenerational nature of *vertical relationships* (Hargrave & Pfitzer, 2003), but in *horizontal relationships* or relationships between equals, each partner in the relationship has the responsibility for self-regulation in order to be able to share balanced and fair intimacy. Furthermore, just as we do not want to be held responsible for someone else's reactivity, we realize the after-effects of someone else taking responsibility for ours. In a related sense, we recognize this as a matter of freedom because taking responsibility for our own emotional regulation is an act of agency. Agency is defined as "the capacity, condition, or state of acting or of exerting power" (Merriam-Webster, 2017). To add some nuance, we think about agency as "the extension or use of power in a beneficial or safe manner" (Hargrave, 2001, p. 34) and in effect using one's power as a means for good, as opposed to exploitation which is the use of one's power for personal gain and at the expense of others. There is a freedom in knowing we can choose to regulate our emotions and to actualize that choice.

Practice Makes Change Permanent

The saying usually goes, "practice makes perfect." But the fact is whatever it is that you practice will become solidified into permanency, even if it is not correct or undesired. You can learn a piano piece incorrectly and practicing it repeatedly will not make it perfect, just permanent, mistakes and all. Therefore, although repetition does not make things right, it does make things stick and this is what we count on in the Restoration Therapy Model. Here is where we apply the concept of neuroplasticity and the wonderful good news that we can learn new patterns that have lasting impact at a physiological and neurological level (Hargrave & Hargrave, 2015).

A Case Study in Identifying and Understanding the Pain Cycle

A couple in their late forties came in for couples therapy to address conflict that had escalated over the last several months and resulted in higher levels of disengagement than they had experienced in the past. Although the relationship had a history of strained interactions, the notable change began seven months prior to therapy when the husband was passed over for a promotion at his job as a hotel manager. The stress of his work situation leading up to the potential promotion had been weighing on the couple for the past year but during the months following their disappointment with the promotion, the level of strain between the spouses increased. The husband worked longer hours, consequently decreasing his involvement in family activities with his wife and the children. Overall, the husband isolated himself from their larger community of family and friends. His increased time at work resulted in his wife bearing more responsibilities at home in addition to the demands of her work as a high school music teacher. When together, they argued incessantly and eventually they cut each other off from day-to-day decisions regarding the children, household purchases, time commitments, and social activities. By the time the couple came in for therapy, they were entrenched in a classic pursuer-withdrawer interaction and were admittedly stuck in finding their way out.

The couple had been married for 19 years and had two elementary school-aged children. The husband was Mexican American and his wife was Irish and German American. Both of their families lived in neighboring towns and had been a regular part of the couple's family life. Until recently, the couple had been involved in community organizations such as the children's schools and had an active social life as a couple. However, the recent strain in their relationship had caused them to isolate and pull away from each other as well as from family and friends.

Joining and Listening for Pain

In the first session, the therapist joins with the couple and listens to their story using the benefits of sound active listening, empathy, honesty, and acceptance (Rogers, 1961). She listens for content, gathering facts and information about the story of their presenting issue, at first allowing the couple to determine the direction of their story. She also observes non-verbal processes including their interaction patterns, body language, affective communication, and overall presence in the room. Not unlike a therapist using any other therapeutic modality, she builds rapport with the clients and assesses for any clinically significant assets as well as concerns, getting her bearings with what the clients are presenting. As an RT therapist, she is also intently listening for points in the story that lead to a deeper understanding of the clients' pain. *In this first stage of therapy the primary goal is to identify pain.*

As she listens, the therapist notices that the spouses sit as far apart on the sofa as possible. They interact directly with one another only when prompted to do so by the therapist and make minimal eye contact, speaking mostly through the therapist. Eventually the therapist will structur-ally (Minuchin & Fishman, 1981) move them in order to facilitate direct interactions. The therapist asks what brings the couple in for therapy and they both agree that they need help with communication. The husband describes his wife as being critical and negative all the time. He states that they hardly see each other anymore because he's working hard for the sake of his family but instead of appreciating him for his hard work, she criticizes and nags him. The wife describes her husband as being absent and indifferent toward her. She agrees that they see each other far less than they used to but when they do he seems distant and uninterested in her or anything related to the family.

Identifying Pain

The therapist has the choice of beginning by identifying the clients' pain by directing the focus of the session on what is happening in the room in the here-and-now, or by asking them to give an example of an interaction in the past week when they felt they were stuck in their communication pattern. Although the therapist knows that the core issue lies at a level much deeper than what is being presented by the clients as a communication issue, she is still building rapport with the clients and decides to move with the client's narrative of the problem, using that scenario as a springboard for digging deeper into the root of their issues.

The wife begins with an incident that occurred two weeks prior when her husband came home from work three hours later than he said he would earlier that day. He had called at dinnertime to let her know he would be late because one of his staff members had a family emergency and he needed to stay at work to ensure everything was covered. He urged her not to wait up for him. The wife stated that although she understood that his position required him to occasionally extend himself, she was particularly frustrated that night because she had to cancel her own plans to meet some friends. She expresses that the root of her frustration at the time was that *she* had to make sacrifices for his work and that, once again, her needs came second to his. She explained that she knows this is not rational; she recognizes that his work emergency was out of his control. And yet, the outcome is the same, regardless of his intentions. At this point the husband gives nonverbal indications of irritation as he rolls his eyes and shakes his head. Finally, he throws up his hands and exclaims, "I can't win!"

The therapist sees that both clients are in their pain cycle as they use attacking and defensive language and maintain minimal eye contact with one another. The therapist looks at the husband and gives him nonverbal acknowledgment of what he just said, but stays in the process with his wife. The therapist has the opportunity to deepen her work with the wife and help her make a connection to her primary emotions by asking focused questions. The therapist slows down the process with the use of her voice (steady pace) and body (leaning forward slightly) as she repeats to the wife what she believes to be a key statement that relates to a deeper pain.

Therapist:	*You* had to make sacrifices for his work and *your* needs came second to his. What message are you receiving when you hear this statement? What do you believe this says about you?
Wife:	(Short pause and slightly calmer tone with tears filling her eyes). That I'm alone and I'm not good enough or worth enough to make sacrifices for. (Pause).
Therapist:	You are alone. You aren't good enough or worth enough to make sacrifices for. Wow, that sounds very painful. When was the first time you remember feeling this way?
Wife:	When I was 11, the summer before I started middle school, my father had a heart attack. I'll never forget how scary it was and how it changed our family's life forever. Eventually he was able to go back to work, but it took at least a couple of years before life felt normal again.
	I have an older brother who is two years older but my mother counted on me to help her around the house and to take care of my father. That year I had to stop all of my music lessons and pull out of all the extra-curricular activities I was involved in with my friends. Although I understood that my mother didn't have the time or energy to drive me around places, I was devastated that my life was being turned upside down. (Pause). None of my friends had experienced anything like this so I felt very much alone. But I also felt like what was important to me—my music and my friends—didn't matter to anyone else.
	(Long pause). I didn't tell anyone what I was feeling because I didn't want to burden my mother and I felt guilty for thinking and feeling these things in the first place. My father almost died and here I was feeling sorry for myself about music and friends. It seemed so trivial and yet, it really hurt.

Although she is in her forties, she was almost immediately able to recall this painful experience that happened 35 years previously and connected it to the pain about her identity that she feels today. Much like the incident she described with her husband two weeks ago, the circumstances were beyond her control and what was asked of her—to temporarily sacrifice her desires and needs—may be understandable, considering the acute crisis of her father's health condition, but nonetheless leaves her feeling unimportant. The violation of her identity that occurred 35 years ago might not be considered to be egregious and did not result from an abusive or unloving parent. Nevertheless, in the midst of what could be described as an understandable situation, the message she received and internalized for 35 years was that she was alone and that she was not enough for whom others would make sacrifices. She described feeling isolated from her friends. She knew they cared about her and she still saw them in school, but it was her first year in middle school and she felt like she was on the outside looking in, feeling flawed and inadequate as a person, and disconnected from the social scene. She felt she had to navigate her first year of middle school alone. The wife states that although she knew her expectations were unrealistic, at the time she remembered wishing her friends would sacrifice some of their activities in order to be with her. She also wishes her mom would have made her brother sacrifice more of his activities so she would not have had to give up so much. She felt alone in all of the losses she experienced.

As the wife shared, her husband barely moved from his position, but he occasionally looked over at her. He was quiet, but engaged. He was listening and the therapist was aware of the imbalance of time and focus on the wife. However, this process benefits the husband as well. He has the opportunity to develop empathy for his wife and an understanding of her pain. He is also bearing witness to her process of identifying pain and will likely find that he is able to identify his own pain with greater efficiency because of what he has observed. Thus, the therapist continues to focus on the wife and in an effort to begin developing her pain cycle, she inquired about how the wife coped with her pain 35 years ago.

Therapist:	When you felt alone, what did you do?
Wife:	With my friends I started to pull away. (Pause). I got quieter and kept to myself more. I would still sit with my friends at lunch, but they would carry on about the things they were doing without me and I had nothing to contribute so I got quiet and waited for someone to notice me.
Therapist:	Did they?
Wife:	Sometimes. But when I didn't have much to say they would move on. (Pause). They never asked about my father. That was really hurtful because they knew my parents. There was this significant thing going on in my life but no one seemed to get it. I was being pulled by my parents to help out at home, but no one seemed to notice. (Pause). My friends weren't outright mean, but it was like they were leaving me behind. (Tears form).
Therapist:	That sounds very painful. (Pause). Even now, as you're describing that time, it still seems to affect you.
Wife:	(Pause). Yeah, I guess so. I'm sort of surprised. I've never really talked about this before so maybe that's why I'm so affected.

Therapist:	Well, thank you for sharing. What I'd like to do now is draw what we refer to as a pain cycle. The pain cycle is a visual representation of our pain and the way we cope with it. So, for example, based on what you just shared, when you felt alone, you coped by pulling away. Am I understanding that correctly? Does this fit? (Drawing while speaking).
Wife:	Yeah, pretty much. It was so long ago that I don't remember all the details but I remember feeling really alone and isolated and pulling away as a result.
Therapist:	Today, when you feel alone, what do you do?
Wife:	I pull away.
Therapist:	And when you pull away, how do others respond?
Wife:	For the most part, they pull away too. My kids might be an exception. They never stop pursuing me! But no one pursues me when I pull away. For example, when I pull away from him (Pointing to the husband) he pulls away too.

In the wife's story, when she was 11, violations of identity and safety emerge pretty quickly. The therapist explores violations of identity (feeling alone and not worth enough) first and later explores the violation of safety. The significant coping response that she has identified at this point is "pulling away." From a Restoration Therapy perspective, this is a shaming behavior. Essentially, the wife withdraws with the desire to be pursued, but her coping behavior tends to be met with the same withdrawing behavior from others, further confirming her pain of being alone, or occasionally, propelling her into other parts of her pain cycle. This information for the woman was tracked by the therapist into the pain cycle in Figure 1.3.

The therapist has worked with the wife to begin identifying her pain cycle, and has established three connections thus far: 1) The connection between her primary emotion of feeling alone and her coping response of pulling away; 2) The connection between her pain cycle in the past at age 11 and her pain cycle in the present being the same cycle; and 3) The connection between her intrapersonal pain cycle and her interpersonal interactions (how others respond). The therapist continues to clarify and sharpen these connections in subsequent sessions while identifying new components of her pain cycle. In particular, the therapist is interested in exploring how the wife copes at home.

Wife:	At home I worked hard. My mother was pretty distraught and disorganized after my father's heart attack so I stepped up and took control. I figured out a system for cleaning the house, putting together grocery lists, preparing meals, and making

sure my father was taken care of, including administering his medications. Although I didn't necessarily do all of the tasks, I created a schedule for our family and made sure that everyone followed it.

Therapist: Wow, that is impressive. You mentioned "you made sure that everyone followed it." What did you do to make sure?

Wife: I created a chart and put it up around the house. I left sticky notes to remind my mother and brother of the tasks they had to do that week or that day. If they didn't do it then I would do it myself. But I got pretty good at keeping them on task and making sure they kept to their commitments. My parents didn't applaud me at the time for my work, but years later I would hear them tell others that they wouldn't have survived without me. It felt good to hear them acknowledge what I did for them.

The therapist helps the wife make the connection between her feeling like the world around her is unpredictable and chaotic and her coping

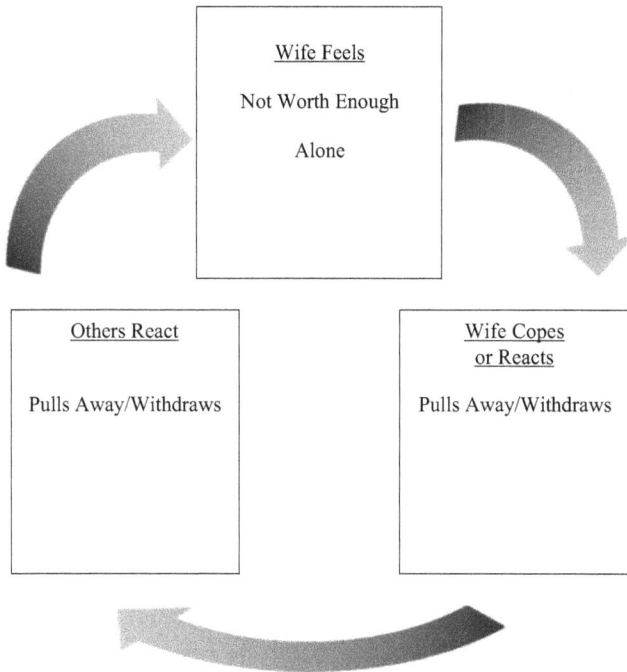

Figure 1.3 In Progress Pain Cycle from Couple in Case Example

behavior of controlling. When they discuss how others respond to her controlling behavior, she referred to more recent experiences and described others distancing themselves.

Wife: Although people agree with my directions or they do what I ask them to do, whether or not they agree with me, it seems like they distance themselves. (Pause). Or at least, there isn't a feeling of closeness or kinship that I wish there could be with, say, my co-workers or family members or friends. In the end, I'm able to get the project or the task accomplished, so at least there's some reward in that.

Here, the wife holds in balance the loss of the closeness with others with the success she has when she is in control. The illustration below shows what the wife's pain cycle looks like with this new information.

The therapist works to clarify and solidify the wife's pain cycle by eliciting stories from her past as well as experiences that occur throughout her weeks of therapy and begins to discuss how different parts of her cycle could be interconnected. The therapist begins by stating how this is a typical pattern with pain cycles in general and focuses on the particularities of the wife's pain cycle.

Therapist: Pain cycles often have multiple parts and are interactive. So, for example, (Pointing at the pain cycle drawn on the white board) as we look at yours we see that when you feel *alone* or *not worth sacrificing for*, you *pull away*. When you pull away, others, especially your husband, respond by *pulling away*. When they pull away then it's much like what happened with your mother when she was "distraught and disorganized" by your father's heart attack. In effect, your mother pulled away from her parental responsibilities, resulting in you feeling like your home-life became *unpredictable* and *chaotic*. At that time, when you felt like the world around you was unpredictable and chaotic, you coped by *controlling* the world and the people around you. This is understandable, but this is what you still do now to cope with feelings of chaos. You control. However, when you control, sometimes others respond by *distancing* themselves and when they distance themselves this results in you feeling *alone*. And we're back to where we began with your cycle.

For the first time, the wife was able to see how her emotional experience and her behavioral coping is patterned and how the interplay between

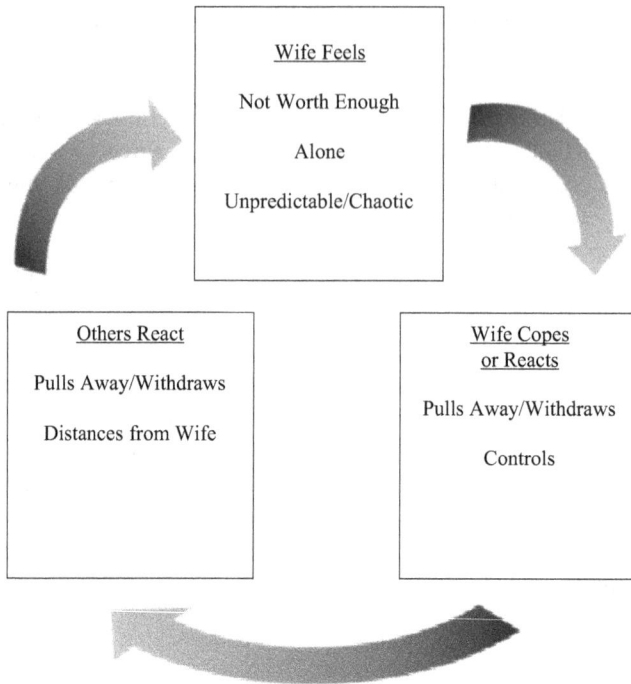

Figure 1.4 In Progress Pain Cycle from Couple in Case Example

these patterns and others' responses create a perpetual cycle of pain as seen in Figure 1.4. One of the most beneficial aspects of the pain cycle is that as a visual representation, clients are able to see and gain insight about their patterns in a new way. We would compare it to the benefit of a genogram (McGoldrick, Gerson, & Petry, 2008). Our clients know their stories and the myriad facts about their family members, but oftentimes they "see" their family narrative in a way they have never seen it before. The intergenerational patterns and the relationship dynamics that are drawn out with symbols, shapes, and lines suddenly take on new meaning for clients. In much the same way, the pain cycle illuminates for the clients in a new way insight about their intrapersonal patterns. This awareness begins the journey of mindfulness and eventually works to create alternative patterns that promote peace and healthy relationships.

Getting to this point with the wife took three sessions and included alternating between her and her husband throughout. As we turn to the husband's pain cycle, we want to reiterate what we stated before about his involvement during the thicker narrative parts of his wife's work. Although

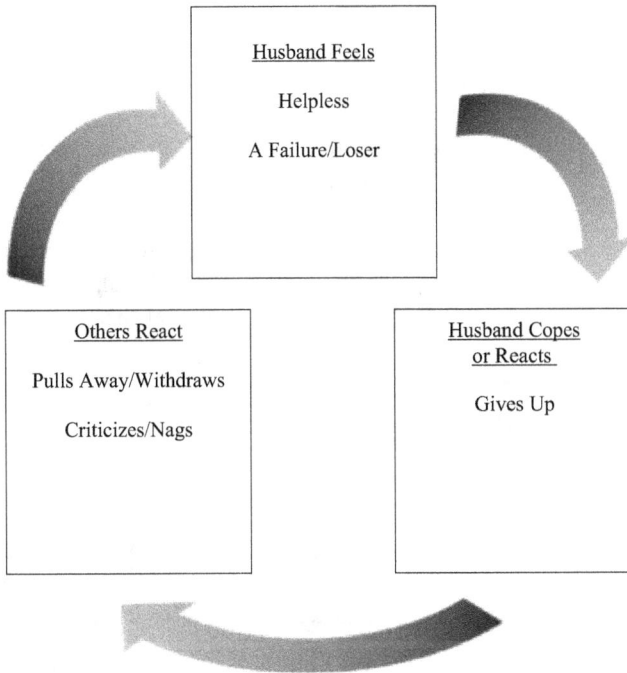

Figure 1.5 In Progress Pain Cycle from Couple in Case Example

the therapist was not working directly with him, he was part of the therapeutic process by way of bearing witness to the wife's work. After the therapist has worked with the wife to construct the first part of her pain cycle,
she turns to the husband to check in with him. The tracking of his pain cycle
is found in Figure 1.5.

Therapist:	I appreciate you patiently listening. I'm wondering what you're feeling right now.
Husband:	I don't know. I've heard a lot of this before so I didn't learn anything new. But I haven't really seen her cry about it. So I guess that part is new.
Therapist:	Hmmm. You didn't hear anything new, and yet as you were listening to her just now it was different because she expressed some emotion.
	What is it that you're feeling right now? In this moment? In this room?
Husband:	(Pause). I guess I feel sad for her. I feel protective of her, like I wish I could go back and help her 11-year-old person.

I think I would have stuck with her or at least found ways to help her.

I also feel helpless, like there's nothing I can do. In the same way that I can't go back to when she was 11, I can't do anything now to make things better.

Therapist: Something you said that really stands out to me is the word "helpless." You said you feel helpless. Can you say more about "helpless?"

Husband: (Pause). Well, it's like I can see that there's a problem and yet there's nothing I can do about it and although no one is blaming me for the problem, I still feel that I should be able to fix it.

Therapist: (Pause). Stay with that feeling and tell me when was the first time you remember feeling that way.

Husband: You mean, helpless? Oh, I feel that often.

Therapist: Do you remember the *first* time you felt that way?

Husband: (Pause). I don't know. (Pause). Probably around the time I was in high school. My parents and one of my uncles owned a restaurant and they were struggling to pay the bills. They were really stressed out and we all could feel it. They worked long hours and I really wanted to quit school and help them out, but they wouldn't let me. I was a really bad student. I always got bad grades and just didn't care about school. I wanted to be at the restaurant helping my family—*doing* something, you know? But instead I had to be stuck in school all day where I was a loser.

Therapist: A loser.

Husband: Well yeah. I felt like a total loser, unable to do anything well. I couldn't help out at home, but I was a failure at school and all along my family's business was falling apart.

Therapist: Do you remember what you did when you felt like you were a loser?

Husband: I just gave up. What could I do? I mean, I wasn't doing well in school but my parents weren't really all that involved because they were so preoccupied with their business, so nothing was really done about it. I failed a couple classes here and there but eventually I finished high school. I really wanted to quit school to help out at the restaurant, but my parents wouldn't let me so I just gave up asking. I hardly saw my parents at home as it was and when I realized they would never let me quit school to help them out, I just gave up. (Pause). I remember feeling like they didn't really value my help. Although they

	made it clear that they wanted me stay in school because they felt that was best for me, I remember being convinced that they didn't value my help and so I just gave up.
Therapist:	(Pause). You've said some really significant things so let me make sure I heard you correctly. You talked about several feelings, that you felt "helpless" and like a "failure" and a "loser." (Pause). These are all pretty strong messages you were receiving about yourself. And it sounds like when you felt those things, the way you coped was by "giving up." And I understand that the giving up came only after you made an earnest effort to be helpful. But in the end, you gave up because you really didn't have much choice. Does that sound right? (Drawing husband's pain cycle).
Husband:	Yeah, that makes sense. And I realize that I give up when I'm not good at something like school, but I also give up when I know I'm right but there's nothing I can do. To this day, I still believe that quitting school to help them would have been the right thing to do but I had to give up asking and let that dream go because there's no way they were going to change their minds. (Pause). So sometimes I give up because no matter how hard I try I just can't do it. But other times I give up because in spite of the fact that I know I can do something, I have to give up because the other person isn't going to budge and it just isn't worth trying anymore.
Therapist:	Is that what you were feeling earlier when you threw your hands up in the air and said, "I can't win?"
Husband:	Yes, exactly. Often with my wife I feel like I just have to give up in order to keep the peace or to just keep from going crazy!
Therapist:	So when you "give up" with your wife, how does she respond?
Husband:	I guess she either keeps to herself and gets quiet or she starts to get really critical and nags me even more.
Therapist:	When that happens, what message do you receive about yourself?
Husband:	Essentially that she doesn't care about me and what I want or what I'm going through.
Therapist:	And so what is the message embedded in what you're saying? When you give and your wife responds by either pulling away or getting critical, what do you believe about yourself?
Husband:	(Pause). Well I feel disrespected, like what I have to say and what I'm trying to do just doesn't matter.
Therapist:	Is that the message that you received when your parents wouldn't let you quit school to help them?

Husband: Yeah, it was really mixed. (Pause). Because on the one hand they would tell me at home that as the son in the family, it was up to me to take care of my siblings and keep the house together when they were away. They would sometimes talk about it being my duty and my responsibility. And yet, when I tried to help out and step up to my responsibilities, they would say, "No, I don't think so." You know, they told me that they wanted me to grow up to be a proud and respectable Mexican man who knew how to take care of his family and yet they were the ones who stood in the way when I tried to take care of them!

With the husband, the therapist moves more quickly into the couple interaction sequence than she did with the wife, but then connects his pain back to the experience with his family-of-origin. Making the connections with him that were made with the wife about the past and the present, emotion and behavior, and his reaction and others' responses is an important part of the work. In this case, when the husband was able to connect his present pain with the pain he felt when he was an adolescent, not only did the pattern of his pain cycle become more clearly illuminated, but he was able to connect it to the cultural narrative that his family endorsed about the roles and expectations for males in the family. We won't expound on this point here, but simply will mention that part of the therapeutic conversation included a discussion about this culturally-based gender expectation and how it played out intergenerationally in his family-of-origin (i.e. How did his father model this role?) as well as his family-of-creation (i.e. How is the husband modeling this for his children?).

The husband brought up another primary emotion that is important to chase down. He mentioned feeling "disrespected." He stated that when he feels disrespected, he performs to please. This part of his pain cycle tended to play out most prominently in his work context. And most recently, when he was passed over for the promotion at work, his response was to prove to his employer why they should have chosen him. Therefore, he worked harder and longer hours. He was available above and beyond what was expected of him and although he was receiving high marks and accolades from his employer and his co-workers, it did not change his position status. This was not a sustainable work situation and it was taking a toll on his physical, emotional, and relational availability at home.

After clarifying and solidifying the husband's pain cycle both spouses were able to recognize their own pain cycles throughout the weeks as they were occurring outside of sessions, the therapist joined the two pain cycles to create their interactive pain cycles. The reason why the therapist did not

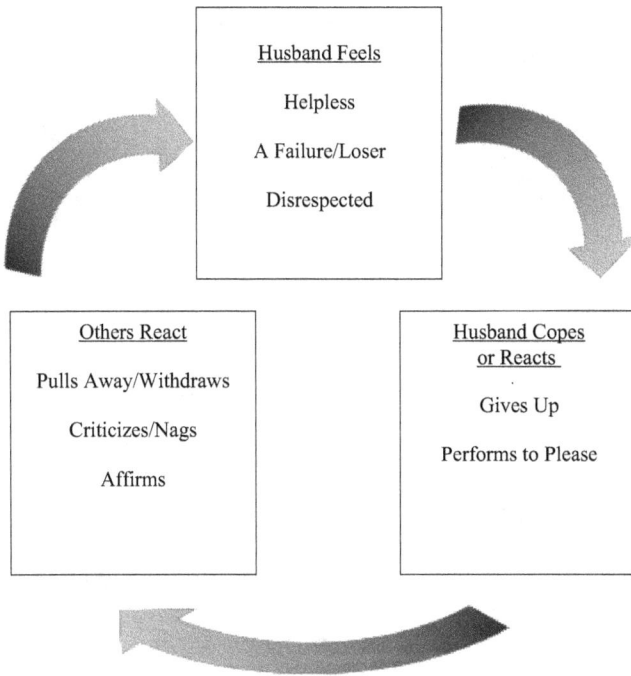

Figure 1.6 In Progress Pain Cycle from Couple in Case Example

do this right away is because it is helpful for them to focus on recognizing their own pain cycles, independent of one another. This communicates two messages that are critical in this stage of therapy. The first message is that their pain cycles are *their own individual* pain cycles. Although they might be familiar with one another's pain, the focus of the attention is to remain on recognizing, understanding, and acknowledging the individual pain cycle. Without prompting, clients will tend to become preoccupied with the other's pain cycle and submit to the temptation of calling the other out on his or her pain. This is unproductive and can counter the work of personal responsibility and ownership of one's own pain cycle. The second important message that the therapist communicates by starting with individual pain cycles is that their pain will show up in all contexts, including, but not limited to, the couple context. It is important that clients understand that their pain is not limited to the couple relationship and that the more aware of it they are in all contexts, the more effective they will be in developing agency and control of it as time goes on.

The spousal interactive pain cycle came together without much effort and is seen in Figure 1.7. The couple were quickly able to see how their

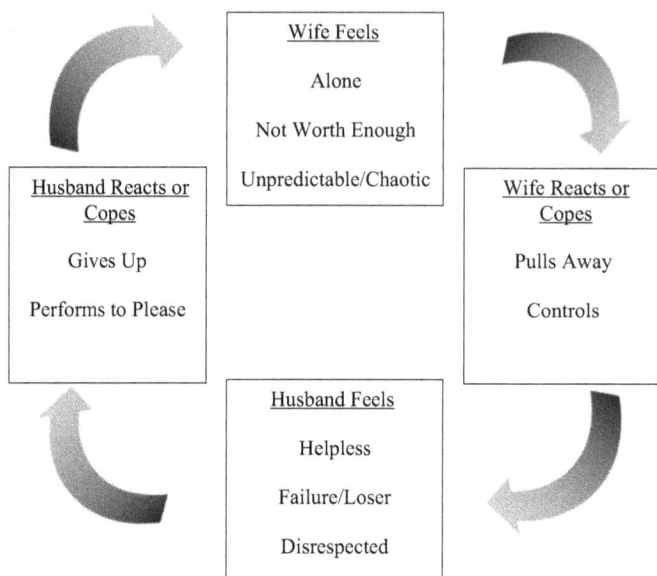

Figure 1.7 Husband and Wife Interactive Pain Cycle in Case Example

behaviors emotionally dysregulate one another and how easily they fell into an interaction sequence that increased their pain and diminished their resources to stay connected. Using the example given earlier in the sessions about the husband coming home from work later than he had planned, the therapist describes how their pain cycles interact to create a harmful relationship environment which violates love and trustworthiness in the relationship. When the husband called to say he would be coming late, the wife's pain about being alone was activated. When she felt alone, she coped by pulling away so that when the husband got home, she was distant and minimally responsive. She pulled away with the hope that he would pursue her, but instead his own pain of feeling helpless and that he had failed her and the children was activated and instead of pursuing her, he gave up. By this point, they were chronically distant and so bridging the divide of distance would have taken more energy than he had after a long day at work. In the days that followed, the distance between the spouses began to evolve into chaos because they were not communicating as much and the logistics of school, work, and children began to feel chaotic and unpredictable to the wife so she began to take control and become more critical of the husband. The more critical she became, the more disrespected he felt at home. He continued to "give up" at home, but then increased his availability and performance at work, where he felt his work was appreciated. The more he was available at work, the less he was available at home and his wife continued to feel alone. It is important to note and make clear with clients that although the narrative of their interactive pain cycle began with the wife in this situation, the cycle can just as easily begin with the husband and that both people have the opportunity and the responsibility to take ownership of their own pain cycles and, in effect, disrupt the cycle.

Restoration Therapy, in many ways, is like a family-of-origin shorthand. It enables the therapist to listen, empathize, and reflect the narratives of clients both accurately and meaningfully in helping them to understand the impact of relationships on identity and safety (Hargrave & Pfitzer, 2011). In RT, we do not ask "How did it make you feel?" but instead make the questions much more specific toward identity and safety. For instance, we ask, "How did it make you feel *about yourself?*" or "What did the action say *about you?*" As well as, "How did it make you feel *about the relationship?*" Utilizing these types of questions, the restoration therapist is able to organize the client and therapy in an efficient manner very quickly and determine the pain that drives untrustworthy and unloving behaviors. We find that most clients feel restoration therapists empathize and understand their stories of pain much more effectively and they feel the power of insight as the therapist is willing and accurate in chasing down their particular stories of pain. As the therapist becomes more familiar with the concepts of identity and safety and gets to know with the words clients utilize to describe their identities and experiences with safety, the therapist not only becomes more expert in chasing the pain but also more efficient in organizing and using the model.

2 Finding Truth and the Peace Cycle

As clinicians, we know that helping a client gain insight into his or her story is a foundational step toward healing. Understanding the client's relationships and the events that have taken place in his or her life, and clearly identifying the primary emotions and reactive tendencies that he or she experiences ensures that the therapeutic work is targeting the appropriate primary emotion and guiding the client toward emotional regulation and behavioral change. However, as restoration therapists, we would argue that insight around the pain is only part of what we need in order to facilitate change in clients' lives. We must also help our clients experience and name the truth about their pain and guide them toward taking responsibility for changing the old behavior. In addition to understanding the pain, we need a path forward. The only way to move toward peace and connection is to understand and *change* the old feeling and coping patterns.

In Chapter 1, we saw how the therapist was able to wisely guide clients toward identifying their feelings and their coping behaviors. This process enabled the therapist to identify the couple's unique pain cycle, which illustrated the underlying feelings and destructive reactions that occur when clients are in pain. While it is certainly important to help clients understand their pain cycles, the pain cycle does not describe how people feel and behave at all times. As restoration therapists, we would argue that it is equally important that clients also have an understanding of who they are and how they act when they are at peace. The therapeutic work of identifying a client's peace cycle not only promotes healing and growth in their life, but it also has the benefit of providing them with a path forward that is clearly defined. In other words, we believe that it is important that clients not only know what *not* to do, but also what *to* do (Hargrave & Pfitzer, 2011).

Identification of the Regulating Emotions: The Truth

Where Change Begins

Most clients seek therapy because they desire change in a particular relationship or area of growth in their lives. It is important to note here that many if not most clients know what the problem is and what they *should* be doing. The therapist that covers this problem saturated story (White & Epston, 1990) over and over again without any framework of focus is likely to do the client little good. As Hargrave and Pfitzer (2011) state, the real art of therapy is helping people do what they know they *should,* but somehow cannot do on their own. In RT, we find that the reason most clients have difficulty in stopping a coping behavior is that they do not deal with or are unaware of the underlying emotional dysregulation which drives the unwanted behavior. The difficult task is moving clients into a position of taking responsibility for this pain and emotional dysregulation which is trapped in their senses of identity and safety. If the therapist can learn to read these primary emotions accurately and help the client own the responsibility for changing the emotion, then the client most often can modify the behavior that they wish to see change (Hargrave & Pfitzer, 2011). Some clients might find themselves wanting their outside circumstances to change in order to feel better. These clients might say things like, "If we could just have a baby, I wouldn't be as negative all the time," or "I think the conflict in our home will resolve itself when we are able to move into a house with more space." Situations certainly do not modify or change the primary emotions connected with identity and sense of safety.

Others might be waiting for the individual who was the source of the painful message to tell them what they wish they had heard long ago. For example, a man whose father was always critical of his performance growing up might find himself still longing for his father to acknowledge that he is good enough and worthy. Although the man's father may have power to be able to speak truth to his son about his son's identity and safety as he was an original caregiver and thereby an original programmer of the man's identity and safety, the fact still remains that the man himself must be open enough to the father communicating a long-believed message and must take responsibility to award it value over and above the previously programmed message. The man still holds the responsibility to *believe* or *have faith in* the truth even if it is spoken by the father. Some clients might even be waiting for God to correct their feelings or circumstances. Although these desires are certainly understandable, we know that regardless of whether or not one's outside circumstances or relationships shift, change requires us to take action. Therapy provides the client with the opportunity to use his or her understanding of the past to become more loving and trustworthy in the future. The change we hope to see in our lives begins with ourselves and, as clinicians, we must press our clients toward taking responsibility for their own sense of peace and emotional regulation regardless of any changes in their outside circumstances or relationships. Thus, the big question for each client is, "How will you choose to live your life if your struggles persist?"

In the following example, the therapist was working with a 38-year-old Chinese American woman. The woman had been struggling with the pain of infertility for several years and had experienced four miscarriages in just two years. The pain of what she had lost and the longing to become a mother led her to seek therapy. Certainly and understandably, the woman wanted her circumstances to change. But what became clear in early therapy sessions was that her sense of peace hinged on her desired outcome. In other words, she could not imagine finding peace or joy outside of the fulfillment of her hope of being a parent. She sought therapy because she wanted to feel better but initially she was unable to see ways in which she could take responsibility for her own feelings. The question for the woman was, "How will you choose to live your life even in the midst of this painful infertility season?" Over the course of the work, the woman was able to move into an empowered position, where she was able to take responsibility for her own sense of peace, rather than being stuck in the vulnerable position of having to rely on the fulfillment of a desire to feel stable. How was this empowerment able to take place? The woman was able to come to terms with her own feelings of not being enough without being a mother and the sense of her own failure. She was able to take the powerful position of recognizing that with or without a child, she was enough as a person and did not have to achieve a successful pregnancy for her identity to be sound. Certainly she was sad and grieved over the miscarriages, but the difference was that she was now able to separate the identity from the infertility. She was able to shift her focus to shaping her talents and gifts toward acceptance of who she was instead of focusing on a performance identity. She found that she was empowered enough to live life amidst the grief by knowing and deciding her identity was not dependent upon a successful pregnancy.

Taking Responsibility

As we discussed in Chapter 1, we all carry messages and ideas about our identity and sense of safety. For many, the most powerful messages came from their earliest relationships: a parent, caregiver, or other family member such as a sibling. For others, the most powerful messages came from individuals outside their families such as peers, teachers, coaches, or mentors. And for some, the most painful messages did not come from people, but from painful events or tragic circumstances such as the death of a loved one or victimization from a crime or natural disasters (Hargrave & Hargrave, 2015).

The messages we carry about our identity and sense of safety are often developed early on and persist throughout our lives. Because this pain was learned early, and these were often messages given to the client by significant people or circumstances, it is easy for the client to assume that these painful messages are indeed true because he or she has little or no power to evaluate and decide what messages should be used in constructing identity and safety. In early development, the child simply has no blueprint of healthy identity and sense of safety and so it is constructed by the messages of others. As White (1997) clarifies, the landscape of identity and actions are the building material of the individual's narrative. Having adopted these feelings as beliefs about themselves or their environment, he or she copes with destructive behaviors in an attempt to survive the pain they feel. Of course, these behaviors are not constructive or helpful to his or her pain in any way. They are merely reactions he or she has learned to employ in an attempt to protect him or herself (Hargrave & Pfitzer, 2011). But while these feelings are certainly real, pain does not tell us the truth about our identity and safety. The hopeful news is that as human beings develop and grow into adults, we have the power and brain development to choose agency and are certainly capable of telling ourselves the truth about who we are and the truth about our safety and empowerment in the world.

Many clients have never considered the possibility that they have the power to tell themselves the truth about their own identities and senses of safety. Many would believe that it is a fundamental requirement of relationships for the relational partner to continue to shape these senses of identity and safety because, simply stated, that is likely all he or she has experienced in life. In other words, since we experienced this formation exclusively from others with no plan of our own, we do not consider the reality that we now do have the power to choose what we believe about ourselves and how to live and negotiate in the world of relationships. It feels strange for the individual to grant him or herself the power to consider the fact that the painful messages he or she has so readily accepted as true, may in fact be lies. The real therapeutic work can begin when the client recognizes his or her empowerment to confront the lie taught and shaped by others and, instead, embrace his or her *own chosen* truth. Consider the example below.

A 28-year-old Caucasian male originally sought therapy for his inability to perform tasks and meet deadlines at work. The man was an extremely bright young man and clearly capable, but had difficulty making much progress on important projects assigned to him. Notice here how the therapist moves the man into a position where he can take responsibility for his own pain and recognize his own agency.

Man:	I don't know what to do. (Pause). I know the deadline is approaching and I just freeze. (Pause). I can't think and I can't seem to make any progress.
Therapist:	How do people respond to you when you are unable to complete the project?

Man:	My boss usually rolls his eyes and sighs. (Pause). When it's a bigger project, he typically yells. One time he said something like, "Sometimes I wonder why I hired you!"
Therapist:	(Pause). That must have been painful to hear. (Pause). How did that statement, "Sometimes I wonder why I hired you?" make you feel about yourself?
Man:	I felt completely worthless and like there is nothing I can do to measure up to his expectations.
Therapist:	You feel worthless and unable to measure up. (Man nods).
Man:	(Pause). And alone … it feels like I am the only one.
Therapist:	(Long pause). Tell me about the first time you can remember feeling worthless, unable to measure up, and alone.
Man:	(Long pause). When I was in middle school I had an undiagnosed learning disability. It went unnoticed in elementary school but the increased workload and level of learning in middle school caused great difficulty for me. (Pause). My grades dropped significantly. It wasn't until my junior year in high school that a specialist discovered that I was dyslexic.
Therapist:	(Nodding and then pause). Tell me the story that stands out as particularly painful when you reflect on this season in your life.
Man:	(Pause). My eighth grade English class was the worst. There was one class in which we were analyzing a particular passage of the book we were reading and the whole class took turns reading one paragraph at a time. It was my turn to read and I asked to pass. My teacher rolled his eyes and said sarcastically, "What's the matter? You forgot how to read?"
Therapist:	(Pause). What did this statement communicate to you about your situation?
Man:	I was being forced to do something I could not do. I was completely unable to measure up to the expectations of my teacher and the standards of the other kids in my class. (Pause). I gave it a try anyway but all of the words were coming out wrong and I was completely tongue-tied. My teacher cut me off and said, "Forget I asked" and the whole class laughed.
Therapist:	You must have been feeling a lot of pain in that moment. What message did these events give you about who you are?
Man:	(Pause). I felt like I wasn't as valuable as everyone else. I felt worthless. The worst part was that I thought my teacher was so cool. I wanted his approval so badly and I felt totally unable to meet any of his expectations. (Pause). I wish I could talk with him now.

Therapist:	(Long pause). What would you hope to hear in that conversation?
Man:	(Long pause). I just wish I could hear him say that he was wrong. I would want him to recognize the talent that I had and to see all that I have been able to accomplish in spite of my learning disability.
Therapist:	I certainly understand your desire to hear your teacher affirm you. (Pause). However, I am concerned that you may not get that opportunity. And even if you did, I fear it would not be powerful enough to correct the feelings that you carry— worthless, alone, and unable to measure up. (Pause). How do you want to be the affirming teacher to yourself that you did not have in eighth grade?
Man:	(Pause). I can't change what happened ...
Therapist:	You are right. You cannot change the events that took place when you were in eighth grade. But you do have a choice as to what message you give yourself about your value and capabilities now.
Man:	(Long pause). Honestly, it never occurred to me that I could do anything about the message my teacher gave me all those years ago. I would want to be encouraging toward myself ... (Long pause). I think there's a part of me that knows I won't get that chance with my teacher. (Pause). So I think I might be asking other people to tell me that he was wrong. It's subtle and I didn't see it until now, but it's like I'm asking my current boss to correct the message my eighth grade teacher gave me all those years ago.
Therapist:	Where does that leave you?
Man:	(Pause). It usually leads me back to those same feelings— worthless, unable to measure up, and alone.
Therapist:	(Long pause). When you think about the possibility of being encouraging to yourself, what does that look like for you?
Man:	(Long pause). It means that I am willing to say the things that I keep waiting for my boss to say to me.

In this example, we see that the man has been carrying strong messages about his identity and his ability to measure up in situations where he feels challenged. While the therapist empathized with his experience and validated his feelings and his desire to hear a different message, the therapist also illuminated the client's own agency. The man had never considered the possibility that he is able to respond to the faulty messages he was given about his identity. Here, the therapist encouraged the client to take an empowered position where he is able to take responsibility for connecting and correcting his sense of being worthless and unable to measure up. The client is now in an empowered position to choose what message he would like to give himself about his identity and sense of safety.

At the time in the client's life when the painful message was first received, it is likely that he did not have the agency to refute the lie or take meaningful action to put a stop to the destructive relational dynamic. But there is great therapeutic possibility when a client recognizes the agency that he has in the here-and-now. Having identified his unique pain, the client has a choice as to whether he will continue to accept the emotionally dysregulating message, or choose to do the difficult but worthy work of taking responsibility for his pain and shaping an emotionally regulating truth about his identity and sense of safety.

The Sources of Truth

As human beings, we have a choice. We can choose to believe and react destructively to our feelings. We can, on the other hand, claim the truth and take action toward living with peace and constructively connecting with others. While the choice is simple, it is not easy. Before we discuss how the restoration therapist approaches this task, it is important to note that there are three sources of truth that can be helpful to a client as they work to identify the truth about their pain.

Others

It is a valid question when we are therapeutically seeking to help the client identify an emotionally regulating truth: "Who is powerful enough to speak into a client's life concerning identity or safety?" There are others in clients' lives who have at least some of this power. Of these "others," original caregivers and parents likely have some agency. After all, most often these people were the original programmers of the client's brain when it came to love and trustworthiness. Of course, even though these caregivers and adults might have power to do additional programming or even reprogramming, it does not mean they will use the power for good. The reality is that many of these parents and caregivers were damaging in their messages of love and trustworthiness and remain damaging in the present day. Still, there are very few others in the lives of clients who carry as much power to potentially speak into the emotionally regulating truths of clients (Hargrave, 2001).

Where it is possible to have these original programmers reshape a client's perceptions of identity and safety, it is wise for the therapist to collaborate with the client to determine if there is the potential to receive a different message. As original caregivers and parents grow and develop, in many cases they become wiser and see clearly how their efforts of love and trustworthiness fell short. Many of these caregivers and parents sincerely desire the opportunity to redress issues with adult children and specifically address questions as well as take responsibility for mis-steps. The therapist can be a helpful resource in not only making these interactions a possibility, but also in keeping the interactions focused on making a difference in the emotionally regulating truth of the client. Essentially, the therapist helps the client and his or her original programmers rewrite new identity and safety programming (Hargrave & Pfitzer, 2011).

Some clients are quick to reject these efforts of others—particularly when the efforts come from formerly damaging parents—because the client is caught in his or her own destructive and reactive violations of love and trustworthiness. As a result, by their own dysregulated reactivity to primary emotions these clients damage others' identities and senses of safety. Victims almost always become victimizers at one time or another (Hargrave & Zasowski, 2016). Often, the therapist can assist the client in seeing his or her own reactive and destructive patterns and thereby become more willing and open to the efforts of previously damaging people who hold enough power to redress wounds to identity and safety (Hargrave & Pfitzer, 2011).

It is essential also to recognize that it is not only parents and caregivers who have this power to shape identity and safety. While it is usually less than family-of-origin members, significant people in a client's life can speak powerfully to a client about his or her identity and sense of safety. Many people will report moments in which another person has spoken emotionally regulating truth in a way that shifted their perspective about their identity or changed their ideas about their own empowerment. Coaches, teachers, and dear friends are just a few examples of people who can profoundly shape a person's ideas about his or her identity and sense of safety. Certainly, relationships can shape our sense of identity and safety in powerful ways.

Spiritual Resources

Second, spiritual resources can be a meaningful source of truth when it comes to one's identity and sense of safety. Of course, not every client has spiritual beliefs or resources that present value or power but, unfortunately, it has become almost a taboo in therapeutic processes to mention spirituality and certainly to use these resources as a therapeutic lever (Walsh, 2009). Doherty (1996) explains that many therapists approach spirituality in a morally neutral way in order not to risk offending a client. We would see this stance as a hindrance to good therapy and particularly Restoration Therapy as we believe therapists need to access any dimension of client belief that holds potential power to shape identity and sense of safety. If a client considers spirituality as important to his or her life, then indeed it should be actively engaged as a resource by the therapist to reshape love, trustworthiness, identity, and safety (Hargrave & Pfitzer, 2011). For instance, many clients will state that their relationship with God offers great wisdom and comfort and that prayer and reading scriptures are meaningful tools in moving them from pain to a place of peace. We have had many clients find hope and comfort in using various journaling exercises around scriptures, prayers, and readings in a way that helps them integrate the truth about who they are and their sense of safety.

As Hargrave and Pfitzer (2011) point out, therapists do not have to be experts on all spirituality or religions in order to make them useful as a resource. If the therapist is willing to be curious and interested—similar to the sensitivity required in a multicultural situation—it is likely the client will be able to teach or reveal exactly how the spirituality could serve as a resource to him or her personally. The spiritual resources that are most helpful to clients point toward empowerment, love, peace, honor, tranquility, trustworthiness, justice, and community. Often, these ideals can be used effectively to help the client gain a sense that he or she is loved and there is a community around him or her that can function in a redemptive and trust-worthy fashion (Hargrave & Pfitzer, 2003).

Self

Finally, because the choice is ultimately the client's when it comes to deciding whether or not he or she will believe the messages of the emotional dysregulation or choose to trust the emotionally regulating truth, the self is the most powerful source of truth. People can be told time and time again by others and by their spiritual resources that they are loved, important, and valuable, but they will only be able to receive these statements of the truth to the extent that they are willing to count them as being true. The ability to accept and reject statements about identity and safety makes the self the most salient and powerful source of the emotionally regulating truth. Until the clients are able to claim the truth for themselves other sources of truth will have a fleeting impact at best.

When a client does take this position of speaking into his or her own sense of identity or safety, it can be powerful indeed. We will discuss these specifics further in Chapter 4 in the applications of the truth, but here it is important to draw attention to the fact that as a person grows and develops cognitively, he or she most times becomes capable of abstract thought. Many times, this ability to think abstractly is described as "the ability to think about thinking." In other words, the cognitively mature person can analyze, be curious about, and even challenge his or her own processes of thinking. If clients have this cognitive ability, they indeed become powerful enough to shape their own identities and senses of safety (Hargrave & Pfitzer, 2011). In times past and still in formal government or court settings, the question is spoken in old English, "What say ye?" In other words, what is your opinion? Our clients have been subjected to the influences of years and years of parents, others, and perhaps even spirituality shaping their beliefs about themselves and their senses of safety. It is essential, in our opinion, for the therapist to finally ask, "What say you?" What does the client say about his or her own sense of identity and safety? The client is the most powerful force in his or her ability to choose, it is time for him or her to make this choice overtly when it comes to the emotionally regulating truth.

As mentioned in the previous chapter, as restoration therapists, we believe that the ability to self-regulate versus co-regulate is essential to a client's ability to grow and flourish in his or her relationship with him or herself and others. Simply depending on resources outside of the self to heal pain around identity and sense of safety will have a limited impact on the client's growth and create a destructive dynamic in his or her relationships. For example, a husband and wife came to therapy seeking couple therapy. In the past few sessions, the therapist had worked with the couple to identify their pain cycles. The husband's primary emotions were: inadequate, abandoned, and alone. The wife struggled with feelings of being unsafe, vulnerable, and out of control. Knowing that the husband was certainly a significant person in the wife's life, it might be tempting for the therapist to use the husband as a resource in telling her the truth about those feelings by giving the husband the opportunity to share what she means to him or to tell her the ways in which she is protected and safe. But as restoration therapists, we believe it is absolutely essential that clients take responsibility for their own feelings and actions instead of relying on others to do this work for them. Certainly there is great benefit to speaking truth into a loved one's life; however, this will be much more powerful once the recipient has taken responsibility for his or her own feelings and is self-regulated. This puts him or her in a better and more emotionally regulated position to receive it as an expression of intimacy and closeness instead of a position of need (Hargrave & Pfitzer, 2011).

Embracing the Truth

There are two universal truths that restoration therapists hold as foundational to helping a client build a healthy sense of identity and safety: 1) Human beings are valuable and important (Rogers, 1961); and 2) Relationships are essential and should promote human growth (Buber, 1958). We believe human beings are valuable because they are uniquely set apart from any other species on the planet. We also believe that we have no way of knowing ourselves apart from relationships. In other words, relationships are powerful teachers when it comes to learning how to operate in the world. We cannot develop successfully or thrive or even survive without relationships (Hargrave & Pfitzer, 2003).

In light of these assumptions and in the face of experiences that have given the client faulty messages about his or her identity and safety, the therapist is tasked with pressing the client toward growth and healing by giving him or her the opportunity to speak into the pain he or she carries. Choosing to agree with the pain messages of the past ensures that the client will continue to operate in the pain cycle. If he or she truly wishes to begin interacting with him or herself and others differently, he or she must embrace a regulating truth. The therapist can play an active and important role in facilitating the embodiment of truth through an experiential intervention. Here, the therapist has some choice around which intervention to employ in helping the client to experience and name the truth about who he or she is and the sense of safety. We will explore each of these options in more depth in Chapter 4, but no matter which intervention the therapist chooses, all of them share a few essential common elements.

Essential Elements of Interventions

To begin, most of the interventions that we would suggest at this point in the therapeutic process are experiential in nature. We believe that in order for the intervention to be effective, the client must experience what it feels like to take an empowered position, emotionally connect with the pain, and make the empowered choice to tell him or herself the regulating truth. This is often accomplished through visualization, where the client can see him or herself at a younger age or as a future or best self having integrated the desired change. Making the interventions experiential is essential given the fact that we cannot simply recite words and expect them to have an impact on our feelings or behavior.

Also, in order for the intervention to be effective, the truth that the client speaks must directly address the specific pain identified in their pain cycle. In theory, most truths a client could name are true about all human beings. All human beings are unique and lovable and everyone is empowered and able to make choices. Thus, it is important that the truth the client identifies speaks to the heart of the pain he or she experiences specifically, making it a regulating truth instead of a statement that is merely true and doesn't have much impact on the client's deepest pain. Unless the truth specifically addresses the pain, it will not be a statement that is emotionally regulating when it comes up against the experience of pain in the future (Hargrave & Hargrave, 2015).

No matter which intervention the therapist chooses, it is essential that the therapist instruct the client to speak his or her regulating truth out loud. This is necessary for a couple of reasons. First, the brain processes the truth differently when it hears the statement rather than simply thinking the statement. Second, speaking the truth out loud keeps the client focused. We can think about many things at once but we can only say one thing at a time. When the client simply thinks about the truth, it is easy for the mind to wander and creates a greater possibility that the client will pull him or herself out of the emotional experience. Finally, saying the truth out loud deepens the experiential element of the exercise. For many, the power in the experience comes when they actually speak the truth. Simply thinking the truth might compromise the strength of the intervention.

The Role of the Therapist

In addition to the critical elements of the interventions themselves, the therapist plays a crucial role in the success of the intervention through the use of injunctions, which includes the therapist's vocal tone, pace, volume, and repetition. The use of a voice helps the client to emotionally connect with him or herself more effectively than if the therapist were to simply use a casual conversational tone. Likewise, it is essential for the therapist to speak slowly when employing interventions that are targeted at identifying the truth. Keeping a slow pace and pausing when appropriate helps the client to digest each moment of the intervention, allowing him or her to emotionally connect where necessary. Raising and lowering volume when appropriate can heighten the intensity of a moment in a way that is helpful to the client's ability to connect with the image during the intervention. Finally, having the client repeat significant statements he or she makes about the truth concerning identity and safety can help the client own these statements as his or her own. The therapist may have the client repeat these statements three or four times, slowing the process down to ensure that the truth is not just a nice statement, but also a regulating, embodied truth. If a therapist becomes nervous or feels unsure about the impact of the intervention, the elements in an injunction are often quickly lost. While we cannot control exactly how a client responds to an intervention, an injunction using the elements of voice detailed above is one of the most powerful tools a therapist has in his or her ability to help the intervention to be as effective as possible.

Table 2.1 Clinical Descriptions of Emotionally Regulated Feelings Related to Identity and Safety

Descriptors clients use when reflecting on truths related to peace in identity	*Descriptors clients use when reflecting on truths related to peace in safety*
Loved, Worthy, Significant, Not Alone, Prized, Valuable, Precious, Approved, Accepted, Wanted, Appreciated, Hopeful, Free	Safe, Secure, Adequate, Sure, Fulfilled, Capable, Empowered, In Control, Protected, Connected, Intimate, Competent, Validated, Enough

Identifying Truth

Part of the skill in becoming a restoration therapist is getting familiar with and able to utilize words that deal with the language of identity, safety, love, and trustworthiness. When it comes to identifying the truth with the client, it is essential that the therapist knows what truths correspond to not only the pain the client feels, but also the emotional truths that relate to identity and safety. In Table 2.1, a listing of these common words associated with regulating truths is listed. These words, mostly developed by clients, are elements that are reflective of a sense of peace instead of a sense of pain.

As mentioned before, at this point in the therapeutic process where the therapist is working to help the client identify truth, the therapist has many interventions to choose from. For this particular case illustration, the therapist chose to utilize the "re-parenting" intervention. This is a classic Restoration Therapy intervention that is highly effective in moving the client to connect with his or her pain, and take an empowered position to give him or herself a truthful and emotionally regulating message. The focus of this intervention is to primarily use imagery to help the client focus on different choices concerning his or her identity and give him or her the power to provide safety, taking the position of a parent to him or herself. This case example is a continuation of a later session of the previous case concerning the man who was having difficulty getting his work done in a timely fashion.

Therapist: (Speaking very slowly). Close your eyes and take a deep breath. (Pause as client takes a deep breath). As if you are watching a movie, I want you to visualize that eighth grade English class exactly as you remember it on that day that your teacher made those hurtful remarks.

(Pause). Notice how the desks were arranged (Pause), where your peers were sitting and where you were sitting (Pause), where your teacher stood …

Man:	All I can see is my eighth grade self sitting at the very front of the classroom. My teacher is right in front of him and my peers are sitting behind him and laughing. He feels so alone ...
Therapist:	(Pause). As you see that eighth grade boy at the front of the classroom, can you make yourself be inside of him?
Man:	Yes, even right now, my face feels hot and my heart feels like it's somewhere at the bottom of my stomach. It's like that worthless feeling is just washing over me from behind. (Pause). I also feel stuck because there is nothing I can do to measure up to expectations.
Therapist:	(Pause). Now, I want you to watch as your adult self as you are now entering the classroom. (Pause). I want you to make yourself be inside your adult self. Looking at that eighth grade you, knowing that he feels worthless, alone, and like he can't measure up, and knowing that you have the power to speak into those feelings. (Pause). What is the message you want to give him?
Man:	(Pause). I would say to him ...
Therapist:	Say it to him directly.
Man:	(Long pause). You're going to be okay. It's difficult now, but things get better.
Therapist:	How does he feel when he hears that statement from you?
Man:	(Pause). He doesn't feel any better. He doesn't want advice.
Therapist:	(Pause). Yes, I think you're right. I want you to tell him what you want him to know about who he is and how he is empowered, knowing that he feels alone, worthless, and like he can never measure up.
Man:	(Pause as his eyes well with tears). You are not only not worthless, you are a prize. And you are very capable ... when a task is difficult, you are empowered to figure it out.
Therapist:	(Pause). He is a prize. (Pause). He is capable and is empowered to figure it out. (Pause). And how do you want to speak to him knowing that he feels alone?
Man:	(Pause). I just want to get down on his level and look him in the eyes and tell him that he belongs.
Therapist:	(Long pause and in a quieter soft voice). Give that a try right now.
Man:	(Comes off the couch and crouches down on the floor while crying). Buddy, you belong.
Therapist:	(Pause). Say it again.
Man:	(Pause and takes a deep breath). You belong.

Therapist:	One more time … really slow it down.
Man:	(Long pause). You belong.
Therapist:	So he is a prize, he is capable and empowered, and he belongs. Can you say those truths to him one more time?
Man:	(Pause). You are a prize, you are capable and empowered, and you belong.

In this example, we see the client able to speak truth about his feelings from an empowered and responsible position. Of course, as clinicians we can never guarantee the success of an intervention, but this particular intervention was successful in part because the therapist was directive and persistent in having the client speak directly to his child self and pressing the client to give a message about his identity and sense of safety with emotionally regulating truth that specifically addressed his feelings of being worthless, unable to measure up, and alone. Notice that the clinician also made ample use of pausing, vocal tone, volume shifts, and repetition. All of these elements work together to support the success of an intervention. Also, while the therapist may have a loose plan as to how the interventions will go, it is crucial that the therapist stays present in the moment and attunes to the opportunities the client gives him or her. For example, the therapist may not have planned to have the client engage in a sculpting exercise by having him get on the floor in a crouched stance and speak to his eighth grade self. But because the therapist was present and alert to potential opportunities, she was able to make the intervention more powerful by using what was live in the moment when the client brought his own ideas to the therapeutic process.

The re-parenting intervention allows the client to speak truth to successive targets that usually begin with a child and end with speaking the truth to their current selves. If it appears that a client may have difficulty connecting to his or her own self as a child or if the client has a particularly close connection with a child in his or her life, the therapist may choose to begin this re-parenting intervention with that child first before moving to self. In this particular case, the therapist chose to begin the process of helping the man to claim his truth by having him speak directly to his eighth grade self. The primary reason for this choice was the fact that the man had already described this vivid moment in eighth grade in which he felt the pain he routinely experiences. In this description, it was clear the man would likely be able to make emotional connection with his eighth grade self during the intervention.

Most people are able to emotionally connect with the image of themselves as a child and are willing to take an empowered position to give themselves a truthful message about their identity and safety. The task becomes more difficult when the client is asked to give their adult self this same message. Often clients will hesitate and make statements like, "I should know better now," or "I was just a kid but I've made so many mistakes since then." Here, it is important that the therapist challenge the client toward taking an empowered position in the here-and-now. Often it is helpful to create an experience around the client giving his or her adult self a message of truth as well. This can be accomplished through a variety of simple exercises such as having the client look in the mirror or looking at a recent picture of him or herself. In this next section of the case example, the therapist moves the man from speaking truth to his eighth grade self to saying this truth to himself in the here-and-now.

Therapist:	You have grown and matured in many ways since you were in eighth grade, but you have identified that you carry the same feelings of being alone, worthless, and unable to measure up even today. I want you to stand up and look at yourself in the mirror. (Client complies and is standing in front of mirror on wall in therapist's office). (Pause). Knowing that the man staring back at you often feels alone, worthless, and unable to measure up, what is the message you want to give *him* about those feelings?
Man:	(Pause). The same thing is true about him that was true about me in eighth grade. It doesn't feel like it all the time, but I know those things are true.
Therapist:	(Pause). Say the truth to the man in the mirror.
Man:	You are a prize. You are capable and empowered. And you belong.
Therapist:	(Pause). (Voice is slow and volume is low). Take a deep breath. Say it again and this time slow it down.
Man:	(Pause and takes a deep breath). You are a prize. (Pause). You are capable and empowered. (Pause). You belong.
Therapist:	Now, turn toward me and say that about yourself.
Man:	(Pause and then smiles). I am a prize. I am capable and empowered. I belong
Therapist:	You mentioned in the previous exercise that your face felt hot and that your heart felt like it was in your stomach. How do you feel now?
Man:	(Pause). I feel totally relaxed. I can breathe and I just feel at ease.
Therapist:	(Pause). Good. What is your body saying to you now?
Man:	That I am a prize. I am capable and empowered. And I belong.

Speaking the truth in the here-and-now is an important step in helping the client to be able to claim the truth in the midst of challenging and even painful situations. Many clients will struggle to have as much compassion for their adult selves as they do for their child selves. But once again, the therapist must be directive and persistent for the client to be able to connect with his or her pain and claim the truth.

Taking Action and Moving to the Peace Cycle

Once the client has strengthened him or herself with the truth about his or her identity and safety, he or she must ask how he or she wants to live differently in light of this truth. When a client is stabilized in truth, it begins to open up new possibilities in terms of his or her behavior. The client is able to experience a sense of rest and fulfillment as his or her pain has been answered with the truth. Here, they can experience true peace in the sense of the Hebrew concept of *shalom*. When the individual is at peace, there is a fulfillment and rest with the absence of pressing need.

You will recall that when human beings are caught in pain, they react and their behavior tends toward a flight or fight reactive response. The peace that results from emotional regulation allows the individual to be at rest. There is no need for reactivity because identity and safety are not threatened. The individual is able to choose his or her behavior rationally and intentionally. Instead of the mid-brain being in the driver's seat when there is stress due to pain, the prefrontal cortex is now driving and has the freedom to choose actions that are constructive, loving, and trustworthy (Hargrave & Pfitzer, 2011). When the client is able to emotionally regulate and embody the truth, he or she is able to exercise agency in taking action to nurture others, value self, engage in relationships that balance give and take, and reliably connect with relationships. Just as there was a pain chart delineating the flow of how dysregulated identity and safety prompt the individual to take reactive or coping actions that violate love and trustworthiness, so also is there a corresponding peace chart that illustrates how the flow of peaceful identity gives rise to constructive and agency driven actions. The peace chart is illustrated in Figure 2.1.

Notice how this chart contrasts with the pain chart presented in Chapter 1 (Figures 1.1 and 1.2). Blame, shame, control, and escape do not occur in a client's life because the client is an inherently bad person. These reactions take place as an attempt to survive and protect him or herself from pain related to his or her identity and sense of safety. When human beings feel pain, they don't react in a painful manner because it is their desire or intention to be destructive they simply cope destructively because they are attempting to survive their pain and their brains are accustomed to coping in this particular

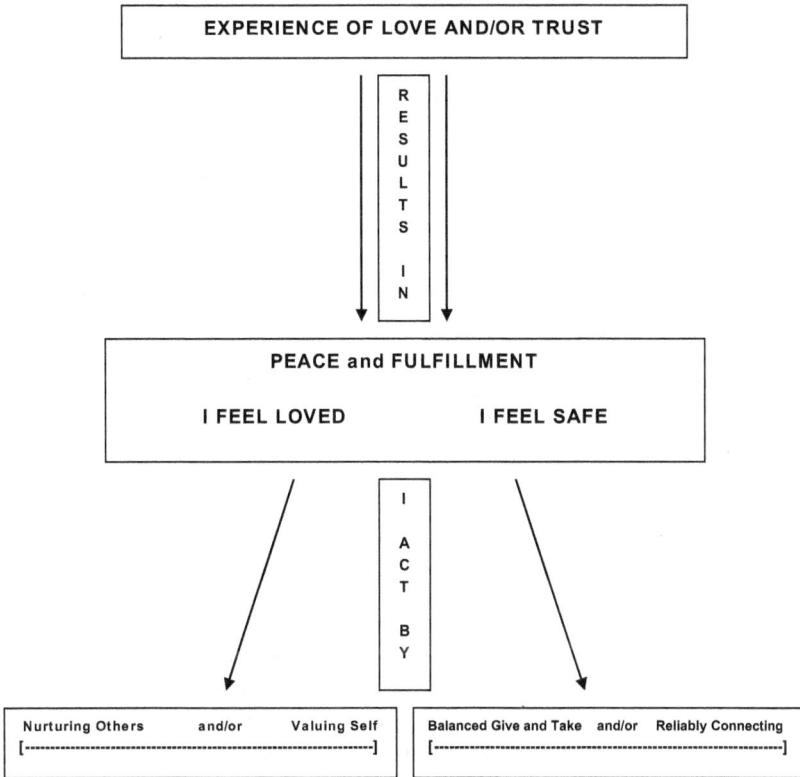

Figure 2.1 Illustration of Peace Chart and Agency Actions

manner. However, it is essential to point out that while we do not believe people are bad and intentionally destructive, the reactivity that comes from the pain is nonetheless both destructive to the individual's sense of identity and safety and also the senses of identity and safety with whom the individual relates. Violations of love and trustworthiness, no matter how understandable given a person's background and resulting identity and sense of safety, *victimize the sense of self and others in relationships* (Hargrave & Zasowski, 2016). This is a hard reality, but a reality that we as therapists and our clients must face when we are tempted to excuse a client from his or her responsibility in the intergenerational exchange of relationships (Hargrave & Pfitzer, 2003).

The peace chart in Figure 2.1, however, offers a different option. When a client is able to claim the truth that he or she is loved, valued, and unique and he or she is able to acknowledge the ways in which he or she is safe and empowered, the client can make different choices in his or her behavior. Here, the client is free to nurture, value self, engage in balanced give and

Table 2.2 Clinical Descriptions of Behaviors Relating to Nurture, Valuing Self, Balanced Give and Take, and Reliably Connecting

Nurture	Valuing self	Balanced give and take	Reliably connecting
Loving	Values Self	Balanced in Giving	Responsible
Encouraging	Respects Self	Balanced in Receiving	Reliable
Accepting	Positive	Vulnerable	Self-controlled
Supportive	Humble	Open	Connected
Inclusive	Optimistic	Engaging	Intimate
Kind	Hopeful	Appreciative	Faithful
Listening	Self-aware	Imperfect	Forthcoming
Patient	Confident	Relaxed	Problem Solving
Compassionate	Other Focused	Spontaneous	Planning
		Lets Things Go	Honest

take, and reliably connect with others. As with pain, clients describe nurture, valuing self, balanced give and take, and reliable connection with a variety of descriptors. These descriptions of behaviors are found in Table 2.2.

It is important to note that change is difficult. Choosing to live differently is a decision that takes effort and is not necessarily a choice the client will suddenly feel like making. However, knowing the truth, he or she is able to make a constructive decision to move toward integrating change in primary emotions as well as behaviors. With practice, one decision at a time, this choice becomes an easier decision to make.

Nurture

When a client is in pain and, thus, in a reactive state, he or she will have a tendency to cope in one, two, three, or all four ways listed above. Some clients will have the tendency to blame others, responding to situations and other people in an aggressive, retaliatory, or punishing manner. However, when a client is able to claim the truth about their pain, they can respond with peace. For someone with a blaming coping behavior in their pain cycle, this will look like nurture toward others.

Obviously, nurture can cover a myriad of connecting behaviors, but we tend to focus on three practical behaviors when we consider the ways in which a client can move toward nurture. First, making the choice to be nurturing means that one can consider the thoughts and feelings of the other and take the time to *listen* to those thoughts and feelings. This behavior communicates that the other individual is a priority and has ideas and feelings that are worth listening to. Listening also offers a gift to the other person in that it provides the opportunity for that person to understand him or herself better (Kieffer, 1977). This behavior creates an environment where new ideas can form and problems can be further clarified as both seek to discuss the issue as a team. But even if no problems are solved and no point of clarity is reached, the listener is acting in a nurturing manner simply by giving the other person a chance to be heard. Of course listening involves other behaviors as well. For example, it is important that listening is not a multi-tasking activity. The recipient should be the only focus of the listener's time. Also, eye contact reassures the other person that the listener is giving his or her undivided attention to the conversation (Hargrave & Pfitzer, 2011).

Another practical step that is included in a nurturing response is being *encouraging*. Encouragement can take a variety of forms. Often, this can look like affirming the very thing that someone most desires to do. We once worked with a client who was a pastor of a local church. During one of the sessions, the client told a story about how one of her parishioners approached her after the service and thanked her for her wisdom and told her that her words made such a difference in a challenging situation she had been facing. These words of encouragement were both affirming and motivating to keep doing the work the client felt called to do. It is equally encouraging when a client is able to name something true about someone's identity (Hargrave & Hargrave, 2015). Statements like, "You are a gift in my life," or "I would choose you again and again," speak volumes to the person being encouraged about who he or she is and the value he or she holds in another's life.

A third practical way of communicating nurture is acceptance. Acceptance says, "I know you and I am with you." Accepting the other person is a statement of commitment that no matter what pain has taken place or what action has been left undone, there is both understanding and a commitment to staying and working it through.

Here, it is important to point out that acceptance is not the same as approval. Acceptance speaks to another's identity. This is not the same as approval as all human beings react in ways that are unattractive and disconnecting. But even if the behavior is not worthy of approval, acceptance communicates patience, compassion, and loyalty to the other. Acceptance speaks to the heart of a person's identity and is key in nurturing.

Valuing Self

As with all reactivity to pain, shame and blame represent more of what a person *does* than of what a person *feels* (Hargrave & Pfitzer, 2011).

Although it is clear that both shame and blame do have secondary emotional features and these emotions can be felt physiologically and observed by others, they are features of reactivity to the primary emotions stemming from identity and safety and are not primary emotions in and of themselves. Therefore, the therapist always must be aware to separate out these reactive emotions from primary emotions. The therapist is wise to always ask, "What is driving or adding fuel to this emotion I am observing?" For instance, when a person shames him or herself, it is usually being fueled by a sense of being unloved, incapable, or alone. The shame reactivity is driven by the primary emotions (Hargrave & Pfitzer, 2011).

Those who are emotionally dysregulated in their identity or sense of safety and react by shaming themselves experience great difficulty in seeing possibilities of self-worth. Instead, the shaming behavior keeps them trapped in hopelessness and powerlessness. Shame is a particularly toxic reaction as it affirms the painful lies about a person's identity. When a mistake is made where an individual feels incompetent, it is easy for him or her to react in shame and to pronounce him or herself as inadequate or even, worthless. In turn, when this person is unable to take responsibility for his or her own pain and longs for this affirmation to come from someone else, his or her feelings of being unloved are reinforced every time another person fails to recognize him or her or say the exact right thing to make him or her feel better. If, however, a person is able claim the truth about their identity and sense of safety, he or she will begin to create the possibility of meaningfully valuing him or herself and taking responsibility to take a positive and empowered position in his or her environment.

Few people would ever speak openly to others about how they are inadequate, worthless, and unlovable. But a shamer does not hesitate to give him or herself these painful messages either verbally or silently on a consistent basis as he or she moves about the tasks in the day.

The first step, therefore, one can take toward valuing him or herself is to commit to saying nothing to him or herself that he or she would not share in the presence of someone else.

Another tendency for shamers is to only listen to feedback that matches the negative messages that play in their own minds and hearts. Therefore, an essential element to valuing self is making a choice to take in affirmation from others. But just like one needs to take responsibility for telling him or herself the truth, agency is also an important element in valuing self.

Valuing self requires that a client take intentional steps to nurture him or herself. This includes naming gifts and talents and being willing to see personal strengths. When a client makes the decision to self-value, he or she is willing to prioritize his or her own needs when it comes to how he or she spends time and how to take care of him or herself with proper nutrition, exercise, and sleep habits. In addition, valuing self makes time for activities that are life-giving and not simply tasks driven by the needs of others or the pressures to be better, do more, or try harder. Valuing self does not mean that one is blind to areas of growth. In fact, someone who is able to value self is able to look at his or her growth areas and hear constructive criticism and not take it as an opportunity to assault his or her own identity and sense of worth.

Balance of Give and Take

When a person who typically controls in his or her pain is at peace, he or she is able to offer a balance of give and take to relationships instead. A person who has adopted the reactive tendency of control is essentially committing to self-dependence and self-reliance. In pain, controllers are absolutely unwilling to place their fates in the hands of others' actions or reputation. The controlling reaction is essentially saying, "No one can be trusted and I am much better off on my own." In the event that they are forced to depend on someone else, a controller will likely manage the other person's decisions and behavior toward his or her own will and desires. Thus, the controller is unable to be vulnerable when they are in pain and refuses to engage in an interdependent relationship (Hargrave & Pfitzer, 2003).

On the other hand, a person who has claimed the truth about his or her identity and sense of safety is able to respond with a balance of give and take. Here, the person is able to be vulnerable and depend on others recognizing that he or she cannot do everything in a relationship and that he or she must be willing to make room for the relational partner to do his or her part. Also, this person is able to acknowledge that his or her ideas may not always be the best ideas and others might have thoughts with merit that should be included in the discussion (Hargrave & Hargrave, 2015).

An assumption that one must recognize as true in moving from control to a balance of give and take is that human beings need others to thrive, and even survive. One cannot function healthfully and completely independently of relational partners. Controllers will try to function alone minimizing their risks, but it is by nature a very unfulfilling and lonely life style. Moving toward a balance of give and take gives a client who tends to control the chance to recognize others' gifts and talents and to look for opportunities to depend on the strengths of others (Hargrave & Stoever, 2010).

A balance of give and take also gives the client the opportunity to focus on what he or she is empowered to do instead of what he or she would like to control, but cannot. Controllers often use perfectionism as a means of trying to protect themselves from unwanted circumstances. But of course, there is only so much they are empowered to do and even with their best efforts perfection is not possible. Certainly, we would advocate a client giving their best effort, but even then, people will fall short and unwanted circumstances will occur (Hargrave & Pfitzer, 2011).

A practical step one can take in an effort to move toward a balance of give and take is to not only listen to others' ideas, but to actually follow through on their advice and desires. This will likely mean doing something that is outside an individual's personal preferences or routines. There is no guarantee as to how the situation will turn out. Taking this practical step, however, is a great exercise for a client to engage in in an effort to move toward this new behavior of employing a balance of give and take in relationships.

Reliably Connecting

Part of the human experience is coming to grips with the fact that no one gets through life without challenges or pain. At some point, everyone will encounter hardship. For some, a natural response to this pain is to check out somehow or escape from the problem or relationship. It can be easy for a person to convince him or herself that he or she just "can't take the stress," or "needs a break" and no one will be harmed by his or her choice to escape from connection and responsibility.

Like the other pain reactions, escape is certainly understandable, but it is decidedly not helpful and is destructive to the person and his or her relationships. People will often justify this reaction by saying things like, "I would only have exploded if I had stayed and, in the interest of everyone else, I thought it would be better if I removed myself." Also, a common statement is, "I'm not hurting anyone when I take a few drinks and come down from a hard day." But when our clients make statements like this, we as clinicians need to be ready to challenge the assumption that escaping is not a destructive coping behavior. Escape does not lead to emotionally regulating pain, it simply numbs pain in an irresponsible way (Hargrave & Pfitzer, 2011).

There are three primary problems with coping reactivity related to escape. First, the escape or withdrawal tends to form a habit quickly and can even become an addiction. Certainly, having a drink to take the edge off their pain can easily form a physical addiction. But we also know that activities like smartphones, social media, video games, and pornography can form strong psychological addictions that are just as damaging to one's relationship with self and others.

A second primary problem with escape is that the person who copes with their pain in this way becomes *reliably unreliable*. As clinicians, we know that building trust in a relationship requires stability and predictability. As human beings, we need someone to show up eight to nine times out of ten in order to trust them (Hargrave & Pfitzer, 2011). Choosing to disconnect in pain ensures that the necessary component of trust in a relationship will not be properly built.

Finally, withdrawing and escaping fosters a passive approach to life, making it next to impossible for a person to take responsibility for his or her life decisions and to own the direction of his or her life path. This behavior usually results in chaos, which brings harm to the individual as well as his or her relationships.

So, the question for our clients who cope with their pain by escaping becomes, "How will you remain engaged and connected even in the most painful of circumstances?" When a person is able to be at peace and respond with reliable connection, he or she gives him or herself the gift of the confidence of knowing that he or she will see the problem through to the end and, eventually, there will be resolution. When a person chooses to escape in their pain, the relief is temporary. Staying connected might be challenging at first, but ultimately it results in a greater peace because issues and problems are resolved. Also, staying connected and committing to working through the issue at hand builds character through trustworthiness and reliability. Making attempts to avoid problems not only solves nothing, but no virtue is developed in the individual who chooses to escape. While life may be hard, great comfort can be taken in the fact that important growth, maturity, and virtue can come from committing to connection (Hargrave & Hargrave, 2015).

While pain is not a welcome visitor in people's lives, it is inevitable and it does offer the opportunity to grow and teach an individual if they are willing to see it and stay reliably connected. In a continuation of the case discussed in this chapter, you will recall that the man identified the truth that he is a prize, capable, and empowered, and he belongs. Here, the therapist utilizes the truth in the previous session to complete the behavioral agency actions that will make up his peace cycle.

Therapist: In your pain cycle, you have identified that you cope with the pain of feeling alone, worthless, and unable to measure up by shaming yourself and withdrawing to escape. (Client nods). You have also been able to tell yourself the truth that you are a prize, capable, and empowered, and that you belong. Knowing these truths, what is it that you would like to do differently?

Man: (Pause). When I shame myself, it's almost like I get really needy. I expect everyone else—mainly my boss—to tell me the things I long to hear and it only makes me feel disappointed and more ashamed when they criticize me or say nothing at all. I now realize that I can give myself the message that I wish someone

	else would give me. When I shut down, the problem doesn't go away, it just builds. I would like to do a better job of sticking with the problem until it's solved.
Therapist:	In what ways do you have the power to give yourself a message of value and stick with the problem?
Man:	I can take care of myself and love myself instead of indirectly asking my boss to do this with his approval. I will also stop staying up all night and skipping meals to prove myself. I can take better care of myself. I can also remain engaged in the project and ask questions when I need help instead of shutting down and hoping it will go away.
Therapist:	(Pause). What will these actions look like this week at work?
Man:	Even if I make a mistake or get corrected by my boss, I will tell myself that I am prized, capable, and empowered, and that I belong. I want to start giving myself the message that I wish my teacher had given me all those years ago. Also, I will do what I am empowered to do and ask questions and ask for help when I need it.
Therapist:	And how will you stay reliably connected and "stick with the problem" this week?
Man:	I can already think of a question that I need to ask a colleague in order to finish my current project. I've been avoiding sending the email. It's all drafted up and ready to go but I haven't been able to send it.
Therapist:	How are you feeling right now when you think about sending that email?
Man:	(Pause). I'll be honest, I am feeling worthless for having to ask the question and I'm questioning whether or not I belong in this job. I feel alone.
Therapist:	And what is it that you normally do when you feel worthless and alone?
Man:	I shame myself and withdraw to escape.
Therapist:	What is the message you want to give yourself about those feelings right now?
Man:	(Pause). I am a prize. And I belong.
Therapist:	Knowing that these statements are true about you no matter what happens, what would you like to do instead of shaming myself and withdrawing to escape?
Man:	I will remind myself of the truth and send the email.
Therapist:	(Pause). Would you be willing to do that right now?
Man:	Here? Now?
Therapist:	Yes

Man: Okay … (Client pulls out his phone and hits send).

Therapist: How do you feel?

Man: (Pause). I still feel those feelings but I know that I am a prize and I belong no matter what happens. It feels good to not listen to the feelings.

In this section of the case example, the therapist moves the client to not only own the truth, but to identify and act upon new behavior. When a therapist sees a chance to help the client practice the new behavior in the here-and-now, he or she is wise to take that opportunity as it allows the client to practice the very behavior he or she hopes to do outside of session. Rather than simply talking about what the man might do after session, it was much more powerful when the therapist was able to help the man regulate the emotion he was having in the moment, and ultimately take the action to send the email in session.

Also, while the client does not yet have the language to articulate the process of moving from the pain cycle to the peace cycle, the therapist walked the client through the steps of identifying the pain cycle and making a different choice with the peace cycle. This gives the client practice with the mindfulness practice of the four steps.

The Peace Cycle

Having claimed the truth about his or her identity and sense of safety, and having identified his or her new behavior, the client now has what is needed to make the cognitive map of the peace cycle. Once again, it is essential that the client's new behavior be articulated in language he or she will resonate with effectively. Ideally, the client is able to produce his or her own language for what he or she would do differently. But in the event that the therapist employs conjecture to help the client name the new behavior, the client must own the language as his or her own. Often, the new behavior will not be phrased as simply nurture, valuing self, balanced give and take, and reliable connection or even as the behaviors described in Table 2.2. Instead clients might use phrases like, "celebrate my strengths" or "collaborate." In these cases, it is important for the therapist not to be rigid with the particular word but rather be pragmatic in observing and reasoning the truth of the statement and the veracity of the new behavior (Hargrave & Pfitzer, 2011).

Like the pain cycle, it is absolutely essential that the peace cycle be written down in front of the client and referred to again and again, both in session and between sessions. As discussed in Chapter 3, the pain and peace cycles are essential in the process of organizing, sequencing, summarizing, and structuring possibilities for change. Clinicians may choose to keep handouts of

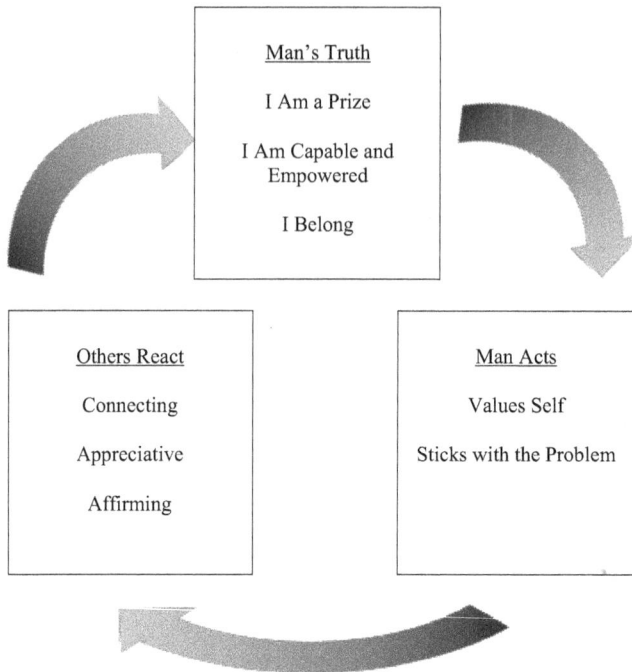

```
                    Man's Truth

                    I Am a Prize

                    I Am Capable and
                    Empowered

                    I Belong


    Others React                        Man Acts

    Connecting                          Values Self

    Appreciative                        Sticks with the Problem

    Affirming
```

Figure 2.2 Case Example of Man's Peace Cycle

pain and peace cycles for therapy sessions or write the cycle on a white board or poster to refer to during session. In the case above, the man's peace cycle in Figure 2.2 was organized and written down to be placed beside his pain cycle in all subsequent sessions.

The peace cycle is meant to describe how a client feels and acts when he or she is at peace and serves as a map for the path forward. The client is now about to not only be able to recognize his or her unique pain cycle, but also to take responsibility to *change* through the cognitive map of the peace cycle.

A Summation About the Practice of the Four Steps

Chapter 6 is dedicated to the findings and work of the four steps, but for readers who are new to the Restoration Therapy approach, it is worth a mention in this context in order to round out the four things we do in Restoration Therapy. We first identify the pain cycle as we did in Chapter 1. In this chapter, we have discussed fully the concepts of identifying the client's emotionally regulating truth, and now we move that truth along with agency behaviors to identity the peace cycle of the client. When the therapist has these contrasting cognitive maps, he or she is ready for the fourth objective in the restoration process of mindfully practicing with the client the four steps.

The purpose behind the four steps is to help the client with a mindfulness tool to be able—even in the midst of emotional dysregulation—to move him or herself from the pain cycle to the peace cycle. As a reminder, these four steps are: 1) Say what you feel; 2) Say what you normally do; 3) Say the truth; and, 4) Say what you will do differently. We must admit that these four steps, like many mindfulness exercises, seem obvious and simplistic. Yet, clinically time and time again we see how they are effective in moving clients to gain the leverage needed to emotionally regulate and put a stop to unloving and untrustworthy actions. It is essential, however, to realize that these four steps take time for the client to successfully integrate into behavioral change. Like the case example above, the four steps start in the therapy room where the therapist touches on the four steps while helping the client give a response to each directive. For instance, "When you think about sending the email, how do you feel?" Eventually the therapist will help the client learn the four steps for him or herself and utilize them in the context of between session work. Further, as the client becomes more proficient at recognizing his or her emotional dysregulation, he or she will eventually become able to transition from pain cycle feeling and reactivity to the peace cycle truths and agency actions. The point is that the mindfulness that comes from the four steps is about a process that takes time to integrate (Hargrave & Hargrave, 2015).

The first step is about the client saying out loud how he or she is actually feeling in the pain cycle. Often, the client will make statements in response like, "I feel angry" or "I feel frustrated" or "I feel like leaving." It is essential for the therapist to recognize that these types of phrases are representative of what the client is *doing* or how he or she is *reacting*. It may be true that the client is angry, but the reality is that these secondary emotions and reactivity are being pushed by the primary emotions. It is important in the first step for the client to name what is actually happening in the primary emotions in order to organize to change the dysregulation (Hargrave & Hargrave, 2015). In reality, the first step is about *actualizing* or the client becoming cognitively aware of the feelings connected to identity and safety (Hargrave & Pfitzer, 2011).

In the second step, the client is dealing with what he or she normally does when feeling the identified pain. In reality, it is about predicting his or her behavior. Saying what you normally do. When clients have the courage to name what they do in terms of coping with their primary emotions, they are actually predicting what they would do if left unchecked. Clients know well the problems and turmoil caused by their own reactivity, they are actually naming their own destructive tendencies. In naming the destructive tendencies out loud, they actually lessen the chance of repeating the unloving and untrustworthy behavior. It is no longer semi-automatic reactivity, it is reactivity that they are mindful of and they recognize the potential consequences of the actions (Hargrave & Pfitzer, 2011).

The third step in the mindfulness process of the four steps is to say the truth. As this chapter well illustrates, when the client actively rejects the dysregulated emotions and beliefs about self and safety and instead focuses on the hopefulness and positive aspects of identity and safety, it infiltrates the brain enabling it to counter semi-automatic responses and regulate faulty beliefs and emotions. It is important, as we have stated before, that stating the truth is not denying the existence of the pain cycle; it simply means the client puts his or her cognitive and empowered self in charge of finding more constructive and beneficial alternatives (Hargrave & Hargrave, 2015).

Finally in the fourth step of this mindfulness practice, the therapist is helping the client first name a behavior of agency based on the primary emotions or a self-regulating truth. As a result, the client is now able to embody those named behaviors into actual actions. In turn, these actions— because they are both loving and trustworthy—reinforce the emotionally regulated truths. As mentioned before, as the therapist looks for and actually encourages these actions in the here-and-now, the more efficient and proficient the client becomes in utilizing the power of the four steps.

Part 2

Advances, Techniques, and Interventions

3 Organization, Sequence, and Structure

We all are aware that clients get stuck in the tangle of their personalities, problems, and relationships. It is indeed a natural and frustrating process for clients as sometimes they cannot verbalize effectively what they feel, nor make sense of their situations and behaviors. But it is just as common for the therapist to get lost or stuck in therapy. Perhaps it is very simple issues like being unable to ask questions that clients can understand. Maybe it is because the therapist him or herself has been dysregulated by something the client has said or done. Perhaps it is because the client is so fast and verbally proficient that the therapist not only cannot keep up with the content, but cannot find a place in the session to get in a word edgewise. Maybe it is because the client is so absent or low in terms of affect that he or she gives little to no response in the session and it feels like floundering. Perhaps it is because the therapist "takes the bait" of something in the content that actually has little or nothing to do with the reason the client came to therapy in the first place.

As therapists, we often get lost because we do not know or understand enough about the backgrounds, pain, or situations of the clients we are trying to help. We become overwhelmed by so much trauma or emotional turmoil or even the complexity of client problems. Many times, as therapists, these problems simply do not look solvable and even when we see hope or answers, we become baffled by our clients being unable to take even simple steps toward change and the resolution of issues. It is easy to get lost in the client story and process and *all therapists* have this experience at one time or another. The question is not about whether we get lost in therapy with clients, rather the question is, "How do we get back on track?"

First, if we are to get back on track, it is important for us to remember that the reasons our clients get stuck or lost is exactly the same reasons we often get lost or stuck. It may appear to be easy to make sense of someone else and his or her feelings, but it is sometimes very difficult for us to make sense of our selves. We all have experienced those times when we do exactly the things that we tell our clients *not* to do or to avoid. We all have been in that situation of being overwhelmed by our issues and problems. In short, we are human just as our clients are human. Being in touch with our own humanity is essential if we are going to stay in touch with the humanity of our client. Awareness of how difficult it actually is to process emotion, make constructive changes in behaviors, and believe the best about ourselves is a prerequisite to working with these same issues in our clients. When we are in touch with our own humanity, we will find it much easier to be patient, understanding, empathetic, and connecting with the humanity of our clients. We may still get stuck in the content from time to time, but we will be able to be present and helpful to the people we desire to help most (Hargrave & Pfitzer, 2011).

Second, if we are going to get back on track with being lost or stuck with our clients, we must be able to find the natural rhythm of therapy. We believe there is a natural weave that clients feel between their beliefs about their identities and senses of safety and their behavioral actions. The ability to connect with the pain in the narrative of the client and then be able to see and understand how that pain flows into the client's reactivity and coping and vice versa is essential if we are going to make the process understandable for ourselves as therapists and understandable for our clients. As Hargrave and Pfitzer (2011) relate, the weave of good therapy in general and Restoration Therapy specifically is the ability to move between two ends of an ellipse. At one end, the therapist must always have connection with the narrative of the client and his or her pain and, at the other end, the therapist must be cognizant of how this pain has played out in the life of the client through his or her action be it destructive, reactive, or constructive and agency driven. If the therapist is going to get on track after being lost, he or she will have to be willing to repeatedly explore both ends of the ellipse. In actively helping the client connect with and explore these two oscillating extremes, the therapist will then assist the client to make movement and gain insight.

The Client Story

Many clinicians believe that the therapeutic work can begin once they understand a client's story. As restoration therapists, we agree that learning a client's story can provide essential information for later therapeutic work. However, we also believe that interventions actually begin in the *process* of understanding a client's story. In other words, how we listen and engage with a client in the early phases of therapy can be just as therapeutic as the interventions we might employ in later sessions. Utilizing wise interventions as the therapist seeks to understand the client's story is crucial in building a strong foundation for the therapeutic process. We have come to realize that as we oscillate from one end of the ellipse to the other as mentioned above, this process is best accomplished through *organization, sequence,* and *structure.*

In order for a client to connect with the therapist and properly engage with the therapeutic process, they must feel that their story is being listened to and understood. As restoration therapists, however, we believe that while a client's story is certainly significant, it is not the most important element when it comes to understanding a client. We believe that most of our understanding of a client is gleaned from the specific messages a client has internalized about his or her identity and sense of safety, the behaviors he or she adopted in order to survive those primary emotions, and the nature of his or her behaviors when interacting in relationships. While the content of a client's story can certainly be useful to the therapist in setting up a variety of different types of interventions, the wise therapist must use organization, sequence, and structure to keep him or herself focused on process, rather than content.

Organization

In listening to a client's story, it is important to not only empathize and reflect the content of the client's story, but also to *organize* the story in terms of messages the client received about his or her identity and sense of safety. Clearly, this is of benefit to both the client and the therapist. When the therapist is disciplined about organizing the client's story, the client is able to not only understand the relationships and events in his or her life in terms of what happened, but also to gain insight into the messages he or she internalized about their personal identity and sense of safety in the environment. Questions that are designed to organize are aimed at the heart of the primary emotions. Here, the client is able to begin to understand not only what took place, but also the feelings they carry as a result of those painful events in his or her life. The benefit of these organizing questions around identity and safety is that clients actually experience the questions and listening as *empathetic connection*. In other words, these questions are not placed in the context of an interrogation or interview, but in the context of the therapist empathetically listening. The questions serve as a method for the client to make deeper and more meaningful connection with his or her narrative. But most importantly, the organization provides the client with a clearer understanding of the *impact* of his or her story on his or her life. A list of these types of organizing questions are found in Table 3.1. Although this list should be helpful to therapists, it is neither complete or exhaustive. Moreover, the therapist should utilize these types of questions within the context of listening to and empathizing with the stories the client relates regarding his or her past or present relationships.

Organization also benefits the therapist as it orients the therapist to where he or she is and protects him or her against getting lost in the details of the

Table 3.1 Questions Helpful in Organizing Client Narratives

- What did this (violation) say about you?
- How did you know you were loved in the home that you grew up in?
- How did you know you were safe in the family you grew up in?
- How did this (violation) make you feel about yourself?
- What did this violation say about relationships or how you must behave?
- What did you have to do (as a child) to make sure things were safe?
- What did you learn about being a man/woman from your parents?
- Can you recall a time when your parents stood up for you or took care of you emotionally?
- What were the rules you followed to make that relationship work?

content in a client's story. Organization keeps the therapist focused to appropriately chase the pain. As the client shares the painful relational dynamics and situations in his or her life, the wise therapist is alert to any opportunity to understand how the client processed the events in terms of identity and safety.

In order to specifically and accurately identity a client's primary emotions, the therapist must be strategic in his or her questions. Questions that are phrased in non-specific language such as, "How does that make you feel?" might yield a specific primary emotion from the client, but will most likely result in a general answer like, "bad," or "not good," which does not provide the therapist with any insight into how the client experienced the event in terms of identity and safety. On the other hand, specific questions with language that is targeted to clarify a client's story around issues of identity and safety, are more likely to result in specific, primary emotions, that serve in appropriately organizing the client's story.

Consider the following example. A 38-year-old female who suffered from severe anxiety was prompted to seek therapy. Early in the therapeutic work, the therapist learned the woman grew up with a father who was an alcoholic and would often and unpredictably go into a blind rage for no apparent reason. Notice here how the therapist utilizes organization in one of the early sessions.

Therapist: Last session, you mentioned to me that you struggle to feel "at ease" in your environment, even when in a place where you are quite familiar. How did you know you were safe in the home you grew up in?

Woman: Safe? I was never safe. Well … at least it didn't feel that way. My dad was an alcoholic when I was growing up and my little sister and I never knew what we were going to get when he walked through the door. He would either explode in anger and start throwing things or he would keep to himself. We just never knew what we were going to get.

Therapist: I can only imagine how painful this situation was for you. (Pause). What did your father's anger and the lack of predictability you experienced teach you about relationships and how you must behave?

Woman: I learned that there was nothing I could do to impact my environment and that even if the house was calm, it was only a matter of time before it would become unsafe.

Therapist: What message did this give you about who you are or your environment when you were in this position?

Woman: There was just nothing I could do ... nothing to do but wait for it to get bad. I felt so exposed.

Therapist: When you say that there was nothing you could do and you never knew when it would be unsafe and that you felt exposed, it sounds like the situation taught you that you were powerless and vulnerable. Am I getting that right?

Woman: Yes, exactly.

Therapist: What were the rules you followed to make this relationship work?

Woman: When the situation was calm, I did absolutely nothing to rock the boat. I was as quiet and as perfect as possible. When the situation became violent, I never argued and just disappeared into my room at my first opportunity.

Therapist: So, you learned to please in an attempt to avoid chaos, and never argue or state your own opinions for fear of making the anger worse. And when it inevitably did get worse, you escaped to your room at your first opportunity?

Woman: (Client nods). Yes.

Therapist: Where was your mother in this picture?

Woman: (Looks down and pauses). She would just stand there. She never even made an effort to stop him or make sure we were out of the line of fire.

Therapist: What did her lack of action say about you and your situation?

Woman: I felt even more vulnerable. (Pause). I also felt like I wasn't important enough to stand up for—like I didn't matter enough to her for her to sacrifice her own safety.

Therapist: Her actions gave you the message that you were vulnerable and that you didn't matter?

Woman: (Client nods with tears in her eyes).

Therapist: When I reflect on the stories that you have shared with me and the relational dynamics in the family you grew up in that you have described, it seems like the messages you have carried with you are that you are powerless, vulnerable, and that you don't matter.

Woman: Yes, I think so. I've never thought about it that way before. Thinking about my childhood has always felt like one big painful mess, but I think that's right—those are the main feelings I carried then and those are actually the feelings I feel most often now.

In this example, the woman provides more detail around the situation she faced in her family growing up. While it might have been easy for the therapist to get lost in the content of the many stories the woman could tell about the pain she felt about her father's unpredictability and mother's lack of action growing up, the therapist remained disciplined in not only empathizing with her story, but organizing her story in terms of identity and safety. Questions like, "What did this say about you?" and "What were the rules you followed growing up to make this relationship work?" specifically target primary emotion and help to ground both the client and the therapist.

Also, notice that the therapist was intentional in repeating phrases the woman had used to keep the question focused. For example, when the therapist was asking about how the woman's mother's behavior impacted her emotionally, the therapist asked, "What did your mother's lack of action say about you and your situation?" rather than simply saying, "What did feel about what your mother didn't do?" The difference may seem subtle, but specific language helps to keep both the client and therapist focused on process instead of content.

You will see that each of these questions is aimed at understanding the message a client internalized about his or her identity and sense of safety. Also, every one of these questions will provide the therapist with a much better chance of understanding a client's primary emotion than a more general question like, "How does that make you feel?"

The Use of Conjecture

There will be times when a therapist may choose to use conjecture in order to help a client name a primary emotion for which he or she is struggling to find the language. However, the therapist must be careful about when and how conjecture is employed. In the example above, we see the therapist use conjecture when the woman was sharing about how there was nothing she could do and she never knew when the situation was going to become unsafe. Here, there was enough specific information for the therapist to name "powerless" and "vulnerable" as primary emotions the client may have been feeling. She did this by repeating the phrases the client had used, using conjecture to name the primary emotion and leaving room for the client to decide if these words best described how she was feeling in the moment. Overwhelmingly, if the therapist names a primary emotion using conjecture that is not quite on the mark, the client will disagree, be quiet, or passively agree without conviction. When this occurs, the therapist gives more time and space to the client in thinking about the primary emotion he or she does feel.

In this case, the therapist's use of conjecture was helpful to the client, but the therapist must be careful and prudent about how and when this intervention is utilized. When the therapist's goal is to identify the client's primary emotion in terms of identity and sense of safety, it is easy for the therapist to become anxious or frustrated if the client struggles to articulate their pain. Then, the therapist will be tempted to use conjecture inappropriately by guessing. There may be a fine line between conjecture and guessing, but the distinction is important. Therapeutic conjecture seeks to simplify and name primary emotion based on reasonable evidence revealed in the narrative that the client might be experiencing a specific feeling. Guessing usually takes place when the client is unable to articulate how he or she feels, and the therapist begins naming a wide range of emotions in the hope that one of them will resonate. While tempting at times, this habit will be unhelpful in organizing a client's story and will likely lead to difficulties later in the therapeutic work. Proper organization lays a strong foundation for the therapist and client to identify the client's unique pain cycle and serves as a helpful technique in ensuring that the rest of the therapeutic work is targeting and regulating the appropriate pain.

Sequence

In addition to organizing a client's story in terms of the primary emotions they experienced as a result of violations of love and trust, the therapist must ensure that the events, feelings, and reactions to those feelings are sequenced. In other words, the therapist must not only understand the messages a client internalized about their identity and sense of safety, but he or she must also understand the reactive behaviors a client employs to survive this pain. In sequencing, the therapist partners with the client in understanding the event that took place, the feelings that resulted, the reactive behavior the client uses to cope, and other relational partners' responses to the client's reactive behavior.

Understanding this sequence helps both the client and the therapist track the cyclical patterns that take place when a client experiences pain. Sequencing

Table 3.2 Questions Helpful in Sequencing Client Feelings and Reactive Coping

- When you find yourself doing those things, what feelings drive the behavior?
  - What do you normally do when you have that feeling about yourself or relationships?
    - How do others react to you when you react in that manner?
  - When others react in that way, how do you feel about yourself or how do you feel about relationships?

certainly benefits the client as he or she feels empathized with and gains insight into the underlying patterns of their behavior. Many clients will report during this type of sequencing that they often experience understanding themselves at a new level for the first time. Clients know there is some type of pattern to their behaviors, but usually are unable to track those behaviors back into the primary emotions. When the client hears the therapist accurately sequence primary emotions and reactive behavior as well as the relational reactions of partners, he or she gains insight into and mindfulness of the previously unarticulated pattern. Also, when the therapist utilizes sequencing, he or she prevents him or herself from getting lost in the content of the client's story. At this point, the therapist must not be afraid to interrupt the client, slow down, repeat elements of the content that the client is sharing, and ask for clarification where necessary. This can be accomplished through statements like, "Let me slow you down a bit to see if I understand" or "Let me repeat this back to you to make sure I have it right." These statements allow the therapist to remain in control of the pace and help to keep him or her grounded in process instead of content. Some questions that are helpful to therapists in sequencing client feelings, reactive coping, and the way others react to the client are found in Table 3.2. Again, this listing is not complete or exhaustive.

The following example is a therapeutic example of how this sequencing takes place. This session is with a young woman who is a junior at college where she has a rigorous academic load in engineering. She sought therapy because of her experience of anxiety and depression that plagued her at college. This section of the case example is from the fourth session.

Woman:	This week has been really bad. It's like I can't stop working even when the work is finished. I pull unnecessary all-nighters, I feel guilty if I do anything that most people would consider "fun." And yesterday, I felt so anxious before my exam and could barely calm myself down enough to take it.
Therapist:	(Pause). It does sound like it has been a really difficult week. (Pause). When you find yourself pulling all-nighters, working

longer than necessary and getting anxious, what feelings drive this behavior?

Woman: I'm just so terrified I am going to be a failure. I hate feeling disappointed and when I do, it's like I automatically feel like I'm not good enough and that I don't have what it takes to be an engineer.

Therapist: So when you experience disappointment, you feel like a failure and that you are not good enough. (Client nods and therapist pauses). Can you tell me about the first time you can remember feeling this way?

Woman: (Pause). Yes ... I had a speech competition in sixth grade. I had worked really hard to write and memorize my speech. Right before I went on stage, my coach pulled me aside and said, "We need a win. Don't let us down."

Therapist: (Pause). What did those words say about who you were or communicate to you about your situation?

Woman: (Long pause). The message I heard was that I have to perform perfectly to be good enough and that if I didn't perform, I would be a failure. That message was pretty consistent in that relationship.

Therapist: (Pause). I can understand how you would feel those things. (Pause). What did you find yourself doing when you felt afraid that you would not be good enough or might be a failure?

Woman: I made every effort to be absolutely perfect. But in doing so, I had no emotion and it was like no one was connecting with what I was saying in the audience. The speech did not go well, so I ended up feeling like a failure and not good enough anyway.

Therapist: (Pause). And what did you find yourself doing with those feelings?

Woman: I just beat myself up internally and out loud to my coach. (Pause). I guess there was a part of me that felt like if I was hard on myself, my coach would be nice to me.

Therapist: (Pause). So when you were beating yourself and shaming yourself for your performance, how did your coach react to this behavior?

Woman: (Long pause). Not how I was hoping. He was just really quiet.

Therapist: When he reacted with silence, how did you feel about yourself?

Woman: (Pause). Again, like I wasn't good enough and that I was a failure. His silence felt like his way of agreeing with the shaming statements I was making.

Therapist:	(Pause). Let me just repeat this back to you, to make sure I have this right. When you feel afraid that you are not good enough, you perform and become perfectionistic. (Client nods). And when you engage in this performance behavior, others appear to have difficulty connecting with you. When you experience this reaction, you feel like a failure and usually beat yourself up. (Pause and client nods). And when you shame yourself, you usually don't get the affirmation you are hoping for, which confirms the very feelings you were trying to avoid in the first place—that you are not good enough and a failure. (Pause). Am I understanding this correctly?
Woman:	Yes, that sounds right.
Therapist:	(Nodding). When you feel like a failure and that you are not good enough, what is it that you find yourself doing today?
Woman:	Pretty much the same thing. I try to perform perfectly.
Therapist:	(Pause). And how do people usually respond when you engage in that behavior in your life now?
Woman:	The same I think … they usually just end the conversation really quickly or stare at me blankly. And it doesn't seem like they really want to share anything about their own lives.
Therapist:	(Pause). And when they respond to you in this way, what is it that you feel about yourself or the relationship?
Woman:	(Long pause). I feel like I am a failure and I beat myself up even more.
Therapist:	So when you feel that you are not good enough, you cope by performing and becoming perfectionistic. And when this fails to work or others respond to you by disconnecting, you feel like a failure and shame yourself. And others' silence usually confirms for you that you are not good enough. Am I getting this right?
Woman:	(Pause). Yes, I think that pattern happens for me over and over again.

As the therapist sequences, she not only asks questions that organize the client's story around issues of identity and safety, but she also begins to understand the client's action tendencies that result from those primary emotions and how others respond to the client's reactive behavior. This line of questioning not only helps the client to understand his or her own destructive patterns, but also prevents the therapist from getting lost in the content of a client's story. In other words, sequencing keeps the therapist focused on the underlying patterns.

One other element that is important to note from the last case example is how the therapist not only sequences the client, but also consistently *summarizes* what the client says. We noticed this technique among emotionally focused therapy (EFT) therapists in the way they summarize often to assure the client that he or she is heard especially when the client is escalating with secondary and reactive emotions (Johnson, 2004). Although EFT uses the technique to provide a "safe and empathetic" figure for the escalated client, we also noticed that summary had the added benefit of tracking the client accurately and keeping the therapist organized and on point. Although similar to sequencing, we believe that frequent summarizations by the therapist sets the stage for both therapist and client to be focused on the task at hand. If the therapist finds him or herself confused or unsure, back-tracking to the summaries and sequencing the therapist is already aware of will most often put him or her back on track. One of our colleagues who is an EFT trainer is fond of saying, "Summary is a therapist's best friend." In terms of clarity and tracking the session well, we indeed do agree.

Working Forwards and Backwards

When sequencing, a therapist can ask questions that work forward and backwards to understand the sequence of feelings and behavior. As was the case with the above case example, clients will often report their behaviors before talking about the primary emotions that drive the behaviors. Here, the therapist can use what the client is reporting and take this opportunity to work backward and "chase the pain" toward understanding the primary emotion at the root of the behavior. The college woman from the preceding case example began the session by talking about the behaviors she recognized to be destructive and unhelpful in solving her feelings of anxiety. The therapist was able to repeat those behaviors back to her and ask about the feelings that drive them. Later in the example, the therapist worked in the forward direction by trying to understand how the woman coped when she feels not good enough or that she is a failure. Working in either direction can be helpful in establishing sequence.

Slowing Down

In using sequencing, it is essential for the therapist to be active throughout the session while listening to the client and to make sure that events, feelings, and reactions are sequenced. In the above example with the woman studying engineering, notice that the therapist did not hesitate to stop the client to be certain that she was accurately understanding the sequence of the client's primary emotion, the coping behaviors, and other responses to those

Table 3.3 Statements and Questions Helpful in Sequencing Client
Feelings and Reactive Coping

- Let me slow you down a bit to see if I understand.
- Let me repeat this back to you to make sure I have it.
- So here is what I understand so far …
- Did I get this correct?

behaviors. In this particular session, the therapist accomplished this through pausing her questions to reflect the sequence back to the client, helping the client to feel heard and understood and this in turn aided the therapist in understanding the feeling and coping patterns in which the client regularly engages. In doing this, the therapist also confirmed with the client that she was getting it right, leaving the client with ample opportunity to make corrections if necessary and to feel empathized with and understood.

It is also important to notice the woman is highly anxious and in the session she spoke very quickly initially. We often train therapists who are unwilling to interrupt a client while telling a story or making a point for fear they will offend the client. The problem is, however, that in many of these cases therapy becomes a monologue with the therapist only listening. Worse still, the client may run from one story and situation to the next and to the next and to the next, most often leaving the therapist unable to remember, much less to process the complex sequences expressed by the client. We often say to our trainees, "If you are not sequencing or summarizing what a client says every two to three minutes, you will become hopelessly lost and your client will become more disorganized." Therefore, it is essential for the therapist to interrupt the client often to ensure the therapist understands the narrative being discussed and the client remains organized. Slowing the client down is good for the client's brain (Hanna, 2014). In Table 3.3 there is a list of statements and questions that can assist a therapist to slow down the process in order for proper summarization and sequencing to take place.

Also, notice that the therapist used both an example from the client's past as well as an example from the client's present life to establish the feelings and behaviors as a pattern. This helps the client to see the fact that not only are his or her feelings and behaviors cyclical in nature, but also consistent across various painful situations. Sequencing is an intervention that lays the groundwork for the client to be able to recognize his or her agency when it comes to making choices about his or her pain. Often, clients were not empowered to make choices when they were young, but are absolutely empowered to make choices and changes in their current life circumstances. Sequencing helps the client and therapist to identify the pattern that the client will make choices about later in his or her therapeutic work.

Structure

Finally, as restoration therapists, we believe that it is not only important that the therapist organizes the client's story in terms of identity and safety and sequences the client's feelings and coping patterns, but also that the client is able to recognize his or her own primary emotions and coping patterns. This is accomplished through structure, which involves writing down the primary emotions and corresponding coping or reactivity that describes what the client does in pain. This written structure is what we call the pain cycle that you have already seen examples of in previous chapters. It serves as a tangible and essential tool for both the client and the therapist to refer to throughout the therapeutic process because it: 1) Provides both the client and therapist with an organizing tool; 2) Provides both the client and therapist with an easy reference in which to understand the current narrative or situations; and 3) Provides a cognitive map that enables insight, contrast, and understanding to the client. It is essential to remember that once a pain cycle forms with an individual, it tends to persist over time and characterizes the feelings and coping behaviors of the client in the overwhelming majority of situations when the client is emotionally dysregulated.

The following case illustration demonstrates how structure can solidify the work of organization and sequence for the client. The client is a 42-year-old Caucasian male who grew up in a military family and his father's position required that he and his family move approximately every two years. Notice here how the therapist uses organization, sequence, and structure in working with the man during an early session of the therapy.

Therapist:	Last session, you mentioned to me that you moved around a lot growing up …
Man:	Yes, my dad worked with the military so it kind of came with the territory.
Therapist:	(Nodding). How did this element of your dad's job leave you feeling about yourself or your circumstances?
Man:	Well, it was really tough being the new kid all the time. I felt no one knew me. (Pause). I was on the outside and constantly looking for ways to belong.
Therapist:	I can understand how you would feel unknown. Help me understand how you felt about yourself or your situation when you were on the outside.
Man:	(Pause and then tears up). I just felt like I never belonged. It's not that the other kids weren't nice most of the time. It's just hard to constantly be the new kid and try to grow friendships that fit in with what the other kids have shared for a long time.

Therapist:	That makes sense to me. So the feelings you carried around growing up were that you felt unknown, and that you didn't belong. What did these feelings teach you about how you must behave?
Man:	I was constantly scanning the crowd for what was required to fit in and connect ... I was desperate to please the other kids so I could feel connected as quickly as possible. I guess I felt disconnected. (Pause). What's strange is that on the one hand, I was desperate to connect with people in my new environment. And on the other hand, I never felt secure in my relationships because I never knew when we would have to move again. Sometimes I would ask myself, "What's the point?"
Therapist:	So when you felt unknown, and that you didn't belong, you learned to please in hopes of connecting quickly.
Man:	(Client nods). Yeah ... (Hesitating) ... I can't say it was the best thing to do ...
Therapist:	How did people respond to you when you were eager to please?
Man:	Most of them were nice enough but I could tell many of the kids just didn't know what to do with my intensity when I was in that pleasing mode so they just avoided me.
Therapist:	I see. And when the other kids avoided you, what message did that send you about your identity or your environment?
Man:	I felt pretty rejected.
Therapist:	(Pause). I can easily see how you would feel that way. What did you find yourself doing to survive that feeling?
Man:	(Pause). I would isolate myself a lot ...
Therapist:	What is it that you were looking for when you would isolate?
Man:	(Pause). I'm not exactly sure but I can remember being really hard on myself and beating myself up a lot. I think there was a part of me that wanted someone to come looking for me too. I would kind of sulk to make people want to come and talk to me. It's not like I was super aware of that but looking back now, I can see that's what I was doing.
Therapist:	It sounds like you shamed yourself and would withdraw to sulk or pout when you felt rejected.
Man:	Yeah, that sounds about right.
Therapist:	How did others respond to you when you were withdrawn and shaming yourself?
Man:	Sometimes someone would try to come and talk to me but most of the time they just let me go.

Therapist:	(Pause). And what message did that send you about your identity and sense of safety when others would just let you go?
Man:	Right where I started. Totally unknown and like I didn't belong.
Therapist:	So let me pause here and just make sure I have this correct. (Taking out a piece of paper and pen to write and draw the pain cycle in front of client. This pain cycle is seen in Figure 3.1).
	When you felt unknown and that you didn't belong, you would please. And this pleasing behavior would often cause others to avoid you, leaving you feeling rejected. And when you felt rejected, you would withdraw to sulk and shame yourself. And when others let you go, it reinforced your feelings of being unknown and that you don't belong. Am I getting this right?
Man:	(Looking at the pain cycle the therapist had drawn in front of him). Yes! You just described my childhood in a nutshell. I had never really put words to it before but this is totally what was going on all the time in my relationships with my peers.

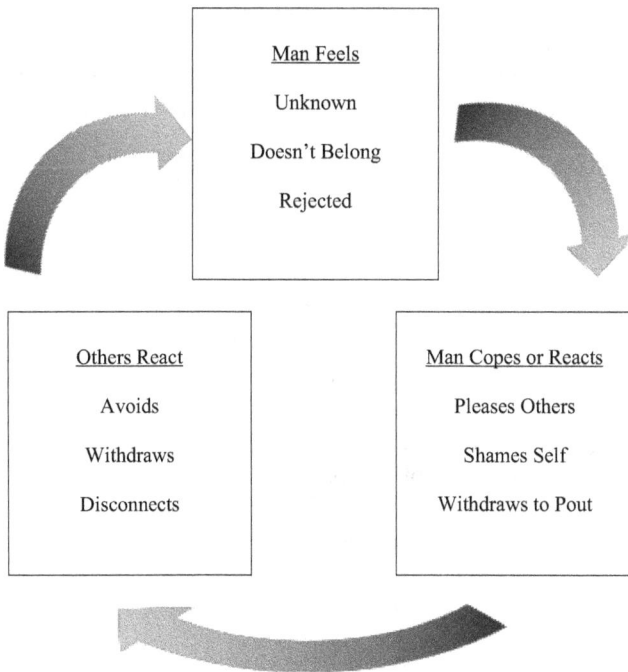

Man Feels

Unknown

Doesn't Belong

Rejected

Others React

Avoids

Withdraws

Disconnects

Man Copes or Reacts

Pleases Others

Shames Self

Withdraws to Pout

Figure 3.1 Case Example of Man's Pain Cycle

Therapist:	Tell me how you see this pain cycle playing out in your life today.
Man:	(Pausing). I have a really good relationship with my wife and kids and I wouldn't say this happens often, but when we do have conflict or go through a painful circumstance, I can see how I contribute to it by engaging in this cycle.
Therapist:	Tell me about the last time you recognize that this cycle was in play with your family.
Man:	I travel for work sometimes and two weeks ago, I was gone for five days. I call every night and talk to everyone in my family, but obviously they share experiences and time together without me when I travel. Sitting here right now, I know this isn't true but in those moments of hearing everyone laughing on the other end of the phone sometimes leaves me feeling like I don't belong. Also, they don't have a lot of context for what I do all day and it's hard to explain so it's easy for me to feel unknown.
Therapist:	So the situation touched the feelings of being unknown and not belonging. (Client nods). What did you find yourself doing to cope with these feelings?
Man:	(Laughing). I became super dad on the phone! I was asking a million questions and making all of these fun plans without consulting my wife first. Thinking about it now and looking at this pain cycle (Pointing to the pain cycle) I can see that I was totally in pleasing mode.
Therapist:	And how did your family respond to you when you were in "pleasing mode."
Man:	The kids kind of went silent and my wife understandably felt disconnected because I hadn't included her in any of the plans I was randomly trying to please everyone with.
Therapist:	And when your wife and kids responded to you by withdrawing and disconnecting, how did you feel about you?
Man:	I definitely felt rejected.
Therapist:	What did you find yourself doing with that feeling?
Man:	I quickly got off the phone and just sort of moped around my hotel room hoping my wife would call, and feeling sorry for myself and criticizing myself for not having a job that didn't involve travel.
Therapist:	(Nodding). How did your family respond?
Man:	(Pause). They didn't call.
Therapist:	(Pause). And what message did you internalize about who you are?

Man:	It just reinforced my feelings of being unknown and not belonging.
Therapist:	(Pointing to pain cycle in front of client). So again, when you feel unknown and that you don't belong, you cope by pleasing others. This behavior tends to lead to others disconnecting from you in some way, leaving you feeling rejected. And when you feel rejected, you tend to withdraw to pout and shame yourself. When you do this, others tend to just give up and let you go, which reinforces the feelings of being unknown and like you don't belong. Am I getting this right?
Man:	Yep, this is exactly right.

Structuring the Peace Cycle

Not only is structuring the client's pain essential to the therapeutic process, but as RT therapists, we believe it is equally important to structure the healing work and growth that takes place during the therapeutic process. In other words, it is crucial to structure the client's cyclical patterns when he or she is in pain *and* when he or she is at peace. To illustrate this, let's skip ahead in our work with the man in the last case example to understand how the therapist uses these same techniques to structure the peace cycle.

Therapist:	We have been talking a lot about how your feelings of being unknown, not belonging, and rejected often led you to please others, withdraw to pout, and to shame yourself. Tell me about a time when you were able to do something different with those feelings—a time when you were able to reach out and persevere in the midst of feeling like you were on the outside.
Man:	(Pausing to think). Middle school lunch was particularly awful when it came to feeling excluded. Most of the kids had been going to school together since kindergarten and sat at the same tables with all the same people every day. My family also moved to that town in November so I started attending that school three months into the year, which didn't help.
Therapist:	I can imagine that was difficult for you and triggered all of those feelings in your pain cycle. What did you do that was different?
Man:	(Nodding). Well there was one day when I was a little late to lunch so everyone had already sat down at their tables. I don't know what came over me but all of the sudden I had this courage to walk up to a table of 11 boys that were already sitting together and I asked if I could join them.

| Therapist: | As someone who tended to withdraw and shame yourself in your pain, that must have felt really different. |
| Man: | It did … it's like all of the sudden I decided that I was worthy of belonging and that gave me the confidence to reach out and connect instead of waiting and hoping that someone else would do that for me. |

At this point in time, the therapist used an intervention called, "Stronger, Wiser, Best Self," which we will explore in greater detail in Chapter 4. However, for the purpose of this chapter, it is important to identify the truths and new actions that the client was able to identify as a result of that intervention. In addressing the pain of feeling unknown, not belonging, and rejected, the client was able to claim the truth that he is known, worthy of belonging, and embraced. Knowing these truths, the client was able to name new and different actions that included staying relaxed, remaining engaged, and valuing himself. Once these truths and new actions were identified, the therapist was in a position to use repetition, summary, and structure to solidify the ideas of Kyle's peace cycle.

Therapist:	So, when you are able to claim the truth that you are known, and worthy of belonging, you are able to relax instead of going into pleasing mode, correct?
Man:	(Nodding). Yes.
Therapist:	How do others tend to respond when you are more relaxed and able to be yourself?
Man:	I think they feel more relaxed too. I'm more approachable and it seems to put others at ease. I think they are more inclined to reach out and be inclusive too.
Therapist:	(Nodding). When others are at ease around you, what message does that feed you in terms of your identity and safety?
Man:	That I am embraced.
Therapist:	And when you know you are embraced, what do you do differently than withdrawing to pout and shaming yourself?
Man:	(Pause). I stay engaged in whatever conversation or activity is going on and I treat myself like I am a person of worth.
Therapist:	So, when you know you are embraced, you stay engaged and you value yourself?
Man:	Yes, exactly.
Therapist:	How do others tend to respond to you when you stay engaged in the conversation and value yourself?
Man:	They tend to be more interested in what I have to say … they ask me more questions about my life, which makes me feel known and worthy of belonging.

Therapist:	Yes, I can imagine that it would! If for some reason others did not embrace you or take an interest in getting to know you, what would be true about you?
Man:	(Pause). Well it would still hurt … but I guess others' treatment of me doesn't change the truth.
Therapist:	Truth that you are … ?
Man:	Known, worthy of belonging, and embraced.
Therapist:	And when you know this is true, what will you choose to do?
Man:	Relax, stay engaged, and value myself.
Therapist:	(Charting peace cycle with pen and paper in front of client. This peace cycle is found in Figure 3.2).
	Let me repeat this back to you just to make sure we have it correct. When you are able to claim the truth that you are known and worthy of belonging, you are able to choose to relax. Here, others typically respond by being more at ease when they are with you, which makes it easy for you to claim the truth that you are embraced and can choose to stay engaged and self-value. When you take these actions, you often find that people are interested in getting to know you, which

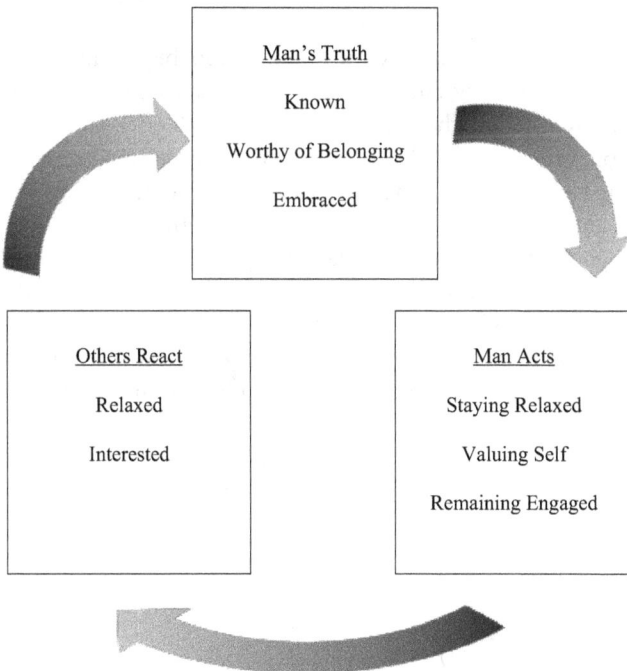

Figure 3.2 Case Example of Man's Peace Cycle

	understandably leads you back to the truth that you are known and worthy of belonging. (Pointing to peace cycle). Does this look like an accurate picture of you and your interactions when you are at peace?
Man:	Yes. Absolutely.

Notice that during this last segment of the session the therapist included others' reactions in the sequence to highlight the patterns in the man's interactions with others. However, the therapist then moves to challenge the man to take responsibility for telling himself the truth and choosing the new behavior *regardless of what other people do.* As restoration therapists, we are always seeking to challenge people toward self-regulation. It is important to recognize, however, that a client's ability to claim the truth and choose new behavior is not dependent on receiving a desired response from others. Although, when a person is living in his or her peace cycle, it is indeed more likely that he or she will receive more connecting responses from others.

The peace cycle serves as a corresponding structure to refer to throughout the therapeutic process. We believe that not only is it important to provide a visual resource for how a client feels and behaves when they are in pain, but also to give the client a visual for the truth he or she wants to claim and the actions he or she chooses—a map for the way forward into a more peaceful and connecting way of living.

As we stated earlier, therapeutic intervention begins in the process of gathering a client's story and narrative. Organization, sequence, and structure are the restoration therapist's basic building blocks of this therapeutic intervention. Organizing a client's story around issues of identity and safety, sequencing feeling and coping patterns, and structuring this information with the pain cycle and peace cycle will serve both the client and therapist well throughout the therapeutic relationship. The late poet and friend, b. f. maiz would often speak to therapists and say, "All good poetry is therapeutic and therefore, all good therapy should be poetic." As the therapist learns the skills of weaving primary emotions to behavior and back again, it turns into a beautiful and poetic tapestry of the client's identity and safety as well as the potential of both.

4   Interventions to Identify Truth and Expand Emotional Regulation

I am a person (Terry) who is actually brave enough to admit I am a bad driver! When I was younger, I used to think to myself, "No, I really am a good driver and I have just had some unlucky breaks while out on the road." But as the evidence mounted, I had to take a hard look at the facts: 13 wrecks and "fender benders" for which I was solely responsible; 14 moving violations while driving; being dropped by my insurance company twice; countless "near misses" where I ran a red light, stop sign, or barely missed another crash because of my inattention to the road. I was a bad driver and finally faced the fact about 25 years ago. I came to a couple of thoughtful conclusions about why I had all these "unlucky" breaks: I traveled too fast and followed other cars way too close. Now I will not say I am a good driver because I am still a bit inattentive behind the wheel (besides, I do not wish to tempt any fate), but I can say that after slowing down my speed significantly and creating more distance between me and other cars, I have not had a wreck since making the adjustments 25 years ago. I clearly recognized the problem and finally took the responsibility necessary. But most importantly, I made the adjustments habitual and solutions *regulated* the causes of my driving problems.

The second objective in the Restoration Therapy Model is to help the client identify and experience a regulating emotion to the pain that he or she feels. In Restoration Therapy, we call this regulating emotion the truth. When we say the truth, it is not some objective perspective or particular philosophy we therapists are rigid about the validity of which we try to convince clients, rather is very much a truth we co-construct with the client in order to have a *useful alternative* to the painful primary emotions they have carried and practiced in their lives for many years. While almost all clients and therapists have an appreciation for hearing the narrative or story of the pain and then mindfully bringing that pain into a coherent and organized map of understanding emotions and client reactivity, the focus of regulating emotions is very much on the perspective of *change* and *responsibility* for future client actions. This is essentially difficult and work that is not nearly as popular as understanding pain. Why is this so? Most of us who practice this approach therapeutically recognize that we are asking the client to do something that requires skills and effort. In other words, we are not just therapeutically understanding the client, we are putting him or her in the position to make a difference in his or her own life and the lives of people with whom he or she has relationships.

A Different Perspective

My colleagues and I who have practiced Restoration Therapy for many years will heartily say that this element of the truth as a regulating emotion to the pain is the most difficult therapeutic objective to attain. There are several elements that make this so. First, most clients have not appreciated the power from which they have learned their basic identities and senses of safety. Powerful people programmed our clients from the beginning of their lives through the way they loved and acted in a trustworthy manner toward these individuals who we now see in our offices. As infants and very young children, our clients simply never had the prefrontal cortex insight to be aware of how their identities and senses of safety were being shaped by initial caregivers. As mentioned before, our caregivers were, in most cases, trying to do the best they could in giving us love and trustworthiness. But even the best caregivers were flawed with their own shortcomings of identity and safety to the point where their own reactivity got in the way of good parenting and a good environment of shaping and programing another human being with love and trustworthiness. In these cases of original programing, our clients simply did not have the choice to decide or influence their own senses of identity and safety and were left to assume that what they were taught and experienced was the final word on important identity questions regarding being loved, worthy, and belonging. As well, they did not have the cognitive ability to challenge the perspective of their caregivers with regard to their safety and questions of reliability, openness, and fairness. Because they thought the original programming regarding identity and safety was true, they were left to develop coping skills such as we have seen in the previous chapters regarding pain: blaming others, shaming self, controlling situations and relationships, or escaping pain by disconnecting and evolving into chaos.

But it is not only the caregivers who did this type of programing with our clients. As children and adolescents, many of the individuals we see in therapy were also shaped by the powerful forces of their peers and others such as teachers, coaches, and people who were considered to be mentors. In many cases, a good number of clients we see actually had very good—despite being imperfect—programming of identity and safety from caregivers and family. But the power of the peer group, teacher, or mentor was able to influence identity just as much as the original caregivers. Imagine a coach who demanded the underling perform and win every time or the music teacher who insisted on absolute perfection when playing any piece for a performance or competition. It is not hard to see how these types of expectations from individuals our clients presumed were powerful could easily influence senses of identity and safety. Even with our clients' advancing ages and cognitive development, it is not unusual at all for these misguided power moves on the parts of other powerful people to have gone unchecked by our clients. Most often, they simply assumed these people had the right to speak into their identity and sense of safety without being challenged. As a result, unhealthy programming given by those other people our clients considered powerful led to the same type of coping and reactivity that caused not only injury to themselves, but also their relationships. For instance, the following is from a session with a 28-year-old client who was seeking help with an eating disorder.

Woman: Actually, I think of my parents as doing a reasonable enough job in loving me when I was little. I always felt valued and prized—like I was the most important thing in their lives. Those years as a child were really happy for me.

Therapist: It sounds like your parents went out of their ways to make sure you felt nurtured and loved and those things tend to build healthy identity. Was there a time when that began to change for you?

Woman: (Long pause). Things started to unravel for me when I was in the sixth grade. I was a target for this group of "mean girls." (Long pause). Every day one of them would comment on something about me like what I was wearing, my body shape, my athletic ability, and even what I ate at lunch. They would make—(Long pause and begins to cry)—these snorting noises like a pig every time they were around me or every time the attention was on me. It was devastating.

Therapist: (Long pause). I can see how it was devastating. To feel and hear that kind of bullying and targeting had to devastate your sense of being okay, valued, and prized and certainly made you feel unsafe.

Woman: (Nods).

Therapist: (Long pause). After receiving so much damaging feedback about what you were wearing, your body shape and even what you ate, how did you survive?

Woman: For a long time, I just tried to disappear and lay low. But after about a year, it was proved to be impossible. So, I started

	dressing more like them, acted like I wasn't talented at athletics, and stopped eating.
Therapist:	So it sounds like these modifications you made—dressing, stifling your ability, and eating very little—made you kind of disappear by becoming like them.
Woman:	(Long pause while looking down). Yes, that is right. I became so good at it that I really became part of their group after about 18 months.
Therapist:	Makes a lot of sense that you would do all these things to protect yourself.
Woman:	I protected myself, but I also lost myself. When I look back, before that year was the last time I felt safe and knew who I was.

There is a third possibility that is powerful enough to program our identities and senses of safety. This is the impact of trauma. It is essential to remember the therapist is not the one who determines whether the severity of an interaction or relationship qualifies as being traumatic. It is the client's perception of the occurrence or interaction and especially the impact of the event on the client's identity or sense of safety that determines whether or not there is trauma (Hargrave & Zasowski, 2016). It is clear, however, trauma does produce disturbances in normal functioning for clients and these can be interpreted as flaws in identity or safety the client is unable or uninformed about challenging. We will discuss more about trauma in the next chapter, but for now suffice it to say traumatic occurrences can be a powerful force in shaping identity and safety.

There is a second reason the truth or the regulating emotion to the pain of identity and safety is difficult to achieve in therapy. Many clients believe this deficiency in knowing the regulating emotion of identity and safety can only be achieved by someone acting to regulate their own pain by either acting in a loving or trustworthy manner. This perception most commonly comes from attachment theory (Bowlby, 1988) where the child looks toward their attachment figure to regulate fears, sadness, and injustices in a loving and reliable way. While most restoration therapists are greatly appreciative of attachment theory and see exactly how it explains how caregivers provide love and trustworthiness in shaping identity and safety with children, many clients will see this need extending to adult relationships where significant others should supply emotionally regulating love and trustworthiness when there is pain to the sense of identity or safety. Certainly, there are appropriate times where adult to adult nurturing is appropriate. In the Restoration Therapy Model, however, we would see helping clients, especially adults, to become *self-regulating* emotionally as an essential element. Although there are powerful people in clients' lives who are able to speak into their identities and senses of safety, frankly, as therapists, we find that most of these are simply not powerful enough to counteract the painful messages surrounding identity and safety from childhood caregivers, influenced adolescents, or vulnerable trauma victims.

Not all of this lack of power is because of the nature or position of relationship, but it is clear to us therapeutically that a spouse has difficulty giving to another spouse the love and trustworthiness that was flawed in a client's childhood (Hargrave & Pfitzer, 2011). The spouse is in a position of *partner*, rather than *parent*. This is especially true when a child tries to meet the identity and safety injury of the parent. Positionally, the child (like the spouse) simply does not have the power or the ability to shape the identity and sense of safety of the parent.

Primarily, however, others have limited ability to affect the painful dysregulated identity and sense of safety because it is difficult to have another person present each time a client feels threat. This reality often runs diametrically opposed to what many learn in a culture. When we feel depressed, confused, unloved, alone, chaotic, threatened, or fearful, we have come to rely on significant others to comfort, reassure, or connect with us to feel better about ourselves or our situations. From an attachment perspective, this framework looks at the client in need of an attachment figure or *safe haven* relationship (Johnson, 2004). Simply stated, instead of maintaining a position of *self-regulation,* we often crave and desire a position of *co-regulation.* At times, this kind of having others meet emotional needs is appropriate as we previously stated. It is, however, more difficult to imagine the efficacy of co regulation when there is also a cultural expectation on individual sufficiency, competency, and autonomy. If a client, for instance, was in a position of business where a superior was highly critical, blaming, and unsympathetic, it would put the client and their position in jeopardy to appear needy, hurt, or fearful. It would likely be unrealistic to have the client go to the superior and try and reason out the situation, clarify expectations, and have the superior co-regulate the emotions of the client. At the same time, it would likely be unrealistic to have a spouse or other safe haven relationship in a position to be present quickly enough to be able to counteract the statements and judgments of the superior because either the co-regulating partner would be limited by the amount of time or the context to present continued support. In the culture of work and adulthood, the client would be expected to be able to regulate him or herself enough to get back to work in a reasonable time frame, meet the expectations of the superior, or decide to leave the situation to seek other employment.

The truth or self-regulating emotion we are suggesting is most powerful in emotional regulation only occurs with immediate availability and sustained exposure. We often say that co-regulation has some strength in providing clients support and comfort and certainly it can provide relief from situations of threat and a sense of aloneness or incompetency, but there is a profound need for the individual to be able to regulate fears, beliefs about identity, and safety through self-resources. If these kinds of truths or self-regulating emotions are non-existent, then the client will run into the cultural limitation of society expecting him or her to act more fully as an adult and, therefore, he or she will become dysregulated by a sense of incompetency. Only when the individual is able to gain the depth of familiarity with his or her own sense of truths associated with identity and safety will he or she be able to mindfully practice the leverage needed to feel competent and confident in self and situation. Co-regulation and connection with safe haven relationships is nice and is good, but in the Restoration Therapy analysis of adulthood, it is most often insufficient to achieve a substantial anchor to guard against loss or threat to identity and sense of safety.

The Position of Power and Authority

In childhood when the sense of identity and safety is being formulated, shaped, and programmed, it makes perfect sense that we would focus on the caregiver of the child to have both the power and responsibility to infuse the child with love and trustworthiness. Caregivers have this remarkable power and authority with their children to be able to speak, act, and connect with those aspects of human elements that set us apart in almost all of biological life. Perhaps, these parents and caregivers maintain some of the power and authority to speak into the identity and safety of their offspring long past childhood and well into late adulthood (Hargrave & Pfitzer, 2003). There is definitely something about the position of parent and caregiver making the programming of love and trustworthiness applicable across the lifespan of the offspring. But at what age or time does the individual start to acquire this power and authority to command and program his or her own sense of identity and safety?

Let us be clear: We believe very strongly love and trustworthiness are relational components and are expressed, experienced, and reacted to in relationships. As such, identity and sense of safety are *relationally dependent*. As, however, human cognitive development occurs throughout childhood and adolescence, individuals are clearly *introjected* in their own minds the perceptions and thoughts of others (Jung & Long, 2018). In other words, as we are exposed to love and trustworthiness in relationships, we begin to cognitively construct our own psyche of identity and sense of safety according to what we see in the experiences, connections, and interactions of powerful relationships. Although caregivers are most often the epitome of power in shaping these psychic introjects for the individual—both positively and negatively—there are other powerful relationships in terms of peers or mentors as well as situations impacting the psychic introject.

In Restoration Therapy, we would maintain that along the cognitive development stage of *formal operations* (Singer & Revenson, 1996), the adolescent and emerging adult begins to think abstractly and, to some significant degree, develops the ability to think about his or her own process of thinking. He or she is able to analyze concepts such as sense of self and identity as part of his or her own perspective and is no longer specifically or exclusively tied to the concrete relationship with others. In short, the individual becomes equipped to start relating to him or herself as a person or being able to have a relationship with self. This relationship with self can be also both positive and negative in influence as the individual gains the power cognitively to become aware of identity and safety and critique issues of loving and trustworthy actions toward him or herself. Definitely it should be noted here that people progress into the formal operational stage of development at different ages with some precocious children exhibiting early signs of formal operations, while for others the characteristics emerge from the late teens to twenties. However, the balance of research indicates the majority of adults approaching age 30 display at least some significant aspects of formal operational or abstract thinking.

The point is, however, that most individual adults begin to have the power to relate to their own identity and senses of safety in both loving and trustworthy ways. The way I think about myself and my situation is not only under the control of what I have learned from my programming and introjects of the past, but can be molded and changed by the way that I think about and relate to myself in the present moment. I, and our clients, have the power to weigh in on identity and sense of safety as adults. It is not only our primary caregivers, mentors, teachers, and peers of the past nor even the situations of our experiences that dictate the current status of love and trustworthiness. Adults have the power to relate to themselves and shape the truths about their own identities and senses of safety.

But wielding power and relating to self with a sense of authority is a very different thing. For instance, my now adult children report back to me that I was a good father particularly in the areas of adoring them appropriately, taking interest in their personhoods, and providing them with a physically and emotionally safe environment. Although both of my children would report (as I would also) that I did not do the job of parenting perfectly, it is clear to them (and me) that I did far more right in the position of "father" than I did wrong. The reality is I was very intentional about fathering as I realized how essential the early stages of caregiving were and the continued influence I had in speaking into their hearts and minds concerning their identities and senses of safety. I sought to nurture every opportunity to build into their lives the beliefs they were unique, desirable, and worthy. Moreover, I strove to be predictable in my behavior, balanced in their experience of justice, and open without secrets. Apart from doing these things imperfectly, I know many of the things I tried to do landed successfully in their programming and they experience many of the benefits of clear identity and safety.

All this I did as a father to my two children all the while having a huge sense of inadequacy about my own worth and value and believing I was not up to the task of relationships a good part of the time. I gave to them what I was in desperate need of myself. How did I father well? I was given enough examples and knowledge to work at the process and as the process became habituated, I grew in my capacity to be loving and trustworthy. But the larger question is why would I not use my examples, knowledge, and growth by experience to give identity and safety to myself? Here is the difficulty with the dysregulating emotions concerning identity and safety that exist in the pain cycle. We become so acquainted and practiced with the process of faulty identity and lack of safety that we refuse to take the position of authority to utilize the power of love and trustworthiness on ourselves. My children are living examples that I used this power and authority to shape their identities and senses of safety, but I was unwilling or unaware enough to never take this position with myself. I suspect that when it comes to our clients, it is very much more often the case that they are unaware that they have this power and authority to treat themselves in a loving and trustworthy manner. They continue to live in the pain cycle of the past because they are unaware that they have the power and authority to do something different that is *self-regulating*. Is it any wonder that as a society we have pinned our hope of improving our faulty identities or lack of safety on the hope that someone—anyone—will come and *co-regulate* the emotions that cause us so much pain? And some people who do love us will often step forward and tell us the truth about ourselves—that we are deeply loved, worthy, and belong and they are there for us—but not nearly as often as we repeat the old messages to ourselves of pain about our faulty identities and safety. If we are to truly emotionally regulate our pain cycle, we must become empowered by our own authority to speak the truth about love and trustworthiness *to ourselves*.

Parents are powerful in that they are the original programmers of our identities and sense of safety. Others are powerful in the mentorship, closeness, belonging, and influence they have exerted in our lives. Even our spirituality is powerful in communicating values about our identities and safety. But as we enter late adolescence and adulthood, we as individuals become the most powerful purveyors of our identity and sense of safety. This is not true because others are weak or unwilling to love us or be trustworthy, but rather that the self is able to actively reject outright any messages that do not fit with current psyche or schema. This reality is tied to the emotional and cognitive bind of past introjects and the repeated influences of experiences in current relationships. Because we are habituated to our old view and painful views of self and relationships, we are sensitized to look for those situations where people do unloving or untrustworthy things that confirm our previous biases toward our identity and safety (Hanna, 2014). What we look for, we tend to find as even our closest friends and companions are not perfect and will do and say things that confirm our deeply held beliefs about self and safety. For example, take the following discussion with a 41-year-old male in discussing his work situation.

Man:	It feels like I can never do or be enough in any situation at work. I work hard and go above and beyond, but they continue to just ask for more and more from me. I can never get ahead. And then when I pull back just a little, I get thrown under the bus by my boss.
Therapist:	You work and work and excel at what you do, but it seems that it never counts for anything, but in fact results in more work and higher expectations. The moment you cut yourself some slack, then someone is there to criticize you. Am I getting it right?
Man:	(Nods).
Therapist:	(Pause). It sounds like a terribly unsafe environment for you. (Long pause). Tell me about the feedback you get from your boss and the things he says.
Man:	He actually knows that I am one of his top performers and tells me so. He says things like I make his job much easier and he counts on me. He does reward me, but the better I do, the more he piles on. Then when I don't do something the way he wants it, he is always there to tell me what I should have done.
Therapist:	(Pause). So it sounds like you get much in the way of positive feedback, but even the positive feedback results in higher expectations. And when you do something that is not in line with his expectations, that is when you get the negative feedback.
Man:	It is not so much negative feedback as it is correction to meet what he had in mind.
Therapist:	I see. So in terms of positive feedback to negative, what would you say the percentage is that you get from your boss?
Man:	Probably 98 percent to 2.

| *Therapist:* | But if I hear you correctly, the positive feedback puts you in a position to have to perform more and so it feels like that no matter the message from your boss, you can't do enough to measure up. |
| *Man:* | That's right. If you just look at it from the outside, it looks like I get all this positive feedback and advancement, but it always leaves me with the feeling that I have to do more and I can never measure up. |

Here you see the quandary of the current relationship. Actually, the man receives much in the way of accolades and rewards and many would interpret the additional responsibilities as a recognition of good work. This man, however, came from a family with a truly unrelenting father by demanding perfection in school, athletics, and career. He still carries the message and programming of his father in his psyche and schema. Even if his boss tries to give an overwhelming positive message, the man consistently looks for the behaviors or situations that confirm his pre-existing belief about the relationship—mainly that there are expectations which he can never meet and the correction is a judgment that he has failed. Perhaps the boss is like the man's father, but more likely the boss would be surprised to find out that the man feels he can never meet expectations and the situation feels unsafe and unfair. The verbal accolades and positive feedback from the boss are rejected by the man and, instead, he looks for the messages and actions which confirm his pain concerning his identity and safety in the relationship.

We believe in adulthood, the self is the most important voice in accepting or rejecting messages about identity and safety. As a result, the adult or emerging adult self is in a unique position to formulate loving and trustworthy actions concerning identity and safety. The reason we state this regulating emotion as the "truth" is, first, it gives clients an active contrast and clarity of choice from the emotions that exist in the pain cycle. As a result, by stating the truth about his or her choice about identity and safety the client is directly challenging the old psyche and schema in the most powerful manner possible. But even further, we believe that human beings have more intrinsic values than just being a social construction of meaning or action. In other words, humans have value in and of themselves which make them loveable, valuable, and worthy of belonging (Buber, 1958; Rogers, 1961). Further, we believe there is an innate sense of justice or balance that exists in the human condition that governs the natural give and take of relationship (Boszormenyi-Nagy & Krasner, 1986). Although it may run counter to post-modern or constructivist ideology, we feel committed human beings actually do possess innate value and are deserving of love and consistent safety in relationships. Human beings *should* have the experience of love and trustworthiness because they are humans (Hargrave & Pfitzer, 2011).

Therefore, when we put an individual client in the position of choosing an emotionally regulating truth, we are doing more than simply asking him or her to shape a constructed sense of self and safety. Rather, we are asking them to make contact with the innate part of their humanness in order to challenge the propositions of *lies* about identity and safety that were programmed into their psyche, whether intentionally or not. It is the innate truth that humans are loveable and deserving of safety and protection and it is this reality that Restoration Therapy asks the client to re-discover or uncover buried in the past lies and faulty schema that tells him or her otherwise. In a sense, we see this desire to be loved and safe as the most essential longing within our clients specifically and humans in general. In proposing the client challenge the old programming concerning identity or safety, Restoration Therapy believes we are enabling him or her to successfully challenge the patterns of the pain cycle and successfully reach into a place of peace where confidence, freedom, love, and trustworthiness flow from his or her identity and sense of safety.

The practice of teaching, organizing, and recognizing the client pain cycle is a powerful first step in making the client mindful and aware of the fault lines in his or her identity and sense of safety. It is true, however, that the pain cycle is a powerful organizing pattern likely dominating the thinking and reacting of the client for many years or even decades. There is still a preference in the brain and our thinking as humans to do what we already have practiced and know well (Siegel, 2007). Given this reality, the practiced pain cycle of the client will persist for a very long time in the thinking and behavior of the client. What we need to be able to do as therapists, therefore, is to make the truth as powerful as possible to make an impact on the pain cycle. Throughout the first decade of practicing Restoration Therapy, we have developed and modified existing techniques in order to consolidate the impact the truth or regulating emotion can have on the client. A review of these techniques we have utilized in identifying regulating emotions dominates the rest of this chapter.

Re-parenting Imagery

The focus of the re-parenting imagery is to experientially put the client in the position of power and authority in determining his or her own perspective of identity and sense of safety. In essence, the therapist places the client in a position of providing a good parenting model to him or herself while challenging the past messages concerning identity and safety. This technique is modified from the empty chair technique made popular in the work of gestalt therapy (Perls, Hefferline, & Goodman, 1951).

Target One of the Imagery

We usually place an empty chair in front of the client and aim to follow interactions utilizing three successive targets or images during the session. In the first target or image, our aim is to call attention to a non-descript child sitting in the empty chair revealing his or her pain regarding aspects of identity and safety. Of course, a therapist with experience will have the discussion about the pain of the child in the empty chair being very close or identical to the feelings in the pain cycle of the client. The central idea of this first target is to give the client an easy or "low shelf" opportunity to identify truths for the child who has little or no direct bearing or connection with the client. The following is from a re-parenting exercise utilizing the first target of a non-descript child with a man who was 30 years old struggling with excessive use of pornography.

Therapist:	As you look at the chair in front of you, I want you to imagine a child close to age 10 sitting in front of you. You don't have to know the child—it can even be a child that you composite in your mind. It might be the child of a friend or a relative. (Pause). Take a moment and see this child sitting in the chair.
Man:	(Pause). Okay, I think I see the child.
Therapist:	(Pause). Notice the child's eyes. (Pause). Hair color. (Pause). What expression is on the child's face. (Pause). What he or she is wearing.
Man:	He's has blue eyes and blond hair. Wearing a red shirt and shorts.
Therapist:	Good. (Long pause). Now the child looks at you and is in obvious emotional pain. (Pause). He looks at you with those blue eyes and says, "No one in my life sees me." (Long pause). "Everyone—my mother—my father—my teachers—my few friends—they are only interested in me doing better. (Pause). Better grades. Better behavior. Better at everything. (Long pause). I am worthless. Unseen. I cannot measure up to anyone. (Pause). I am worthless. Unseen. I can't measure up." (Long pause and then stands off to the side of the man). You know how he feels because you have felt the same way. What can you say to this young boy with his blue eyes, blond hair, and red shirt about him feeling worthless—unseen—unable to measure up?
Man:	(Long pause). I would say to him …
Therapist:	(Interrupting). See him in the chair and speak directly to him. Worthless. Unseen. Can't measure up.

Man:	(Pause). You are okay. I certainly see you. It isn't important whether you meet the expectations. Succeed or fail, you are okay.
Therapist:	(Pause and then speaking to the empty chair). You're okay. I see you and understand you. Your success or failure does not matter because you're okay. (Pause). In looking at his face, what does his face tell you?
Man:	(Pause). He feels better but he still feels worthless.
Therapist:	(Pause). He still feels worthless. What can you say to him?
Man:	(Pause). You are important. Priceless. You are okay whether you succeed or fail.
Therapist:	(Long pause). Important. Priceless. Okay whether you succeed or fail. (Long pause). What does his face tell you now?
Man:	(Pause). It connects more. All he wants is to know he is important and that he is okay.

In this example above, you have a classic illustration of the first target work of re-parenting. The therapist works hard to connect the man with the imagery of the boy and then utilizes pain and feeling words that are very close to his own pain cycle that was identified in previous therapy. Notice also how the therapist slows the technique down to further draw the man in to the imagery. As well, notice how the therapist repeats the words used often to contrast the truth or emotionally regulating words with the pain words from the pain cycle.

In this initial re-parenting target, it is usually not so emotionally charged as it is focused and organizing the truth. The man in this example is able to identify and sharpen the words that he projects the young boy will need to hear in order to make a difference. When he identifies truth and emotionally regulating words that he longs to hear, he is able to imagine the 10-year-old being comforted by his words. Although the imagery here is powerful, it usually carries less emotion because the child sitting in the chair is not representing a real child at this point. This actually assists with the success of the client in the first target of re-parenting in that the therapist is counting on the innate belief of the client that every child is important and priceless, is deserving to be seen apart from performance. With the first target in the imagery successfully identifying the regulating truth, the therapist is ready to proceed to the next target in the re-parenting.

Target Two of the Imagery

The second target in the imagery still involves the empty chair, but this time the child who will be sitting in the chair will be the client as a child. This involves a dramatic shift in the emotional investment of the re-parenting because the client knows the ins and outs of this child very clearly. This makes the emotional impact of the imagery much more intense and often more dramatic. In this target, the client is not only identifying truth words that make sense, he or she is now taking on the responsibility of actually parenting the child (him or herself) in the way he or she wants to be parented. The example below, from the above case later in the session, illustrates how this emotional impact can be much deeper.

Therapist: Good. I like very much how you identified those elements that would make a difference to that 10-year-old, blue eyed boy. (Pause). Important. Priceless. Okay whether you succeed or fail.
(Pause). Now I would like you to look at the chair again. This time, however, the child in the chair is not just any child, it is you as a 10-year-old boy. (Long pause). I want you to see yourself as a 10-year-old. (Pause). Notice how he looks and what he is wearing. (Pause). Notice his eyes—his hair—the expression on his face.

Man: (Long pause). All I can see is how I look in my fourth grade picture—my school picture. My hair is long, almost down to my shoulders. I have this blank, vacant stare with absolutely no smile. Solemn. (Pause). I have seen that picture in my mind's eye a thousand times

Therapist: (Pause). When you look at him here and now—with his shoulder length hair and blank expression—what is he feeling?

Man: (Pause). He is feeling so lost. He doesn't fit or belong. All he does is fail and disappoint.

Therapist: (Long pause). Lost. Doesn't belong. Fails and disappoints. (Pause). You remember how you felt when you look at him. (Client nods head). (Pause). So feeling that way, what did he do to cope with such an awful feeling?

Man: (Long pause). He just would check out and not try. He would do just the bare minimum until he could play video games.

Therapist: (Long pause). Lost. Doesn't belong. Fails and disappoints. You know that territory and those feelings well. (Pause). What does this 10-year-old you need to hear from you as an adult?

Man: (Pause and feels emotional while shaking his head). I don't know. I don't know what he needs to hear from me. To tell the truth, I've got nothing for him.

Therapist:	(Pause and moves to stand beside him). I hear you. It makes sense that you are not really sure if you have anything for him or not because you carry these same feelings now. (Pause). Worthless. Unseen. Can't measure up.
	(Long pause). But here is the truth. (Points at the empty chair). He needs to hear something from you. Even if you are going to tell him you don't have anything for him—even if you are going to confirm to him that he is lost, doesn't belong, and fails and disappoints—you at least need to take the opportunity to say something to him.
Man:	(Long pause and tears come to his eyes. Looks at chair). I know how you feel. (Long pause). I can tell you that you are going to survive this and that what you hear from everyone has more to do with them than who you are.
Therapist:	(Pause). You do know how he feels and your advice to him is heartfelt. But my question is, does the advice make him feel better or address the worthlessness or failure he feels? (Man pauses and shakes his head). (Long pause). So what does he need to hear from you that will address his feelings of being worthless—unseen and alone—a failure.
Man:	(Long pause with tears). It may be hard to believe, but you are priceless to me. (Pause). No matter what others say, you are not a failure. You are just you and you are okay the way you are.
Therapist:	(Long pause). Priceless. (Pause). You are okay whether or not you succeed or fail. (Pause). Say it again to him.
Man:	(Pause). You are priceless to me. You are okay no matter if you succeed or fail.
	(Long pause). I think I saw his expression change a little.
Therapist:	(Long pause). He probably sees that you believe these things about him. (Man nods).

There are several aspects of this last example of the second target in re-parenting imagery that warrant attention. First, notice the therapist utilizes some of the same techniques of pacing and repetition to slow down the process of the imagery while, at the same time, intensifying the emotion in the room. Johnson (2004) points to this emotional heightening using similar techniques in emotionally focused therapy. Second, notice that the man realizes the difference in the emotional intensity when the child in the empty chair represents himself. There is a common bond between a person as an adult and the same person as a child because both feel the same things with the same amount of intensity. When the man reports that the child "feels lost," he is reporting on himself, he also feels lost. The experiential component, if the client connects, makes it highly unlikely that the client can separate the emotions of the child in the empty chair from the emotions he or she feels. Although intense, the emotional connection actually adds to the prospect of making a dynamic impact of the truth. No longer is it just about identifying words, it is about making deep emotional contact with the feelings both the pain and the truth provoke.

Third, notice that after the man rightly identifies the feelings of himself as a child, he proclaims that "he's got nothing" for the child. This is not surprising at all. Earlier in the imagery target, the therapist wisely asks what the young version of himself did when he felt lost, like he didn't belong, and like a failure. The man reports, that he "checked out and would not try." In feeling overwhelmed by the responsibility of offering parenting to himself, he recapitulates his own coping in his pain cycle by checking out and not trying. Notice here the therapist raises the emotional stakes by answering the man's effort to check out. The therapist points at the chair and says, "he needs to hear something from you," even if that "something" is negative or even an affirmation of what others tell the child. Here, the therapist is aware that the overwhelming majority of the time, individuals will not confirm these painful messages but instead make a sincere effort to speak to the pain of the child in a constructive way. It is important to note, however, that when individuals in this re-parenting imagery speak destructive messages to the target, it is most likely a result of the intense pain the individual feels as a result of his or her pain cycle. In these cases, the experiential exercise demonstrates the therapist needs to back-track and hear more stories about the client pain in order to understand and empathize with the reason for the client taking a destructive action.

Finally, it is important to notice that the client's first effort at speaking to himself as a child takes the form of advice. Here, the therapist rightly appreciates the client's empathy and effort, but more importantly points the client toward speaking in a language of regulating truth. Many times, clients in this second target of re-parenting imagery will speak advice to the younger version of themselves. This advice, although well meaning, has little to no power to emotionally regulate pain. Therefore, the therapist helps the client refocus efforts by calling attention back to the pain and giving him another chance to speak a regulating truth. This type of sharpening, clarifying, and shaping is very common as the therapist helps the client develop deep, connecting, and emotionally regulating truths.

Target Three of the Imagery

A fair question regarding the re-parenting imagery often emerges as students are learning the techniques of Restoration Therapy. They often ask, "How often will the re-parenting imagery be successful in identifying the client truth regarding identity and safety?" Through clinical observations, we observe success with target one imagery about 75 percent of the time. This number is high because we are asking the client to identify truths with children with whom they have little to no emotional tie and, therefore, it becomes a more cognitive experience. It is as if we are asking the client to have connection and compassion philosophically with a child that has pain. Answers and effort seem appropriate to the client because of the overwhelming fundamental belief that all children deserve to be loved and to be safe and protected. In the second target of re-parenting, however, the emotional stakes go up and what makes philosophical sense to the client no longer makes as much sense because they *know* and *relate to* him or herself as a child. Success on initial efforts in clients speaking to the empty chair representing themselves as children usually range from 45–50 percent. It is easy to see in the previous example that if the therapist had stopped with the initial effort to get the man to speak truth to himself as a child, the target two in the re-parenting imagery would not have been successful. However, the therapist in the above case is skillful and continues to work with the man both clarifying, comforting, and confronting. With this kind of organizing efforts in the second target, the therapist can usually produce a successful identification and connection with the truth about 70 percent of the time. Utilizing the third target in the re-parenting imagery, the client is usually more acclimated to the emotional intensity of the work if he or she was successful with target two imagery. Therefore, there is a carryover effect that if a client can identify and speak the truth with emotional connection in the first two targets, he or she can speak and connect to the truth about 65–70 percent of the time in the third target imagery.

It is also helpful to reckon with the prospect of timing when using imagery work. We have found clinically that the client connects best with experiential imagery about three times during therapy. If used more than three times, the responses of clients are increasingly less emotionally connected as the process becomes more predictable or even rout. Therefore, we have found it wise to limit the imagery work with a client to about three times during the entire course of therapy. But we have also found that this "three times" guide holds true only when you use the imagery in separate sessions. Often in the re-parenting imagery, therapists are able to utilize target one imagery in about 10–12 minutes of a session. Most often, they proceed directly in the same session to work on target two imagery for about 15 minutes. This often leaves the therapist with around 20–25 minutes to accomplish the third target imagery all within the same session. The imagery in the three targets is definitely tied together and is often most effective in building connection and identification if all done in one session. It should be noted here, however, that achieving the three targets in one session is certainly not a requirement and will often be spread out over two or perhaps even three sessions. It is important for the therapist to use his or her therapeutic intuition concerning how much intensity and work is useful and helpful to the client in each session. With this said, there is an advantage in doing all three targets of the re-parenting imagery in one session. One is the dramatic heightening and impact of consolidating the truth from one target to the next. Another is that clients do not tire of the imagery nearly as fast when it is concentrated in one session. We often say that when therapists do the imagery of re-parenting on all targets in one session, it is experienced by the client as one session of imagery work. Therefore, the client can easily respond and be impacted by other imagery exercises once or twice more during the course of therapy.

With the scaffolding of the imagery in target one, the client and therapist have identified the possible words of truth that perhaps will have the power to emotionally regulate the pain that exists with the client in his or her pain cycle. Further scaffolding in the imagery of target two puts the client in an emotional context experientially to be able to connect the emotionally regulating truth while he or she takes the position of parent with his or her younger and more vulnerable self. The third target in the re-parenting imagery involves using the empty chair so the client can now see him or herself as he or she is today and speak the emotionally regulating truth into him or herself. The following example is the third target of the re-parenting imagery from the case discussed above. All three targets were covered in one session.

Therapist:	You have done a great job. You have identified and connected with this reality that as a 10-year-old, you are important, priceless, and okay whether you succeed or fail.
	Now I would like you to go one step further. First, move into the empty chair that is in front of you. (The man complies). I want you to just be you for a moment as you are today. Think back over this past week. (Pause). Think of a time where you really were tied up in your pain cycle. (Pause). Can you tell me about that time?
Man:	I know exactly when it was. I had a really bad day at work and I was planning how I could take a break to look at porn to get my mind off the issue. I started loathing myself for making the plan and then progressed into feeling more and more hopeless. I felt like I wanted to tell my wife, but then was afraid that if I told her, it would just upset her more. Then I started feeling more depressed and didn't feel like I could find a way out so I just gave into the urge on my break.

Therapist:	You were having a bad day at your work and it set you on a course to want to escape by looking at porn. As you made a plan to escape, you started this self-loathing and it felt hopeless. As you looked at the situation, you wanted to be honest and tell your wife to break the pattern, but you were frightened it would make things worse for her and upset her. You beat up on yourself more and felt hopeless enough to just give in to escaping using porn. Did I get it right?
Man:	Yes. In the meantime, I did nothing at my work.
Therapist:	(Pause). The bad day at work, what was going on that day?
Man:	I had some contacts and calls that I absolutely needed to make, but I didn't feel prepared with the information to be able to make the calls. I just had stalled out.
Therapist:	(Pause). And what were you feeling when you were unprepared and stalled? (Therapist is pointing to the client's pain cycle).
Man:	(Pause). Feeling like a failure—couldn't measure up.
Therapist:	And when you were loathing yourself and afraid that you would upset your wife, what feeling was driving shaming yourself?
Man:	(Pause). Again, not measuring up but also feeling worthless and alone.
Therapist:	(Pause). You can still feel it now.
Man:	(Long pause). Yeah. It still is there and something I am always fighting.
Therapist:	(Long pause). Okay. So go ahead and move back to your chair. (Man complies and then long pause). Still looking at the empty chair where you were just sitting, I want you to see yourself sitting there just as you were a minute ago. (Long pause). I want you to remember the story he told about his bad day. I want you to hear him say, "I feel like such a failure. I am worthless and alone. I can't measure up." I feel like a failure. (Pause). I am worthless and alone. (Pause). I can't measure up. (Long pause). What is it you can say to him?
Man:	(Long pause). I don't know. (Pause). It seems those things are true.
Therapist:	(Pause). I understand that you feel those things also. But just like you had the courage to be a parent to yourself as a 10-year-old a little while ago, this version of yourself needs to hear the same truth about who he is.
Man:	(Pause). It was easier to believe about the 10-year-old. It is hard here because there are so many layers of screw ups.

Therapist:	(Pause). Look at yourself in the chair. (Long pause). It is still you. (Long pause).You still need to hear the truth about yourself from someone who cares and understands you.
Man:	(Long pause and then leaning toward the chair). You are important and priceless. You are okay whether you succeed or fail.
Therapist:	(Pause). Say it again to him.
Man:	(Long pause and feeling much more emotional). You are important and priceless. You are okay whether you succeed or fail.
Therapist:	(Pause). One more time.
Man:	(Takes a deep breath).You are important and priceless.You are okay whether you succeed or fail.
Therapist:	(Pause and then speaking to the empty chair). If he was able to really hear that he was important and priceless and that he was okay no matter what (Pause) what do you suppose he would have done on that really bad day.
Man:	(Pause and takes a deep breath). He would have studied specs and then made some calls. (Pause). He would have called his wife to report how he was doing.

There are several things that warrant discussion in this third target of the re-parenting imagery. Notice first that the therapist has the man take the seat of the empty chair and has him relate a recent story about his pain. This is essential because now the client is not dealing with a distant memory of past feelings and beliefs, he is dealing with something that is close and very much impacting his life in the here-and-now. Second, the therapist also uses the pain cycle worked out in previous sessions to help the client not only identify coping behaviors that he states, but also track down the emotional pain he feels that prompts those coping behaviors. Third, when the client questions whether or not he can say or believe the regulating truths about this grown version of himself, the therapist uses the scaffolding from the previous imagery to connect the 10-year-old boy to the feelings of pain that still exist within himself. Fourth, once the man speaks the regulating emotional truth to himself in the empty chair, the therapist further connects and deepens the emotional experience through having the man repeat the words twice more.This not only makes the emotional impact of the imagery broader, it drives these foundational regulating truths into the man's memory where they will not be so easily forgotten. Finally, notice that the therapist then checks the work to see if the spoken regulated truths actually emotionally regulate the pain of feeling worthless, alone, and like a failure. The therapist asks, "What do you suppose he would have done on that really bad day?" The man's clear response of actions not reflecting escaping, shaming, or giving up is a clear sign the he feels emotionally regulated enough to make constructive choices.

Re-parenting imagery work is powerful and deep, but it is still only a beginning place to help the client acclimate toward emotionally regulating him or herself. Many times, clients will say something like, "I can say the truth, but I have trouble believing it." This is totally understandable as the individual is faced with counteracting messages and programming from the past perpetuated in the pain cycle. Immediate belief is not so essential based on an imagery exercise. Much more essential at this stage is the *familiarity* with the regulating truths and the ability to take on old habituation in the pain cycle with effective counters. As the work proceeds and the client becomes familiar with the regulating truths, then the therapeutic work focuses more on the *faith* that if the client continues to lean into these truths through practice in confronting the pain cycle, the truths will become more foundational to identity and safety. With familiarity and faithfulness of practice, the client will begin to *accept* and *believe* that these regulating truths concerning identity and safety are the real and strong messages he or she wants integrated into him or herself. It is like a parent with a child. When a parent becomes familiar with the precious gift of another human being, he or she is faithful to build affirmations, encouragements, and acceptance into the child's identity. As the parent practices this faithfulness, the power of what he or she says takes root and becomes a reality in the child's identity and sense of safety. This is basically the position a client takes when he or she engages the work of the re-parenting imagery.

The re-parenting imagery is not for every client. Because the imagery is often emotionally charged and deeply connecting with the past, clients who have past trauma and particularly *post-traumatic stress disorder* may not be good candidates for this type of imagery work. As always, the therapist must be cautious to carefully assess the traumatic history of the client and gauge whether or not the client experiences instances of flashbacks or disassociation during any kind of imagery work. In general, if a client has a highly traumatic past, we usually chose not to utilize the re-parenting imagery technique.

The Use of Timing, Voice, and Repetition in Imagery Techniques

It is obvious from the examples used in the re-parenting imagery above, both the client and the therapeutic work greatly benefit from the therapist increasing the emotional impact of the experiential activity. We have already pointed out the work of Johnson (2004) and the work of emotional *heightening* in emotionally focused therapy as a means of clarifying and enhancing the emotional responsiveness of the client. We also would point out here that the use of imagery particularly when one uses voice, timing, and repetition is similar to *hypnotic induction* and *hypnotic injunction*. As used in hypnosis, *induction* is the setting, environment, and influences the hypnotist promotes with a subject in order to make it more likely the subject will cooperate or change in line with the *injunction* or the direction/instruction of the hypnotist (Burrows, Stanley, & Bloom, 2009). In using Restoration Therapy, the therapist uses his or her pacing, voice, and repetition to pull the client further into the imagery and also the emotion of the experience.

The first technique we use to influence the emotional experience in imagery work is to slow down the *timing* or *pacing* of verbalizations and directions. Although pacing means something quite different in hypnosis, in Restoration Therapy we find that when the therapist changes the timing and pacing of words, clients usually respond by being focused and open to the next words or instruction. In the following example, the therapist uses timing and pace to bring the focus together in a very specific way so the client is able to block out all other competing thoughts.

Therapist: As you look at the child—and see—directly into—her— heart. You see—clearly—the pain—she feels. She cannot name the pain. Only—you—are here—to name—the pain— for her. What. Is. Her. Pain?

When a client experiences this type of focus through the therapist utilizing timing and pacing in his or her clinical work it is very rare that the client is not touched emotionally and able to respond effectively in the imagery.

The second way we enhance the emotional experience in imagery work is for the therapist to use *volume* and *tone* to more readily bring the client into emotional awareness. Although tone has to do with the pitch (high or low) of the voice, volume has to do with loudness or softness of the voice. For instance, the following is from a session where the therapist uses her voice to evoke the emotional feel of the imagery when the client was a young, school-age girl.

Therapist: (Very soft and higher pitched voice). All you wanted, was to have your mother see you as the best you could be at running. (Pause). (Louder and much lower pitched voice). But that isn't what she saw. (Return to a very soft and higher pitched voice.) What did your mother's criticism communicate to you about who you were?

Again, there are very few therapeutic situations that we have observed where a client does not feel a deeper emotional impact when the therapist manipulates his or her voice in the manner illustrated above. The emotional impact in turn connects the client more with the imagery and clarifies the feelings and contexts which make the contrasting truth more accessible.

The final way that we broaden the emotional connection and impact of imagery techniques is to bring important elements of pain, story, or regulating truth into sharper focus using *repetition*. This repetition, especially combined with a slower pacing, allows the client and therapist both to emphasize and organize essential elements which in turn make it beneficial in the imagery practice. The following is an example of how the therapist utilizes repetition in order to clarify the work of painful feelings as well as broaden emotional connection with the pain the client feels.

Therapist:	It sounds like you felt a sense of injustice in dealing with your husband. It spread from there until you felt little regard from him or contempt as well as a lack of respect. (Pause). Just listen to these words as I repeat them and see if it matches what you feel. (Pause). Unjust. Unloved. Disrespected. (Pause). Unjust. Unloved. Disrespected.
Woman:	(Long pause). I don't know if it is unjust. I think I just feel controlled and unimportant.
Therapist:	Say those two words again.
Woman:	Controlled and unimportant.
Therapist:	(Pause). Controlled. Unimportant. (Pause). Do these words describe what it feels like when you feel this pain in the relationship?
Woman:	Yes.

Notice here how the therapist uses repetition to bring the client to a point of focus, as if to "try on" the description of the feelings. This leads the woman to name the pain she feels very accurately and much more accurately than the therapist. The therapist then immediately adopts the words and repeats them back to her to consolidate the sharper description and meaning. This use of repetition is very useful to the therapist throughout the therapeutic process with a client, but particularly salient in helping the client describe feelings of pain and corresponding truths that will emerge in the peace cycle.

Stronger, Wiser, or "Cured" Self-Imagery

Haley (1993) describes a technique from Milton Erickson that was often used in the beginning stage of therapy. In the intervention, a client was asked to imagine how long therapy would take in order to "get better" or be "cured." After setting some cues of what the world would look like in the future based on the time frame the client suggested, the person would then be asked to describe in detail what would be different about him or her and how he or she would be able to recognize that there was a "cure" or improvement. As the more specifics were added to the description, clients were often asked about the advice or direction the "cured" self would give to him or herself in the present moment at the beginning of therapy. It was one of Erikson's unique abilities to help people utilize their imaginations to access possibilities for change and being different.

We have been inspired by this technique for years but began to utilize it specifically in helping the client imagine his or her own emotionally self-regulating truths. Although people always carry painful feelings concerning their identities and senses of safety, they are not always in pain and certainly do not always cope by acting on the pain by violating others in misusing love and trustworthiness. In short, people are not always emotionally dysregulated. In their regulated states, we often see people's natural gifts and talents emerge, their caring and connecting natures as well as supremely loving and trustworthy enactments in their closest relationships. As we are fond of saying, "You are not bad all the time, you are only bad when you are bad." In other words, people are only bad when they are actively emotionally dysregulated and in their pain cycles.

These examples and beliefs encouraged the development of another imagery technique where the therapist encourages the client to make contact with him or herself when he or she was emotionally regulated and experiencing the full fruition of gifts, talents, empowerment, and connections. Clients come to therapy usually at their worst when they have undesirable symptomology or relationships are dissatisfying and conflicted. In actuality, however, they have experiences where they are quite remarkable people. Our goal and the focus of this intervention is to use imagery to help the client become aware of different choices that are available to him or her concerning identity and the power to provide safety from the perspective of a future "cured" self or a wiser "cured" self from the past. In executing the imagery, the therapist will utilize many of the same techniques in the use of timing, voice, and repetition. The therapist initially asks a client to think of the time in their past when he or she was his or her "best version" of him or herself, or project into the future when he or she will be free of the concerns and issues that brought him or her to therapy. In both cases, the therapist will eventually work the imagery to the point where this stronger, wiser self or the "cured" best self will speak into the pain feelings the client currently experiences with emotionally regulating truths. In the following case example, a 42-year-old man who had been depressed for what he reported was 18 months sought therapy. He was currently under the care of a psychiatrist as well, but was responding only minimally to medication prescribed for his depression. His pain cycle emerged in the first seven sessions and is found in Figure 4.1.

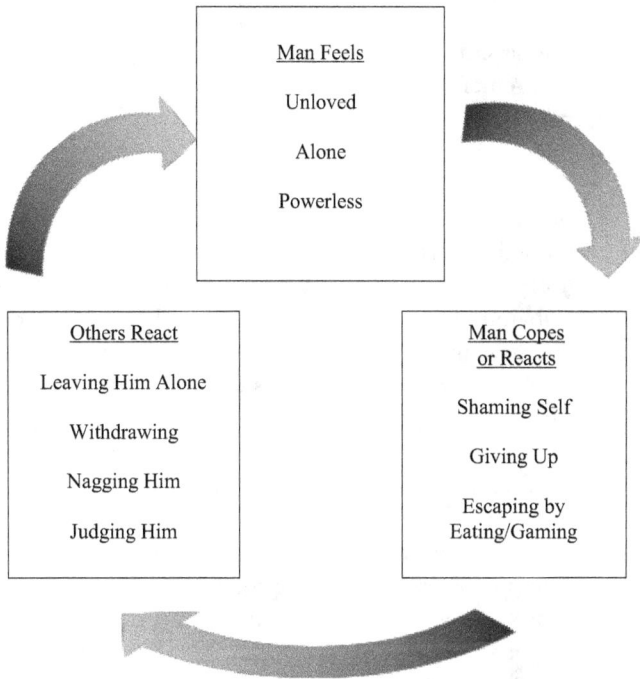

Figure 4.1 Pain Cycle of Depressed Male in Case Example

Therapist:	I was thinking about you in preparing for our session today. I know you have been depressed a long time. (Pause). Eighteen months when you are depressed can seem endless. One day can end up seeming like it is just the same thing for a month. (Pause). I know it is painful and you feel powerless, alone, and unloved.
Man:	I do. Hearing you say it that way makes me feel even more powerless.
Therapist:	(Pause). I can imagine so. It can be easy for others and even me sometimes to not see you accurately because we drift into thinking that depression is somehow equal to your identity and self. (Pause). But I know that is not true. I know you well enough to know that you are deeply human with sensitive and caring characteristics.
Man:	It is easy for me to think that I am just depressed all the time and I just go away—numb out with eating or video games.
Therapist:	(Nods and pauses). It is easy to forget that you are still in you. The you that was not depressed—that is full of gifts,

talents. (Pause). The you that is sensitive, caring, and makes a difference in people's lives. (Pause). I was wondering before our session when I was thinking of you, when was a time you remember that best version of yourself? The strong and wise self that wasn't burdened or covered over with this depression.

Man: (Long pause. After several minutes, a small smile creeps up on his face). I know this is hard to believe, but actually I have trained as a triathlete.

Therapist: (Very surprised). Really. Wow. You really did triathlons?

Man: (Obviously pleased and smiling). Yes! Well, there are various distances in triathlons. I was at the sprint distance for about a year before I stopped. It is about half the distance of an Olympic competition.

Therapist: Man. How far are those distances you were covering?

Man: Half mile swimming, 12 miles biking, and a little over 3 miles running.

Therapist: Half of a mile swimming. Twelve miles biking. Over 3 miles running. (Pause). That is impressive.

Man: (Looks away). It seems like an age ago, but it was only three years ago.

Therapist: Three years ago you were swimming a half mile, biking 12 and running over 3 miles. Do you have a mental image of that race?

Man: Yea. I was down in San Diego.

Therapist: Can you see yourself there? What were you wearing during your run?

Man: I like blue and gray so my swim suit and biking shorts were gray with a blue helmet. (Pause). During the second transition I put on blue shorts with a gray tank and gray hat.

Therapist: (Smiles). Wow. And the blue shorts and gray tank is what you finished the race in.

Man: I did. Number 172 pinned on my chest.

Therapist: (Pause). You can see it. I can tell. What did you look like when you finished across the last line?

Man: I know exactly what I looked like. A buddy of mine took a picture of me finishing. I had my hands up in the air with my head back. Man, I was glad to finish that one. (Smiles).

Therapist: (Stands up). Show me what you looked like when you finished. (Man stands up and has his arms extended up with hands open and head back with eyes closed). Hold that pose for a minute. (The therapist also gets in the pose and stands with the man).

	(Long pause). Tell me, when you are in that position and remember what it was like to finish, what did it say about you?
Man:	(Pause). It said that I am a finisher. I worked hard and accomplished the goal. I remember thinking on that race, maybe someday I could do a full triathlon.
Therapist:	(Pause and both still in the position). A finisher. Accomplished. Empowered to go the distance. Is that right?
Man:	Yeah.
Therapist:	(Pause). Come over here beside me for a minute. (Man complies). Now look at the space where you were on the couch a few minutes ago. (Pause). See yourself sitting there. (Pause). Know what he feels. (Pause). Remember what he thinks about himself. (Pause). Unloved. Alone. Powerless. (Speaks again in a softer, higher pitched voice). Unloved. Alone. Powerless. (Pause). Now, take that pose of finishing the triathlon. (Man and therapist both take the pose). What does this you—the finisher—accomplished—empowered to go the distance— say to the you on the couch?
Man:	(Long pause). Wow. How did you let yourself get here?
Therapist:	(Pause). It makes sense, right? He didn't get from you to there in one big leap. He got there by feeling powerless— unloved—alone. Powerless. Unloved. Alone.
Man:	(Long pause). You are not powerless. All you have to do is the next right step. You have done it before.
Therapist:	(Pause). If he did it before, is he powerless or empowered? Tell him.
Man:	You are empowered to take the next right step, even if it is small.
Therapist:	Say it again.
Man:	You're empowered to do the next step.
Therapist:	And what about his pain of being unloved and alone.
Man:	(Pause). People are there for you, that care for you. It is your isolation that leaves you alone and then you start thinking you're unlovable.
Therapist:	(Pause). You are empowered for the next step. You are loved. You belong. (Pause again). You are empowered for the next step. You are loved. You belong. (Pause and in a louder, deeper pitched voice). Say it to him.
Man:	You are empowered to do the next step. You are loved. You belong.
Therapist:	Now, sit back down. (Man complies). Tell me, what did the accomplished finisher in his blue shorts, gray tank, and hat say to you about feeling powerless, unloved, and alone?

Man:	(Pause). I am empowered to do the next right thing. I am loved and I belong.
Therapist:	(Softer). Say it again.
Man:	I am empowered to do the next right thing. I am loved and I belong.

There are several things to make note of here. In starting the session, the therapist first draws the contrast of the feelings that exist in the pain cycle. This not only clarifies the painful feelings and increases empathy for the client, it puts the therapist in the position to clarify that depression has not been or will not be a characteristic that defines the man's identity or sense of contribution. Next, the therapist engages many real and vivid images of the man competing in the triathlon before a question is asked about the feelings of the stronger, wiser self. This increases the experiential component of the imagery and makes it much more likely the man will be able to contact the more regulated emotions he had when he finished the race. The therapist also has the client engage in an embodied position that he clearly has in his mind's eye of the triathlon. He is much more likely to remember the feelings of triathlon day than his depressed feelings from this embodied pose. Finally, notice how the therapist clarifies, sharpens, and finally consolidates the emotional regulating truths through restating and repetition. During this imagery technique, the man hears either the therapist or himself say the self-regulating truths no less than six times. Not only does this drive the point of the emotionally regulating truth into the man's memory, it also provides the opportunity to see if the man exerts any protest in rejecting the words.

Using the Two Screen Method Imagery

Symington (2015) developed the two screen method as an imagery technique to primarily assist clients in focusing on mindfulness information that reduces anxiety and depression. In the technique, the developer discusses the imagery of having the client imagine a movie theater where simultaneously he or she is exposed to the large front screen with mindful words and images that are calming and reassuring and also to a side screen (on a side wall) that has images or words that are emotionally dysregulating. The primary aim of the technique is to help the client mindfully focus on the images on the front screen which are comforting and calming while learning how to ignore, accept, and be unaffected by the side screen images (Symington, 2015). In other words, the mindfulness comes down to a choice of where the client chooses to place his or her attention.

We have adapted the two screen technique to utilize images and words on the side screen that are most representative of the pain cycle. In placing it on the side of the theater imagery, we acknowledge the pain cycle and the influences that are present in the client's life. We also emphasize, however, the client has a choice of whether or not to place his or her attention exclusively on the pain cycle side screen. On the large front screen in the movie theater imagery, the therapist helps the client walk through a process of constructing images and words that are consistent with the truth or regulating emotion which produces a feeling of peacefulness and congruency, usually produced in the peace cycle.

As we have seen previously, the therapist utilizes all the skills at his or her disposal in summarizing, creating contrast, embodiment, repetition, and utilizing voice in making the imagery more powerful in the experience of the client. Notice in the next case example how the therapist creates the imagery in the two screen technique by first setting the scene, focusing on the pain cycle emotional dysregulating words, developing imagery that fits with the pain cycle, and moving the image of the pain cycle to the side screen. Further, the therapist helps the client develop emotionally regulating words or the truth on the front screen and place them with constructive and emotionally regulating imagery. When the client successfully completes the two screen imagery, the therapist helps him or her take attention away from the side screen influence and focus instead on the front screen.

The example here is a therapist working with a 50-year-old female who came from a traumatic and neglectful background. She reported symptomology of being overcome with anxiety about something happening to her young adult children and had frequent outbursts of anger toward her husband and children. She reported to the therapist in the initial sessions that her children saw her as being "over-involved" and "manipulative." The woman had successfully identified her pain cycle in the five previous sessions as seen in Figure 4.2. The section from the example is from session six.

Therapist: We have discussed your background several times so far and how coming from a family where your father was absent and your mother was neglectful resulted in these feelings of being consistently unsafe, unprotected, and unappreciated. (Pointing to the pain cycle). And when you feel this way—unsafe—unprotected—and unappreciated—you cope or react by trying to control or manipulate the situation where you will feel safer. As you have said before, "I try to not only have my ducks in a row, I try to get everyone else and their ducks in a row."

Woman: (Smiling slightly). That's right. I try and take care of everyone's business so I will rest easier.

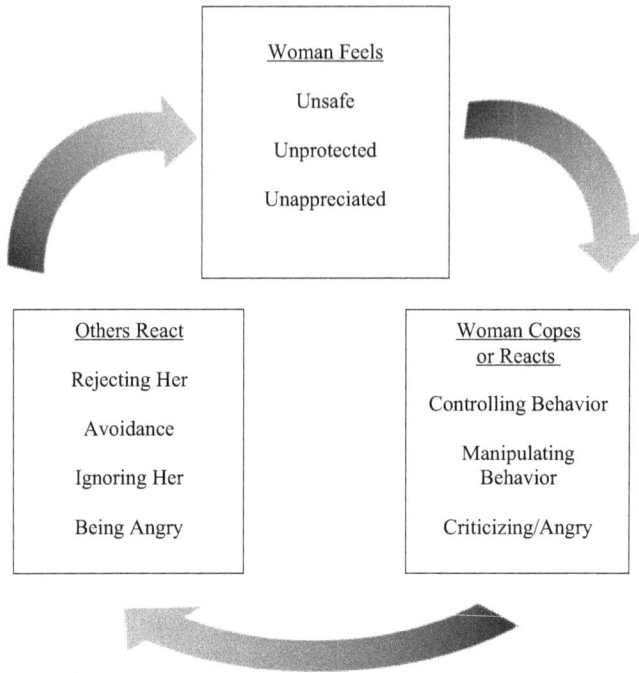

Figure 4.2 Pain Cycle of Anxious and Angry Woman in Case Example

Therapist:	(Pause). And when they reject your ideas, avoid or ignore you, that is when you are most likely to feel unappreciated which often leads to you getting critical or angry.
Woman:	Yes. I didn't realize that pattern before, but I have been doing that cycle one way or another since I was very young.
Therapist:	(Nods and pauses). Today, I would like to work on an alternate cycle with you. Let me move this chair in front of this open wall and I would like you to sit in this chair. (Woman complies with the therapist's request).
	(Pause). I would like you to imagine that you are sitting in the center of the row in the middle of your favorite movie theater. There is no one there except you. (Pause). No noise except the noise you make. Nothing on the screen but a white blank. (Pause). Tell me about the theater where you are sitting?
Woman:	(Long pause). Lights are dim and the room has blue drapes on the walls and side of the screen. It is a stadium type theater where the chairs lean slightly back.

Therapist:	Very good. (Softly and slowly). On the blank screen, I would like you to have the words I am going to say come on to the screen. (Pause). Unsafe. Unprotected. Unappreciated. (Long pause). Unsafe. Unprotected. Unappreciated. (Pause). Can you see the words on the screen? (Woman nods). Tell me about the words—what kind of font, capital letters, colors, and any movement.
Woman:	(Long pause). They are plain black words, but they have fuzzy edges and shadows. They are not moving, but appear and fade out one right after another.
Therapist:	I see. (Pause). And as you see those fuzzy edged words with the shadows that fade in and out, tell me where they appear and fade on the screen. Unsafe. Unprotected. Unappreciated.
Woman:	(Pause). The screen is black now and words are a gray white. Unsafe is over on the left. Unprotected is on the right. And Unappreciated is at the bottom.
Therapist:	And do they all appear and fade at the same time or do they go in a sequence?
Woman:	In a sequence. Like they are on a loop.
Therapist:	So as you look at the black screen (Pause). You see the word Unsafe appear on the left. (Pause). Unprotected appears on right as Unsafe fades. (Pause). Unappreciated appears at the bottom of the screen as Unprotected fades. (Pause). Then Unappreciated fades as Unsafe appears again and we go through the same sequence. (Pause). See those words run through three times. Unsafe. Unprotected. Unappreciated. (Pause). Unsafe. Unprotected. Unappreciated. (Pause). Unsafe. Unprotected. Unappreciated. (Pause).
Woman:	(Nods her head with each word the therapist repeats).
Therapist:	With those words continuing to appear and fade in sequence, I want you to imagine an image, set of images, or a video clip from your life that represents what you feel when you see those words. Unsafe. Unprotected. Unappreciated.
Woman:	(Long pause). I see it in black and white. A little girl—me—at age five standing in the corner of the barren kitchen. The apartment is on fire and smoke is everywhere. (Long pause). I am there by myself and I realize there is no one to save me—I curl into a ball sitting on the floor. That is the image I see—sitting on the floor in the corner with smoke engulfing the room.
Therapist:	(Long pause and very soft voice). And no one—is there to save you.

Woman:	(Starts to cry). And no one is there to save me. My father long since left and my mother was out doing her thing.
Therapist:	(Long pause). Now take a deep breath. (Pause). This is the image of your pain. The five-year-old you curled up in a ball in the corner of the kitchen and smoke engulfs you. You can see how you feel. Unsafe. Unprotected. Unappreciated. (Woman nods).
	Now as you see that image on the screen, I want you to shrink it down from the movie screen size to the size of a television size screen. (Pause). Is the image to a television size? (Woman nods). I want you to take that image on the television screen, and put it on the side wall of the movie theater. (Therapist points to the side of the office). (Pause). Looking at that image on the side, see it just the way you saw it before with the five-year-old in black and white, sitting in the corner with smoke coming in the apartment kitchen. The words appearing and fading, Unsafe—Unprotected—Unappreciated.
Woman:	(Looking to the side). I see it.
Therapist:	(Pause). Deep breath now. Return to the blank movie screen. It is all white again and blank. Nothing is on it. But the screen with the previous image is still playing on the side. That image is always there. It is the image of your pain cycle that has been playing and will continue to play out in your life. Look to the side so you can remember that image is there. (Woman complies). You see the image of the five-year-old you and the feelings of Unsafe, Unprotected, and Unappreciated.
	(Long pause). But when you look back to the blank screen, I want you to first place words there that describe you and your life when you are most at peace with yourself and your family.
Woman:	(Pause). I see the word "Belong."
Therapist:	(Pause). Very good. Look at the side screen and see the words again. Unsafe. Unprotected. Unappreciated. (Woman complies). Now look back at the big screen where the word "Belong" is now there. What other words do you see?
Woman:	(Long pause). Cared for. (Pause). Secure.
Therapist:	(Pause). Belong. Cared for. Secure. (Pause). Belong. Cared for. Secure. (Long pause). Describe the words to me.
Woman:	(Long pause). Those words come out in all different colors like red, yellow, and orange. (Pause). They kind of pop out like they come out of a fountain.
Therapist:	(Pause). See those words flow out of the fountain in different colors of red, yellow, and orange. Belong. Cared for. Secure. (Pause). Belong. Cared for. Secure.

	(Long pause). And as you see those words, is there an image or set of images that comes from your life that fits those words?
Woman:	(Long pause). I can see my family and me on the beach around a fire. It is a little chilly and we are laughing, smiling, and singing—like old campfire songs.
Therapist:	(Pause). And the words—Belong—Cared for—Secure—where are the words in the clip?
Woman:	They are coming out of the fire and moving up and out like smoke would. (Pause and then sudden gasp).
Therapist:	You saw something?
Woman:	No, I just realized that both of my images have to do with fire and smoke. (Heavy sigh with tears coming to her eyes). One fire was the worst day when I was alone and afraid—one fire is the place where I find everything that is good in my life. (Long pause amidst tears). Isn't that weird?
Therapist:	(Pause). It really makes perfect sense that you have come from such an unsafe situation and have found yourself now in the secure place of belonging.
Woman:	(Pause). It is amazing.
Therapist:	(Pause). Now see the image on the front screen one more time and describe it to me.
Woman:	My children and husband are on the beach around a fire laughing and singing. The fire light shines on our faces and the words come out of the fire like smoke, but there is no smoke.
Therapist:	And those words coming from the fire?
Woman:	(Pause). I belong. I am cared for. I am secure.
Therapist:	And now remember the side screen that is always playing. Describe what you see there?
Woman:	I see my five-year-old me curled up in the corner of the kitchen of the apartment. All in black and white. The words Unsafe, Unprotected, and Unappreciated come on and fade out again and again.
Therapist:	Very good. Both images will remain with you now, but the peaceful image is the one we will keep building on to keep you in touch with the part of you that belongs, is cared for, and is secure. It will help you when you feel the pain cycle coming on.
Woman:	I really want to spend more time in the peaceful image.

In this case example, we have a clear illustration of how the therapist builds the two screen imagery using Restoration Therapy. The therapist first builds the emotionally dysregulating words from the pain cycle and helps the client associate imagery. Then the therapist moves the pain cycle image to the side and shrinks it in size while drawing attention to the reality that the pain cycle will continue to be a part of the person's life. Further, the therapist moves back to the front screen and helps the client develop words and images that will be associated with the truth and become more emotionally regulating when the client is trapped in the pain cycle. Finally, the therapist contrasts the two screens many times and this helps the client clarify the perspective of truth and peace.

Notice that the imagery in the two screen method is not as intense as the re-parenting imagery or the stronger, wiser, "cured" self-imagery. This reality makes this imagery technique much more appropriate for those who have experienced trauma and usually does not carry the emotional impact to retraumatize the client. For instance, the reason that this woman was alone in her pain cycle image is because her mother had left her at home with two space heaters on while she was out on a date. It was only one instance of a traumatizing lack of care the woman experienced by having no one who would consistently provide care for her and, instead, she was left and neglected in harm's way. While remembering these times of neglect, the woman would often be emotionally traumatized and dysregulated. Here, however, the woman is dealing with a static black and white image that removes the neglect and volatile incident enough from the trauma for her to be able to speak about it more objectively while still benefitting from the contrast the pain cycle provides. Usually in using imagery to experientially help clients get to regulating truths, re-parenting is the most intense process therapeutically, wiser and stronger self being less intense, and finally the two screen imagery.

Other Techniques to Help Clients Access Truth

We believe, as stated before, the experiential imagery outlined in the three previous techniques assist the client in moving from his or her pain into more of the framework of regulating emotion. The more powerful the imagery and experience, usually the more powerful and embodied the experience of truth will be for the client and therefore it will be more regulating to the client pain. Many times, however, clients' emotional familiarity, faith, and eventual belief builds. Some clients feel particularly uncomfortable with imagery and so it is often most useful to start with the client identifying possible regulating truths in a cognitive manner. This can often be as simple as helping a client contrast cognitively words that are opposite to the descriptions of the feelings found in the pain cycle. We often speak of this process as "test driving" different truths to find ones that hold promise to be self-regulating to the client pain. We also often provide a word list for clients with a variety of feelings that reflect pain, coping words that reflect reactivity to pain, and truth words that may have the potential to regulate the emotional dysregulation the client feels. Does this cognitive identification bring the client to the point of *believing* a truth emotionally? Probably not in and of itself. But we find that when a client starts practicing with a word of emotional regulation in the context of his or her pain cycle, it will often create an atmosphere of mindfulness where he or she is able to take more constructive actions. As the client increases constructive instead of destructive actions, there is a much greater chance that they will lead to an experiential and more emotional aspect of the regulating truth becoming a reality. In this way, cognitive restructuring or familiarity with words combined with mindfulness has a building power to eventually yield regulated and peaceful experiences. These peaceful experiences, in turn, reinforce the truths as more regulating. The client using this cognitive methodology usually builds self-regulating truths to emotional pain little by little over a longer period of time.

Another alternative to building imagery is to utilize a client's relationships or spiritual resources as a way to start the process of mastering emotionally regulating truths. Even though we maintain that the "self" is the most powerful source in identifying and consolidating emotionally regulating truths, the initial identification of these truths is often helpful when considering the client's relationships as well as his or her spirituality. For instance, a therapist asked a 38-year-old man who was consistently drinking every day to the point of intoxication, "Before you were consumed by alcohol, your wife saw something in you that she wanted to be in her life. What did she see in you?" After long consideration, the man stated that his wife considered him a wise man who was a hard worker and was extremely thoughtful. This provided the therapist an initial grounding for the man to rationally consider the possibility that he was a wise, hard worker, more concerned with others than himself. Although the man was heavily utilizing shaming himself as a coping mechanism, he began to cognitively assent to this description as being accurate. As he started feeling wiser and more thoughtful, his experiences started building confidence in regulating truths.

Further, if the client has a spiritual belief that is important to him or her, this often provides a place to begin cognitively connecting with the truth and building it into eventual embodiment. For instance, a 20-year-old woman who considered herself a devoted follower of Christianity was having difficulty connecting to any truth about herself. She often talked about praying to Mother Mary and Jesus. The therapist encouraged her in session to simply pray for one minute to Mother Mary and Jesus concerning the truth about her identity and then to listen for any possible answer for two minutes. The woman took a moment to pray silently and after three minutes, the therapist called her back to the session. When asked if there was anything to report she said, "It was amazing. I started listening and all I could see were these words—sort of like voices but not—saying I was beloved and precious." Again, this gave the therapist ample opportunity to start utilizing these identified words from her spirituality to work with her to familiarize herself with the thought that she indeed was beloved and precious. Eventually, the woman consolidated the truth that she was deeply loved and essential. As the therapist encouraged these self-regulating truths, she eventually took actions which were more self-valuing and connecting to others. In turn, these experiences laid a further foundation and scaffolding to explore more embodied truths.

As we have mentioned before, the phase of Restoration Therapy in identifying the emotionally regulating truth is perhaps the most challenging in the work of this model of therapy. It regularly takes therapists who are well trained in the methodology five to six sessions to get this phase of therapy consolidated. It is not unusual, however, for the therapist to spend many more sessions in the process of helping the client lean into or believe the truth about his or her identity or sense of safety. It is always good for the therapist to be aware that like the pain cycle, the need for leaning into the emotionally regulating truth appears again and again during the therapeutic process. We usually think of the four things we do in Restoration Therapy—identifying the pain cycle, identifying the truth, identifying the peace cycle, and the practice of the four steps—as being recapitulated in almost every session in one way or another. In some ways, it is like the cattle rancher who was asked about his work, "Even when everything else is done, there is always fence work to do." In Restoration Therapy, there is always work the therapist must be prepared to do on understanding and chasing the pain the client feels, working with the truth the client will need to emotionally regulate the pain, identifying and experiencing the constructive actions in the peace cycle, or practicing the four steps into mindfulness so the client is prepared to be self-regulating. All of this work is important in Restoration Therapy, but as the regulating truth is essential to the process, it represents our "fence work" which always needs work and attention.

5   The Truth About Safety

Most people have an instinctive belief in the value and uniqueness of human beings. This is not a hard concept to sell to clients especially when they are thinking about others and a general philosophy of other people. We have a cultural heritage of valuing children and have no problem buying into the heuristically sound framework that we all come into the world with a need for bonding, connection, and attachment. We believe that Bowlby (1988) and others were absolutely correct when they stated that it is essential for a child to have experienced these attachment relationships with a parent or carer in order to develop his or her own emotional repertoire, capacity for emotional regulation, sense of self and identity, and the groundwork for future interactions and relationships. Ainsworth, Blehar, Walters, and Wall (1978) greatly extended the work of attachment by delineating the different types of relationships between child and caregiver in the following categories: securely attached, anxious ambivalent/insecurely attached, and avoidant/insecurely attached. Other researchers identified another type of style called disorganize-disoriented/insecurely attached. This attachment model extends into adulthood as adults who possess a positive sense of self and a positive sense of others have a secure attachment style whereas people who do not have these positive senses of self and others are dismissing, preoccupied, and fearful (Bartholomew & Shaver, 1998). The point is that people easily recognize and it is confirmed in the literature that early attachments are essential in developing a healthy identity and relationships and these early influences affect people for a very long time in their lives. These realities build in a sense to people that humans are *entitled* and *deserving* of value, love, and recognition of uniqueness.

When, therefore, a therapist asks a client to consider identifying a regulating emotional truth concerning identity, he or she may have difficulty believing that he or she is deserving of value, love, and recognition of uniqueness, but philosophically there still is usually agreement that he or she *should* be able to identify with those qualities about him or herself because he or she is part of humanity. Again, a healthy and emotionally regulated identity may be difficult for clients to believe but it is not a hard sell for the therapist to head them in the direction of speaking into themselves to overcome any shortcomings in the early attachments.

Although this general and philosophical assent to the value of humans is reliable when the therapist helping the client with the truth about identity issues, it is definitely *not* true with helping the client with safety issues. We may be able to easily agree that all people are deserving of love and have worth, but we cannot say the world and relationships are always safe. This is because safety depends so much on *predictability, justice* or *balance,* and *openness* in relationships. As we saw in Chapter 1, trustworthiness in the relationship translates to the individual as safety. However, people as caregivers, our experiences with mentors, and any personal traumatic experiences have a direct impact on how we determine trustworthiness in these three areas.

High Threshold of Predictability

In order for relationships to be considered trustworthy, humans require a very high degree of predictability. As Johnson (2018) has stated many times the one core question that people ask about a relationship is: "Are you there for me?" Essentially, this is what predictability means. Will you as my caregiver, spouse, important or influential person, sister or brother, or even the natural occurrences in the world show up in a reliable and predictable fashion showing that I can count on your love, behavior, and experiences to fit with what I know? This reality is not like gambling with money on a game where we would gladly accept a winning hand 50 percent of the time. Because it is in the context of relationships where our identity and safety depend on predictability, we require a much higher degree of reliability. How high does this percentage have to be? Our clinical findings keep pointing us to the figures of 85–90 percent reliability. In other words, we as humans can accept something less than perfection because we know that all humans and situations are not perfect, but we do not lean into a relationship and consider it safe unless a person or situation is the same or predictable a threshold of about 9 out of 10 times. Think of it this way, how many of us would give our money to a contractor to build us a house who was only successful at completing the structure 80 percent of the time? As humans, we are bound to the idea that if we are to *trust* a person or situation to the degree where we feel *safe,* the behavior or outcome of the experience has to be very predictable and reliable. If the predictability is lower than the threshold, then people simply will not trust the relationship or situation and will seek to withdraw. If they are forced to participate in this situation, they will likely always feel under a cloud of fear or doubt and will certainly not feel safe.

We all experience people who do not meet this high threshold of reliability and predictability. It may be lower because our caregivers themselves came from unsafe and untrustworthy backgrounds and they simply failed to give us what was needed and deserved because of their own destructive coping. The lack of predictability may be low because our mentors, teachers, coaches, or peers came from similarly destructive backgrounds and they have never really learned how to be consistent and reliable themselves. Or, finally, we live in a world that is notoriously unpredictable in terms of financial security, natural disasters, and circumstances beyond our control. Even at 90 percent reliability, relationships and the reality of life can bring harm to us and it can devastate our sense of safety. The more relationships and situations become unpredictable, the more we will likely disengage, withdraw, manipulate, or become aggressive in the name of caring for ourselves.

Justice and Balance

All relationships require at least two people who are engaged in mutual giving to and taking from one another. This is a philosophical reality that was first articulated by Buber (1958) in the *I and Thou* relationship. In other words, we have an innate quality that is born into our relational expectation from birth that we require people to provide us what we need and, as we grow, we become capable of giving to the other what he or she needs from the relationship. This is essentially a balance of giving and taking that, if continued in a predictable fashion, results in a trustworthiness where relational partners can depend on one another. The consequence of this trustworthiness over time communicates to me that, first, I can freely give to another without threat, manipulation, or fear because I know he or she will reliably give back to me (Boszormenyi-Nagy & Krasner, 1986) and, second, that I can feel safe in the growth of the relationship knowing that it is good for the *I* and good for the *Thou* (Hargrave & Pfitzer, 2003). Both of us get what we need from one another in a balance and justice driven by mutuality and trustworthiness. In relationships between friends, for example, both relational partners rightly expect to give to each other whether it is through listening when there is a need to be heard, caring and taking care of when there is hurt, or celebrating when there is joy. Laughter, sadness, joy, and empathy are all part of the language of giving that we expect in the balance of give and take in our best friendships (Hargrave & Hargrave, 2015).

Even in friendships as well as in deeper relationships, there is an expectation or *entitlement* we feel that we get from relationships. In the case of relationships between equals such as partner relationships or friendships, as we give to the other or the *Thou* we feel entitled to receive the same consideration and experiences from the giving of the other. Our giving,

Table 5.1 Illustration of Ledger Balance Between Spouses

Obligation to GIVE to spouse	Entitled to receive or TAKE from spouse
1. Love	1. Love
2. Care and Nurture	2. Care and Nurture
3. Performing household responsibilities	3. Performing household responsibilities
4. Contribution of work or money	4. Contribution of work or money
5. Reliable and faithful to relationship	5. Reliable and faithful to relationship

in other words, entitles us to the receiving in a relationship (Hargrave & Pfitzer, 2003). Where does this sense come from? It is logical and certainly arguable that this sense of relational balance is *innate* in us as humans just as our need for bonding and attachment is innate (Boszormenyi-Nagy & Krasner, 1986). It is like an internal gyroscope that directs us by balance and justice to know when we have over-given to the relationship or have under-benefitted from our relational partner's giving (Hargrave & Hargrave, 2015).

All relationships have this element of give and take and the expectation to be just and balanced. For example, consider the relationship ledger of give and take between spouses. As seen in Table 5.1, as one spouse gives some of the essential intrinsic and extrinsic elements to the relationship, he or she is entitled to receive the same elements or at least similar elements from the other partner.

If this spousal relationship goes on for a substantial period of time, the fair balance of give and take produces the resource of trust or safety in the relationship. If, however, one spouse does not do his or her fair share in the obligation to give, the other will feel the pain of injustice, unfairness, or lack of injustice which, in turn, will drive destructive reactivity in the form of aggressiveness, manipulation of the spouse, or withdrawal from the relationship (Hargrave & Pfitzer, 2011). Just as trustworthiness and safety tend to beget free giving in the relationship, injustice or imbalance tends to beget destructive reactivity making safety and trustworthiness impossible.

The above example is from a horizontal or *symmetrical* relationship of giving where what is expected on one side of the ledger is balanced by the giving or receiving on the other side of the ledger. There are also vertical or *asymmetrical* relationships of giving and taking that exist between generations (Hargrave & Pfitzer, 2003). For example, the relationship that exists between a parent and a child. From the parent's perspective, the giving to the young child can be seemingly endless and very demanding as he or she is, at times,

Table 5.2 Illustration of Ledger Balance Between Parent and Child

Obligation to GIVE to the child	Entitled to receive or TAKE from the child
1. Love	1. Nothing
2. Nurture	
3. Time	
4. Respect	
5. Care	

totally responsible for the physical, emotional, cognitive, and social develop-ment of the child. In turn, what does the parent receive?

As seen in Table 5.2, the parent actually receives nothing from the child because the child is not *obligated* to give back to the parent for the sake of the relationship. We would certainly agree the parent gets something from the job of parenting such as the joy of seeing a human develop, the priv-ilege of receiving connection and response to his or her giving, and the respect and admiration that may come from the child eventually. The point is, however, that the child is not obligated to give these things to the parent for the parent's good. The giving of the parent to the child is meant to be asymmetrical.

We might look at this ledger and feel this sets the stage for the parent to be unsafe in an untrustworthy relationship and likely to result in destruc-tive reactivity on the parent's part. The overwhelming majority of parents, however, do not see this ledger as unfair or unbalanced in any way. In these asymmetrical relationships, balance, justice, and fairness are built in an intergenerational manner. In order to understand the nature of these relationships, it is necessary to think of the parent once being a child. Presumably, he or she was given the love, nurture, time, respect, and care from his or her caregivers the same way that he or she is now giving those same things to his or her child. The parent did not have to give the love, nurture, or care back to his or her parent, he or she simply had to take in and absorb the benefit of the care into his or her identity and sense of safety. But as the parent has now grown, developed, and matured into an adult, he or she is now in the giving slot to provide the next generation of the intergenerational lineage with the love, nurture, time, respect, and care that was given to him or her. It is balanced and just through the alternating gen-erational framework of give and take (Hargrave & Pfitzer, 2011).

There is something that is profound and beautiful when this type of intergenerational justice and balance works well in contributing to the legacy of healthy families. Likewise, it is equally discouraging and tragic when trustworthiness in these asymmetrical relationships is absent. For instance, consider the story of a 41-year-old, small business owner who was extraordinarily angry and intimidating with his family.

> I was always the one responsible. My mother left my father when I was eight and managed to immediately overdose. My father was strung out all of his life and so I was figuring out how to take care of my sister before I was ten. For a while, I would just steal whatever I could but eventually got caught by a guy who cleaned pools and cut grass. He put me to work and I was able to earn enough to eventually take care of my sister and move us away from my father. He was a dangerous guy for us and would steal everything we had. When I left, I never let him know where we were and never contacted him again. By the time I was 16, I had learned how to trim trees and landscape places and could act old enough to get a place for me and my sister. It is what I have been doing ever since. Everything I ever had was either stolen from me or given by me to someone—and my kids wonder why I'm angry all the time?

As this man makes clear, he did not receive love, nurture, and care but instead was immediately given the responsibility of taking care of himself and a sibling. In this untrustworthy situation, he was unsafe and did what he could to manage a life for himself and be responsible for his sister. But obviously, he is deeply resentful what was stolen from him both physically and emotionally. Having been deprived of his just entitlement that has never been filled, he feels destructively entitled or that he has a "right" to his anger and intimidation. He takes care of his children physically and financially, but also makes his resentment and anger clear to them. Thus he robs his children of a sense of healthy identity and safety just as sure as he was robbed as a child of the same. The intergenerational ledger or transfer of justice is not balanced and trustworthy, but instead inflicts injury and curse on the subsequent generations (Hargrave & Pfitzer, 2011).

No matter where we grew up or the status of our current relationships, all of us have experienced the imbalance and injustice of relationships. Perhaps it is because we were on the end of being cheated out of our just entitlement or perhaps, just as likely, we were on the end that was over-benefitting from a relationship in which we felt unable or unwilling to give back in a balanced fashion. Either way, all of us have experienced a lack of trustworthiness and safety due to the reality of injustice or imbalance. As people are not perfectly reliable and predictable in trustworthiness, neither are they perfect in executing balance or justice. Consequently, the reality is that relationships and the world are not a safe place all the time.

Honesty and Openness

We do not know about you, but it seems to us that we live at a time in history when honesty and openness have never been more confusing. Ourselves, we live in a nation where the press keeps an "inaccuracy count" of how many times the president misrepresents something or out and out lies about a situation. In the same way, any story about a politician or the government that is negative is immediately denied or decried as being "fake," even when the facts seem indisputable. The whole and vulnerable truth about any situation we hear about in politics, entertainment, work, or education seems open to debate. "Spin" has become the new substitute for reality and "alternative facts" have become the tentative mooring for what used to be factual reality.

We can be as post-modern or constructivist as we like about this current situation or "reality," but the facts are that people do not feel safe with relationships that are not open and honest. As Hargrave and Pfitzer (2011) point out, we question the truthfulness and reliability of any relationship. When we look at our relational partner, we know they are flawed in some way no matter their skills, talents, and abilities. Every person has faults and therefore we cannot ignore the fact that these faults affect the reliability of the relationship. But more important than the question of trust and safety is how the relational partner represents him or herself in the face of these imperfections. Does he or she reveal these faults honestly and vulnerably? Does he or she try to cover over these "problems" to make him or herself appear better or beyond reproach? Does he or she excuse his or her problems and faults in an honest manner and try to make appropriate changes? If the answers to these questions do not reflect openness and honesty as well as an effort to change, we as relational partners will be left in an untrustworthy and unsafe place. How would we know "the real" person with whom we are having a relationship? Doubt casts a shadow on relationships and usually results in withdrawal or self-protection.

One of the issues that disturbs us greatly in our field of marriage and family therapy is the misunderstanding about change and acceptance. Many interpret acceptance, for instance, as a prescription that since people are imperfect by nature and may have issues in their pasts, we should accept one another as they are. This misleads people to assume that I must accept relationships as they are with no expectation of honesty, vulnerability, or change. Relationships, therefore, encounter this wall of individuality where each partner stays on his or her own separate side and "accepts" that which is not seen and does not change to accommodate further change and intimacy. We believe this to be a gross mis-reading of the idea of acceptance (Jacobson & Christensen, 1998; Gottman & Silver, 2012). We believe these authors do not promote acceptance as a means of foregoing the need for openness, honesty, and intimacy but rather acceptance as a means of changing focus of the potentiality of the relational partner to become more trustworthy and recognition of the positive direction in which the relationship is moving. The change of focus to acceptance of imperfections does not result in lack of change; indeed, acceptance in this context promotes relational change. Unloving and untrustworthy relationships are, in our opinion, unacceptable because they damage individual identity and safety. Openness and honesty allow relational partners to see each other accurately with flaws, gifts, and talents alike. They promote the framework of moving an individual from hiding from the relationship and becoming less intimate to being focused on where he or she can do better, make changes, and become closer to the other (Hargrave & Pfitzer, 2011). In this manner, relationships can become safer not because people do not have flaws, but because there is knowledge that mutual growth is being sought.

However, the reality is that people do misrepresent themselves through lies, deceit, and denial. Complete openness and honesty is hard for any relational partner because it risks the fragile identity of the person. Many feel this threat as they are ashamed or defensive about actions they have taken, prejudices they carry or fears that they will be exposed and humiliated by others. Sometimes these misrepresentations or secrets are very real actions such an infidelity between partners, betrayal in order to look good to a social group, or stealing or lying for nothing more than personal gain. Other times these misrepresentations and omissions of honesty are imagined such as a relational partner believing that he or she is so inadequate or unloved that he or she would never be found acceptable by any person. Either way, however, the secrecy, lack of openness, and dishonesty violate trustworthiness and therefore eventually seep into a global lack of safety. Worse still, there is no sure and absolute way that an individual can know the degree to which a relational partner is not open or honest and is left with the difficult reality of trying to exist in situations or relationships that cannot possibly be totally safe.

The Problem with Living in an Unsafe World

Hopefully, we have shown that there is no easy answer to living in a basically unsafe world. Not all relationships and situations are unsafe or damaging all the time, but all relationships fall short of the threshold of being trustworthy all the time in terms of predictability, justice, or balance and openness. There is no cultural or philosophical underpinning or scaffolding that makes this reality "safe" just because we say it is or we wish to believe it is. Tragedies occur such as earthquakes, tsunamis, and inundations. Errors happen such as crashes, mis-judgments, and mis-calculations. Devasting losses pile up through shootings, terrorism, disease, and malfunctions. One only needs to hear the local news on any day to get the clear perspective that the world is unsafe. We must, as therapists, face this fact with integrity when trying to help our clients come to emotionally regulating truths concerning trust-worthiness and safety.

For example, take the story of Terry's wife, Sharon. She was the fourth of four children and the only girl. Born in southern California, her father was accomplished in advertising and her mother was a lovely woman who stayed home to raise her and her brothers. It really seemed like a California dream as we watch the reels of film from her childhood. Her brothers and dad playing baseball. Her brothers and dad playing tennis. Her brothers and dad going to Disneyland and hanging out with the neighbors who just happened to be famous actors and stars. At some point in the film, in rolls a stroller with Sharon in who is being loved on, prized, and passionately embraced by her brothers and dad. It looks so beautiful, loving, and safe at this stage of Sharon's life. We are sure that her family was not perfect, but it certainly looked enviable. Then the wheels came off in her family.

Unknown to her or anyone in her family, Sharon's father was bipolar. Although he spent most of his life in what could be described as a hypo-manic phase, he had two significant bouts of depression. Unfortunately, while his manic phases were perfectly manageable, his depressions were very hard indeed. During his second major depressive episode, he took his own life. Sharon was three at the time and her mother was left with four children to raise on her own. She moved the family to Texas to be close to an older brother and somehow managed to start bringing the family back to a place that seemed normal.

A little over a year later, Sharon's oldest brother came home from school reporting that he was not feeling well with flu like symptoms. He was put to bed and kept home from school the next day, but by the evening, her brother reported that he thought something different was wrong. Sharon's mother called the doctor immediately and made an appointment to meet him first thing the next morning. Unfortunately, however, Sharon's brother died in the night of acute leukemia. He had gotten sick so fast that he passed away before they knew what was wrong with him. The once happy, loving, and trustworthy family of which Sharon had been a part was tra-gically changed in a bit over a year.

Sharon's mother was a remarkable woman in many ways and was able to pull the family together in such a way that Sharon and her brothers reported they were happy even amidst their wounding. They were moving to not only survive, but had some clear aspects of thriving and moving on with life. They had great family vacations and celebrated each other's athletic, academic, and social success. But Sharon reports that the grief and the unpredictability of life had changed her family in such a way that it was clear that control was a fleeting thing. Life was always a threat, not because of family irresponsibility but because it could mete out blows that could threaten survival in an instance. Indeed, the family was not done with the blows of life.

Nine years after her oldest brother's death, Sharon's next oldest brother was a senior at the University of Oklahoma. He was a wonderful young adult, was well loved in his fraternity, and popular because of his skills and talents. On Mother's Day in 1970, Sharon's family received a call that her brother and his date had not returned home from their date the night before. Immediately, the family drove to Norman, Oklahoma only to be told when they arrived that Sharon's brother and his date had been found murdered and locked in the trunk of his car. Life had already cast big shadows of unsafe and tragic situations, but for the family, this proved to be the biggest tragedy of all. Life and the world had proven themselves to not only be unsafe, but brutal and uncaring even at the most vulnerable of times. It is not difficult at all to see why Sharon developed the pain cycle seen in Figure 5.1.

As understandable as this pain cycle looks after reading the story, it is highly emotionally dysregulated and indeed presents challenges to the effort of living in loving and trustworthy ways. As a therapist, it is not hard to

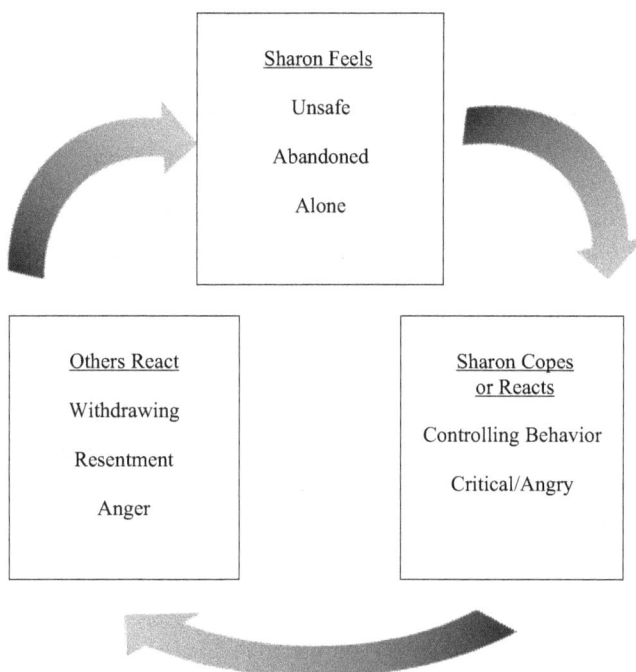

Figure 5.1 Pain Cycle of Sharon

be empathetic and understanding. However, empathy alone will not suffice to emotionally regulate. The therapist must confront the tragic events—whether those events come from the lack of safety because of family of origin, mentors/peers, or influential others, or life and the world itself—with some kind of truth that holds integrity. It will not suffice to say something trite such as, "Life is safe most of the time" or "Those people who have harmed you in the past cannot harm you now." A freeway does not turn into a sidewalk just because a person unwisely tries to cross the road and dangerous and untrustworthy people do not magically become loving and trustworthy just because a client choses to take the risk of engaging with them. Life, risk, and the pain they potentially can cause is real. The therapist must help the client deal with the truths of integrity that the client can buy into as self-regulating to face the unsafe world with courage and the capacity to live.

It is a huge therapeutic challenge to be able to help people with legitimate fears and anxiety because we do live in an unsafe world where people and relationships can result in tragedy. This is why, by the way, many restoration therapists unconsciously lean more towards doing work with the identity issues of the client: it is simply easier and has firmer answers than the truths that exist with and are necessary to regulate lack of safety issues. As therapists, when we see these profound violations of safety, we tend to feel small, powerless, and inadequate. We have a tendency to shy away from these issues and prefer to be with or comfort the client. This does have a place in therapy, but eventually therapists must turn their attention to helping the client—no matter how profound the tragic or traumatic violation—to move toward an emotionally self-regulating truth. To do less is to keep the client in a permanent place that holds on to the remnants of the victimization. Learning truth in the face of lack of safety is one of the keys in moving victims to a place of being whole and peaceful survivors. How then, do we come to the point of addressing an emotional regulating truth when it comes to the issue of safety? Here are the truths we have learned thus far that have the power to emotionally regulate a client in the face of lack of safety: 1) The client is empowered to do something in his or her situation; 2) The client is not alone in the type of violation he or she has experienced; 3) The pain the client experiences through lack of safety and tragedy eventually yields strength and empowerment.

Helping Clients with the Truth About Safety

Empowerment of the Client

Although we can readily acknowledge that we are never totally safe, we are usually far from being totally unsafe. Just because a client is not powerful enough to make him or herself safe in relationships or the world, he or she is far from powerless. The first step, therefore, in claiming some sort of emotionally self-regulating truth is to help the client to feel and act on the *empowerment* available to him or her. Human empowerment is essential and possible if we are going to help a client stabilize trustworthiness and safety in an unsure and unsafe place.

For instance, we have heard a variety of stories from people unfairly and inhumanely incarcerated in concentration camps during World War II. No part of their lives was under their control and seemingly they were devoid of any power. Yet many survivors of the brutality tell a similar story to the one in a camp where eventual survivors tore a small strip of cloth from a garment and hid it on their persons. When they received a meager portion of watered-down liquid euphemistically called "soup," they would drink it down except for a small portion and then soak the strip of cloth and wash themselves. One survivor was convinced that when a person stopped washing, he or she had given up hope and would soon die (Levi, 1986).

Why wash? It was certainly not because these prisoners could ever get clean, but it was rather a statement of empowerment. It was as if the survivors were saying, "In the midst of this impossible and tragic situation where I could be killed or die in a thousand different ways, I choose to stand here and symbolically do what I can do. If I survive, I will tell the story of what happened here and how we survived despite the inhumanity that has devastated me." A strip of cloth and symbolic washing was actually a deep statement of empowerment. Even if it appears that nothing can possibly be done, in this example you see in reality empowerment means that we can do what we can toward safety, stability, and protection.

Clients who feel unsafe often report a feeling of powerlessness or a sense of being out of control or being controlled. It is as if the unsafe situation contaminates the individual's ability for empowered action as the client begins to believe that since he or she was unable to protect him or herself in a particular situation before, he or she doubts that he or she has any power at all. For example, the following story is that of a 32-year-old man who felt depressed and powerless after he had been fired from two jobs in a row.

Man:	I just have lost any sense of faith in myself that I can work and have a successful career.
Therapist:	(Pause). You have lost two jobs in succession and it makes you doubt that you can work and be successful. (Pause). Help me understand your first job situation.
Man:	There really is not that much to tell on that position. The company was a start-up and simply could not come up with

	the cash to keep going. There are remnants of a few people still there but it is really about making sure the ship sinks right.
Therapist:	So on the first position, it really wasn't about you. The company was going under and you were laid off with most everyone else?
Man:	That's right. Really, I don't feel bad about what I did at that job at all but it is hard that it happened to me nonetheless.
Therapist:	That makes sense to me. The fact that you have lost two jobs makes it feel a little like you have a target on your back even though the first job had nothing to do with your performance. (Man nods).
	Help me understand your last position.
Man:	That one is much tougher. (Pause). I thought I was producing good work but every time I thought I was doing well on a project, I was pulled off to work on something else. Then when I would make progress on that project, someone would get angry that I was not working on the original project.
Therapist:	What were you told in these situations?
Man:	Really not much. I would be chewed on by my boss saying that I needed to be more efficient and quicker, but the kind of work I do is running numbers and analysis that are hard to track down. Just to get the numbers I need is a whole project in and of itself.
Therapist:	So what happened after you were chewed on by your boss?
Man:	I would work harder and more hours, but it was like I was juggling knives with three and sometimes four things going at one time. I was having a harder time getting anything completed and more and more work was being piled on me. I was not happy but my boss certainly was not happy. I was not pleasing anyone.
Therapist:	How did you feel when you were getting more and more work piled on and your boss was chewing on you?
Man:	Hopeless. Powerless. Like I could do nothing right. (Pause). I used to think I had some great skills but now ... now, I don't know if I have what it takes to get anything done. I feel so weak.

This particular man had impressive skills. He came from a great business program at a top university and had no trouble securing a position when he finished. He worked for a top company in his internship and held three other positions on his way to managing a team. Up until the time he was let go from his first job, his boss consistently complimented his work and was impressed with his versatility to produce and analyze business data. But the last position was very dissatisfying and he was unable to please his superiors or himself, so he began to doubt everything about his skills and his adequacy. This same feeling of powerlessness and inadequacy began to be imputed to his previous position where he was laid off, so the start-up's failure became his failure also. As a result, he feels powerless in his abilities to perform and his own skills and talents despite the fact that he has demonstrated power and competency before. Many clients make the same attributions to themselves whether it is in their work, school, relationships, or accomplishments. How do we get clients to enable themselves to be more powerful?

Challenging the Accepted Message

It is truly shocking to us as therapists how many individuals feel consistently that they don't measure up or are a failure. At first glance, this may look like an issue of identity but, more often than not, we find that it is actually driven by safety issues. The reasoning goes something like this: 1) If I cannot perform up to expectations, I have failed in what I am supposed to do; 2) If I fail at what I am obligated to give and I cannot correct it, I will also let my relationship partners down and I will fail at relationships. This is the reasoning of a *performance driven* person and is common among high achievers in academia, athletics, business, and almost any setting. The problem is, of course, that much of the performance driven life style gives rise to an enormous amount of anxiety and depression. Think of an elite athlete who attains a personal best height in the pole vault. If he or she is performance driven, the joy of doing a personal best will be extremely short lived because he or she will only feel as good as his or her last performance. When it comes time to vault again and he or she falls short of the personal best, it will result in a sense of failure and can easily lead to reactive shame or anxiety. This is all driven out of the desire to always be able to do his or her part and if he or she fails, it will feel much harsher than disappointment. This is not to mention how he or she feels when comparing him or herself to the others in the competition or the very best athletes at the sport.

This is just as true for academia and business. We have seen this performance driven anxiety and depression quickly turn into *performance driven identity*. In order to illustrate this, let us take a look at a case of a 19-year-old female who was overwhelmed with anxiety and depression when she went to college. Notice here how the therapist gentle guides the woman to challenge the message of performance to an empowered alternative.

Woman: (Almost panicky). I am faced in every class where there are other students smarter than I am. The school where I came

	from, I always knew that I was among the smartest. Here, I just don't know.
Therapist:	(Pause). And tell me what it would mean if you were not the smartest.
Woman:	I don't know. I am so fearful I will fail to live up to these standards I have always been able to meet. If I fail, I will disappoint so many people. I know I am making myself more anxious, but I can't stop thinking about whether I will be able to do this and every time I start wondering, I make myself more anxious and I am unable to do my work. (Starts to cry).
Therapist:	(Long extended pause). I understand how it starts this endless cycle of feeling like you might not measure up that fuels the anxiety. (Pause). Then the anxiety makes it hard or impossible to do your work. And when you don't do the work, you feel like you won't be able to measure up.
	(Long pause). Tell me, who taught you to be such a high performer and have such high expectations of yourself?
Woman:	(Calmer now). I guess it has always been expected of me. I mean … (Pause). I don't really know.
	(Long pause). My parents didn't overtly put any pressure on me. They just seemed so pleased when I would do well. I sort of took on the idea of performing well academically as my thing.
Therapist:	(Long pause). Many times I see this. Parents don't put overt pressure on their children to perform. So what messages did they give you about yourself and your relationships?
Woman:	(Long pause and a bit surprised). Hmmm. You know, that is a little strange. I am not sure I got many messages about myself. (Pause). Most of what I remember we talked about was what I was doing in school and things. They gave me direction and would process things, but I don't think they gave me many overt messages apart from advice and direction.
Therapist:	(Pause). So they didn't put pressure on you. They gave you direction and you all would talk about what was going on with school and relationships but they didn't talk overtly about messages of who you were as a person and what their relationship meant to them.
	Certainly I am not suggesting that your parents did something wrong, but I am still wondering in that context how you got the message that you had to perform at such a high level.
Woman:	(Long pause). I guess I am realizing right now that my school and activities were all we really talked about. I mean, they would always tell me they loved me when they dropped me

off at something, but we really never talked about what they thought of me.

Therapist: (Long pause). So you got the message, your doing was more of the focus or more important than your being?

Woman: (Pause). Yes, I think so. I don't think they meant it that way.

Therapist: (Long pause). Certainly. But it sounds like that always processing your school work and activities, giving you direction in those things and being excited when you performed well, left you with at least a heavy message that your performance was the thing that mattered most about you. Even though clearly they were not trying to give that message to you overtly.

Woman: (Long pause). I think that is right. I've never really asked myself where this focus on performing comes from. (Long pause). I think I have always believed that I am what I do.

Therapist: (Pause). It makes sense how you came to that conclusion. (Pause). So think for a moment, what message do you wish you would have received from them now that you know this performance focus has led you to so much anxiety and depression?

Woman: (Long extended pause). I think I would want them to engage me more around what I thought and what they were thinking more. I mean, I know my parents love me and I mean a lot to them—but we spend so much time talking about work and how I am doing.

Therapist: (Pause). So the message you were wish you would have received …

Woman: (Pause). My doing matters very little. My being is what matters.

Therapist: (Long pause). And if you were to give that message to yourself while you were sitting in the class with all those smart people in the room, how would it change your anxiety and depression?

Woman: (Long pause). I would like to try it. I think it would change it a lot.

Taking Protective Actions

When clients feel unsafe because there are trustworthiness violations due to unpredictability, injustice, or lack of openness, they often disempower themselves by passive approaches: either by refusing to take the time necessary to anticipate unsafe situations and possible protective actions, or they have a vague hope that relationships, people, or harmful situations will miraculously change. We find it very common among people who experience untrustworthy situations and lack of safety to make statements like, "There is nothing I can do" or "I just don't want to think about it anymore because I don't know what to do." These types of powerlessness statements often come from clients who have a coping reactivity of *escape* and we often interpret these statements as methods of "numbing out" or moving away from attentive responsibility. People who are reactive in a controlling manner most often do not have issues of taking responsibility and protective actions, but rather they try and control too much of the relationship and people. Their main issues in empowerment, therefore, usually focus on issues of setting appropriate boundaries for others and themselves. Clients who use the reactivity of escaping are most often the individuals who are neglectful or feel unable to take appropriate actions for protection. How then do we assist people in taking these protective actions and therefore increase their empowerment in an unsafe world?

First and foremost, it is important for the client to understand predictable sequences that lead to being violated in the area of trustworthiness. As Hargrave and Zasowski (2016) make clear, moving a client to be able to be powerful enough to interrupt destructive sequences involves him or her gaining *insight* into how the violations occur. Most people who suffer violation are unaware of the sequence of what the other relational party does and how they in turn react. We believe the best process in therapy is when the therapist helps the client detail a destructive sequence so he or she will be able to recognize empowered choices that can be made during the process of a future damaging action. The combination of both the insight into destructive sequences and the work and practice of the client in taking an empowered position in turn makes it much more likely that he or she will gain a sense of regulating truth or empowerment even in an unsafe relationship. For example, the following is from a case of a 38-year-old woman who was a mother of three who was in the midst of divorcing her husband of 12 years. Like many who are in the process of divorce, she was particularly ambivalent about whether or not she was finished with the marriage and vacillated back and forth on whether to try and reconcile or to divorce. As a result, the woman would cope reactively not only by shaming herself but also being very passive in her reactions toward the relationship with her husband and her parenting responsibilities. Her pain cycle is seen in Figure 5.2.

Therapist:	Tell me about the last time you found yourself in this pain cycle. (Showing the woman her pain cycle drawn out).
Woman:	(Pause). This last week—two days ago—I was in it again. I was having a hard day taking care of the kids and was feeling

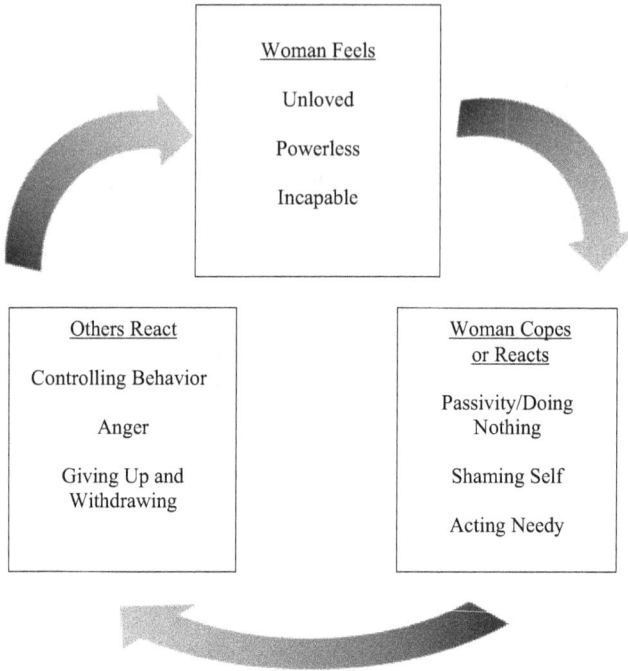

Figure 5.2 Pain Cycle of Woman in Case Example

this general sense of being incapable. I started questioning whether I was a good mother because I am too weak and not on top of things. I started projecting out about being a single mother with three kids and no one being there for me—feeling unloved.

Therapist: (Pause). You were feeling incapable and started shaming yourself about your mothering. Then were feeling like you were unloved. So what did you do then?

Woman: I did what I do—I called up my husband and started telling him I was unsure about the divorce and could we talk.

Therapist: And what happened next?

Woman: He did what he does. He got angrier and started saying things like, "You were the one who started this thing—you are the one who is making our lives miserable." Then he starts telling me all these demands he has about being more decisive and more active in taking care of our kids and being more involved as a wife.

Therapist: (Pause). And how do you feel then?

Woman:	(Long pause and starts crying). I think he is right and think I am the one who is making us miserable.
Therapist:	(Long pause). I understand. But what I am asking is what were you feeling before you started shaming yourself by thinking your husband is right about you?
Woman:	(Pause). I was feeling unloved, powerless, and incapable.
Therapist:	(Long pause and then pointing to the pain cycle). And what did you do next when your husband said these things to you on the phone?
Woman:	(Long pause). I just said nothing and was thinking to myself that he was right about me. Then I started drifting off thinking how much I hate myself in this marriage and how much I dislike how he makes me feel.
Therapist:	(Pause). And so you were feeling incapable and unloved so you call your husband and tell him you are not sure about the divorce. He gets angry at you and condemns you and then begins telling you all the things you need to change. You feel worse now feeling unloved, powerless, and incapable, so you passively listen to him and shame yourself more. (Long pause). What happened next?
Woman:	He just gives up and slams down the phone and says, "I can't help you out!"

It is important here to recognize the sequence of events not only in the pain cycle, but also in the interactions which promote the woman to be disempowered in her situation and feelings. It is helpful to either go over the sequence many times or to utilize the circular questioning to come up with an interactive sequence of the exchange. In this case, the therapist utilizes a drawing of the sequence to increase the client's awareness and point out how she can make alternative empowered choices. The sequence the therapist drew is below in Figure 5.3.

Therapist:	(Showing her the above sequence). When you look at how this sequence occurs, tell me about how often you have this type of interaction with your husband.
Woman:	(Pause). I have it a lot. Maybe our whole marriage this is how it happens. I feel really incapable or unloved or something, then I want him to solve it somehow so I won't feel that way. I start being needy.
Therapist:	(Pause). With your husband then, the sequence takes off because he immediately moves to get angry or tell you what to do or both.

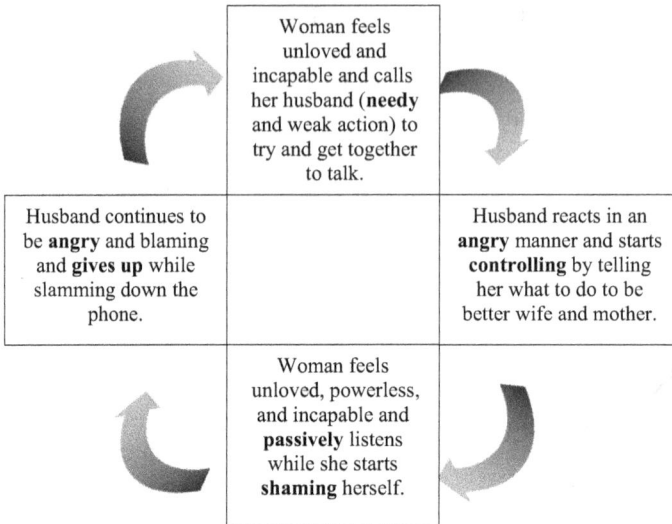

Figure 5.3 Interaction Sequence of the Conversation

Woman:	Sometimes he just tells me what to do and tries to fix me, but that doesn't feel any better and I get quiet and passive.
Therapist:	(Pause). I understand you feel powerless and incapable and those feelings drive you to be passive, needy, and shame yourself. (Pause). But if I were to ask you in this sequence to become empowered enough to take another action, where would you chose to do something different?
Woman:	(Long pause). Of course I could not call him when I felt those initial feelings, but I don't know if that is realistic for me. (Pause). If I could do something different at the point where I know he is angry and telling me what to do instead of being a passive observer—that would be better.
Therapist:	Good. Let's try that then. You play your husband on the phone during this conversation and I will play you.

At this point in the session, the therapist role plays with the client to help her first see what an empowered position would look like in this unsafe and unpredictable relationship. When the woman demonstrated the husband's anger, the therapist would make empowered statements like, "I am calling so we can talk some about our relationship because I have some legitimate doubts." and "I am working on my own feelings and taking clearer actions and so I will decide how to eventually handle my responsibilities." Each time the therapist would make an empowered statement, the woman would report that it sounded better to her than what she normally did in conversations with her husband. After processing the initial role play, the therapist had the woman take the role of herself and the therapist played the husband. The therapist asked her to make as many empowered statements at the strategic point of the conversation as she could when the husband was angry or controlling. The first role play had many starts and stops as the therapist would coach the woman in sharpening empowered statements. The rest of the session was practicing these empowered statements and getting to the place where she was familiar with interrupting the sequence with her behavior.

In the following session, the woman reported that her husband had called her and after some initial discussion, he began to tell her what she needed to do. She said, "I immediately thought of those empowered statements. I made several of them—maybe not as many as I should—but it did change the conversation. He backed off some and even said, I know it is not helpful for me to try and control you. But the main difference was I felt better and a little more powerful." In the rest of the session, the therapist not only consolidated the empowering statements, but worked with the woman in terms of starting with emotionally self-regulating truths based on her experience with her husband. She successfully identified a position of being "empowered to take action" and "loved" as essential truths that would help her take more appropriate actions than passivity, neediness, and shaming herself.

It is important to mention here that learning to take protective actions to increase empowerment in an unsafe world does not just apply to relationships, but also often involves empowering self to protect against trauma or catastrophes. For instance, clients often come to therapy because they are fearful of crime. In most of these cases, the therapist will discover that the client is aware of crime in his or her area but has a position of "anemic hope" that it will not happen to him or her. In cases such as these, the therapist helping the client name "empowerment" as one of his or her regulating truths and then moving him or her to take actions that are appropriate and effective in deterring crime reinforces his or her truth of empowerment. Things like securing a security system, improving lighting, making observations before going outside, going out with companions instead of alone, having gang "tagging" promptly removed, developing a neighbor watch system—all of these actions contribute to the experiential truth of empowerment. Do these actions guarantee that a client will not be a victim of crime? Certainly not. Actions do not guarantee safety in an unsafe world. But the empowered actions reinforce the essential truths that in an unsafe world, I am not in total control but neither am I powerless to do anything. These kinds of empowered choices, decisions, and actions help clients do what they can even in facing natural disasters such as earthquakes, hurricanes, tornadoes, and even global warming. We remember the story of one couple as they were sitting in their home as the flood waters were creeping up in their house. After they had moved all the furniture and objects they could, they sat in a small fishing boat on their porch making insurance and contractor calls to start the repair process. They were well prepared for the eventuality of a flood damaging their home, but this empowerment enabled them to take actions even while the flooding was occurring.

Setting Appropriate Boundaries

As mentioned before, although some people struggle with recognizing destructive sequences and taking appropriate and empowered protective actions, others struggle with setting appropriate boundaries around themselves and others. Of course, when a client is not setting boundaries around damaging relationships, it can be helpful for the therapist to coach empowered boundaries that not only protect, but also promote self-efficacy. For instance, a 27-year-old man was struggling with his unpredictable family.

Man:	It is really tough. I do miss my family, but every time I call home they are asking me for something. Usually money.
Therapist:	And so, how does that feel when you are calling for connection and it comes back that they ask for money.
Man:	I feel really used and just withdraw and want to avoid them. Of course I feel bad also because I do have more than they do, but it is because I'm working really hard.
Therapist:	What would happen if you took another position with them around phone calls. (Pause). For instance, if when you called you told them on the front end that you missed them and wanted to connect because you were feeling low or down. Or, another option might be, every time the conversation goes to asking you for something, you have a ready reason to get off the phone and end the conversation. You don't have to permanently cut off, you are just cutting off for that day.
Man:	(Pause). My first reaction is, can I do that? (Pause). I guess there is no reason I couldn't.
Therapist:	Again, I'm not asking you to cut off or even to make up needs for yourself. I am saying that by having a sound plan to address the pain beforehand, you are empowering yourself to set a boundary around your family where you would feel safer.
Man:	I can start imagining how that would work for me and help me feel better about the relationship I do have with them.

In this situation, the man practiced some of the boundaries with the therapist in anticipation of speaking with his family. He utilized both of the suggestions from the therapist. By the next session, he reported to his family at the beginning of the conversation that he was a little low and just needed to hear his family's voices. He stated, "The whole time was spent on asking me about me instead of telling me about them."

However, most of the empowered boundaries we work on with clients are in situations where the client is far more controlling and tries to extend his or her power to take responsibility for things that are not appropriate and rightly belong to the relational partner. In these situations, it is not so much that in an unsafe world we are trying to help the client *empower him or herself by doing something*, rather in an unsafe world we are helping the client take an empowered position of I can only *do those things that belong to me*. The following case example involves a 52-year-old couple in therapy for marital issues. The couple had been married for 26 years and had two children in college. The focus of the illustration here is work with the wife as she was feeling particularly anxious since the children left home and had become more demanding concerning her husband's and children's behaviors. She came from an unstable background, both of her parents were "social drinkers" to the point where she was often in charge of the family responsibilities. The couple pain cycle is shown in Figure 5.4.

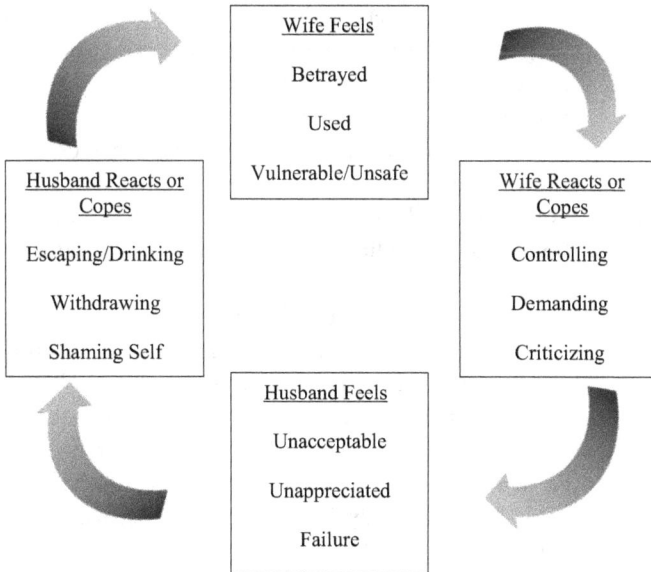

Figure 5.4 Husband and Wife Pain Cycle in Case Example

Therapist:	You seem to talk about what your husband and children should be doing a lot as well as solving problems for them.
Woman:	(Pause). This is one of the problems. I think I am being helpful to them and they think I am just nagging. I do not tell them anything that isn't for their own good.
Therapist:	(Pause.) I am sure that is the case. When they do not respond to you or just ignore what you say, how do you feel?
Woman:	Well, I feel unappreciated at first, but really I feel worried about them.
Therapist:	Worried. That relates to the feeling of being vulnerable or unsafe?
Woman:	Yes. (Pause). I want the people around me to be safe and I don't know if I can live with myself if I don't tell them what they need to do.
Therapist:	(Pause). So even though you are doing it for their own good, there is a part of what you do to try and head off your own vulnerability, anxiety, and lack of safety?
Woman:	(Long pause). I suppose that is right.
Therapist:	(Long pause). So when you feel vulnerable or unsafe and anxious and you cope with these controlling behaviors, it is some about taking care of your family but mostly about trying to cope with your own lack of safety and anxiety. (Pause). That makes sense to me knowing that you have been put in that situation from a very early age in your family to be the one charged with making everything come out right.
Woman:	(Pause). I always have been thinking it is my job to make everyone safe. (Pause). I don't think I've ever considered the fact that maybe I do these things because I don't feel safe when my family is unsafe—or what I consider to be unsafe.
Therapist:	(Long pause). As you consider it now, what do you think about that controlling behavior being tied to your own lack of safety?
Woman:	(Long pause). It doesn't make much sense because they don't really listen to me about the things I want them to do. I can tell him (Pointing at her husband) to stop drinking because it is ruining his health 24/7 and it doesn't make him stop drinking. (Pause). I think he even drinks more.
Therapist:	(Pause). It is tough. You are trying to do the right for your family, but you really have limited power. You cannot keep them safe in a world that is unsafe, but, more importantly, you can't make their choices for them.
Woman:	How do I live with that?

Therapist:	It is mostly about going after your feelings of vulnerability, anxiety, and lack of safety. You are only empowered to address your own feelings. You are empowered to make your choices. When you make peace with that reality, you can let others make their own choices and take their own actions.
	(Pause). For instance, it might look like this. I am powerful enough to do something about my own vulnerability and safety, but not powerful enough to make my husband take care of his own health. He must choose to do his part because I have no power to make him stop drinking and take care of his health. (Pause). If he dies, that makes me more vulnerable, but I am powerful enough to figure out my life if the worst happens. I will not and cannot control choices that only belong to him.
Woman:	(Pause). I know that is right, I just don't know how to believe it.
Therapist:	(Pause). Sure. You've been feeling vulnerable and unsafe and controlling a long time. It mainly has to do with practice. Try saying something like I said to your husband.
Woman:	(Long pause). I know I can't control you. You will make your own choices. I am not powerful enough to make you stop drinking. What I can do is do things that belong to my choices.

This is the first proclamation or the first consideration the woman gives that she is only empowered to do what belongs to her and cannot do this for her husband or children. As the therapist worked with her to sharpen her statements and speak the empowerment position she was taking to her own vulnerability and lack of safety, she began to learn a regulating truth. This was not a shallow regulating truth like, "If I let them make their own choices and take care of their own business, it will be okay." On the contrary, she recognized this would bring her additional vulnerability. She regulated the painful feeling with the reality that in being empowered only for her part, she would not "nag" or drive away her family and, even if "the worst happened," she might be grieved or sad but she would be empowered enough to take the next step in living life.

We are Not Alone in an Unsafe World

At the end of the day, none of us gets out of life alive. It is one of the great realities of life that ties all living things together and somehow makes us a part of one another. We all die and everyone who is dear to us will die.

Whether by traumatic circumstances or of "natural" causes, there is something about death that is sad and tragic. If you have ever been present when a person dies or have seen a corpse, then you know the sad and tragic reality of how one moment the person is able to engage, be present, and involved and the next moment their body is simply void. The same is true with any kind of loss or trauma. One moment there can be stability and a sense of security and the next moment—a devastating financial loss of a job or house, a brutal victimization through hate or crime, or the cheating or infidelity of a spouse of a friend—and life is somehow devoid of what was present just an instance before. It is also testimony to the fact that the world is not a safe place and although we can mediate some of the effects for a while, the hard and difficult truth is that pain will eventually find us all. We all understand grief and trauma at some level, some of us just don't yet know that we understand.

Another fact that is both surprising and difficult for us as therapists to realize is that when people experience these losses and traumas, they often feel like they are totally alone and no one can possibly understand the devastation of problems they feel. All of us are subject to this loss, pain, and trauma, but somehow when we are the ones experiencing it, we isolate ourselves. It is actually worse than simple isolation for the one who experiences the loss and there is also real and palatable resentment toward anyone who dares say, "I understand." Although it is totally reasonable to have these types of grief reactions to loss and trauma and comfort is called for, extended isolation, depression, and anger takes a toll on the person who has experienced the violation. In some instances, these actions and feelings will become habitual and destroy relationships.

The reality is, however, despite the painful loss and trauma, there are many who have passed this way before in exactly the same type of trauma or loss. It is not desirable or pleasant in many cases, but the telling of our stories of pain to witnesses while still in a world we are unable to trust—and then in turn hearing their stories—is essential for our survival in an unsafe place. Why? Because even in the midst of grief, loss, and tragedy, we are made to be relationally dependent. Relationships do not make the world safer in terms of loss and trauma, rather they make the world more manageable and tolerable despite it being unsafe. As mentioned before, isolation from others when we experience the pain of lack of safety inevitably leads us to depression, anxiety, anger, or extreme escapism as reactive coping mechanisms. Such was the case of a couple who had been married for 18 years with one surviving child. Their eldest child, a daughter, died of complications stemming from a bacterial infection. The couple came to therapy seven months after the child's death and had been working with the therapist for six months. Much of the previous therapy was focused on stabilizing and listening to the couple's grief and keeping them focused on connecting with one another.

The couple, however, were enormously resistant to the idea of seeking out group resources such as Compassionate Friends. Notice here how the therapist gently confronts the couple toward a more regulating emotional truth about their aloneness and isolation and moving toward a support group.

Woman:	(Very flat emotional affect). I think we function from day to day just moving from one thing to another, but we don't really talk of anything of consequence. (Pause). It is like we drift from one activity to the next—work, cooking, even caring for our daughter. It is like we are empty shells.
Therapist:	(Pause.) Some days you just stumble through. I hear what you are saying.
Woman:	I wonder if there will ever be a time where we are happy— just for a moment. We're like shells with nothing in them.
Man:	(Staring straight ahead). That's because we are. We are the same people, but we aren't. We are kind of shadows of ourselves. I think we know too much of what life can do to you to ever expect to be happy.
Woman:	(Long pause). I know you feel that way. (Pause). I feel that way too. It is so brutal to just keep living without her.
Therapist:	(Long pause). No one is exactly like you—even parents who have lost a child to death. (Long pause.) I'm wondering if they would report anything similar to you both after 13 months of their child's death.
Woman:	(Long pause). I'm sure they would feel something like we feel. But even as I say that, I can't imagine anyone possibly understanding the hurt we feel.
Therapist:	(Long pause). No one is like you and everyone's grief is different. (Pause). What I was asking was not would they understand you, but rather would they feel something akin to what you both feel?
Woman:	(Pause). I think they probably would.
Man:	(Still staring straight ahead). I don't care what they feel. I just don't want to be lumped into a group. I don't want any books or anyone to tell me they understand. I don't want anyone to try and explain anything to me as to why this happened to us. There are no answers to something like this.
Therapist:	(Long pause). Of course you are right—there are no answers. Certainly these are always your decisions how you go about managing this tragedy.
Woman:	I just don't know what good it would do us to know other people who also were grieving.

Therapist:	(Long pause). I remember a story told to me by a friend. He said a little girl was late coming home from school and was scolded by her mother. "Where were you?" the mother said. She explained that she passed her friend on the way home who had broken her doll. The mother said, "So I suppose you stopped and tried to help her fix her doll?" "No," she said, "I stopped to sit by her to help her cry."
	(Pause). You all have been through so much pain and there are no answers for such pain. Others have been through this kind of pain of losing a child. There are no answers for them. (Long pause). But I do think when you feel like a shell of yourself with so much pain, it is helpful to hear each other's stories so you know that in the midst of hurting and hopeless, you are not alone.
Man:	And what good will that do?
Therapist:	(Pause). Not anything directly. It is just hard to face the pain alone and keep it all to yourself. Sharing stories of pain doesn't fix the pain, it just assures you that people will face the situation and feel it together.
	(Long pause). It is similar to the stories you told me about your daughter's last days. (Long pause). You told me you did not leave her side? Of course you stayed right there with her. Why did you stay?
Man:	(Long pause and now making eye contact). I didn't want her to be alone. Not even for one moment. (Pause). I wanted her to know that I was right there with her. (Woman nods).
Therapist:	(Long extended pause). I know how you love your children, but I also know from those types of stories that you all are caring people. (Pause). When you are around other caring people in pain, you don't fix anything, you simply become strong enough to face the pain together.
Woman:	(Pause). So you are saying that it is not only for us, but also others.
Therapist:	(Pause.) Some of both. (Pause). But I know when you have touched intolerable pain like you all have, you also have been changed. Facing that pain is tough anytime, but more difficult when you have to do it alone.
Woman:	(Long pause and then speaking to the man). I don't know. Maybe we should go once to just see.
Therapist:	(Pause). You all have the right to decide how you grieve. It is just an idea at this point to consider.

Man: I really don't want to go—but at the same time, I think it is
              something we should try. (Long pause). I know if I isolate too
              much I will drift even further away and I don't want that to
              happen.

The couple did go to a support group for grieving families two weeks
later. They both reported that although neither wanted to go at first, they
began to see how they had much in common with people there who had
lost children to death. Although they did not share their stories about their
daughter initially, their resentment of such groups decreased significantly
and they experienced the guarded sensitivity of the group leaders to do
only what they were ready to do. As expected by the therapist, the couple
eventually began to experience the process of the group of not lessening
their grief, but instead making the grief and pain a bit more bearable. This
allowed the therapist to begin utilizing the idea of not suffering the pain of
their daughter's death alone as an emotionally regulating truth to the reality
and injustice that faced their family. As the husband would eventually report
in therapy, "Our pain will forever be there for our daughter, but we are at
least able now to face the world and be hopeful about our parenting and
remaining child. We are different than we were, but we are beginning to have
a soft inside again."

Pain and Tragedy Eventually Produce Strength and Virtue

Anthropologists have discussed for many years now that the original native
population of the Americas migrated via a land bridge from Asia across what
is now the Bering Sea. In this much colder environment, the migrating population was left unexposed to many of the viruses and potential infections
that were commonplace among the comparatively denser population of the
Eurasia continent and the much warmer temperatures. In many ways, it was a
population and environment that became sterilized from the ravages of disease
that had existed in other regions of the world over the centuries. Of course
this native population had viruses and diseases that spread among the people,
but the effects were likely much more isolated due to the vastness of the land
mass and the lack of density of population.

When the Europeans first started coming to the Americas, they brought
with them new diseases that were devastating to the native population
because they simply had no antibodies or resistance to these new strains of
viruses. Perhaps as much as 90 percent of the original native population was
wiped out due to this first contact with the European population. Europeans
also died of the diseases they brought, but not in the overwhelming numbers
common among the native Americans. For instance, in the infamous bubonic

plague of the fourteenth century, estimates of population deaths range from 50 to 60 percent. It was not because the Europeans were stronger, but rather many individuals and their immune systems had previous experiences of being around the viruses and more of them had antibodies that were adapted to the disease. Thus, although the native population of the Americas existed in a much healthier environment than Europeans for centuries, the result of the diseases were much more tragic because of the lack of exposure to the specific unhealthy viruses of the visitors. Friedrich Nietzsche (1977) once said, "That which does not kill us, makes us stronger." At least as it pertains to our physical bodies and the ability to fight off disease, this very much appears to be true.

But there is also veracity in the statement as it applies to us emotionally. Victor Frankl (1984) strongly believed that the way people accept suffering as a part of the reality of living gives him or her the opportunity to add a deeper meaning to life even in the most excruciating circumstances. The concept of *post-traumatic growth* is positive psychological change occurring as a result of adversity or challenges and results in a higher level of functioning. Much research bears out the reality that many people who experience trauma see themselves as stronger now as a result of the pain and difficulty they have experienced (Tedeschi & Calhoun, 1996; Tedeschi & Calhoun, 2004).

There is little doubt that many do not experience this type of growth. Many people feel weaker after physical injury or disease just as many individuals feel lingering unhappiness, pessimism, and hopelessness as a result of emotional trauma and pain. In other words, Nietzsche was only partially correct. So what makes the difference between those who turn trauma and lack of safety into growth versus those who stagnate or become weaker? Brooks (2015) makes an interesting distinction between what he calls our "resume virtues" and our "eulogy virtues." Our resume virtues relate to the skills and talents we can place on our resumes as a report of what we can do. Eulogy virtues are much deeper in that they reflect our character, values, and beliefs that people will recall at our funeral. Virtues such courage, humility, generosity, kindness, joy, gentleness, compassion, peacefulness, honesty, goodness, self-control, patience—these are the types of virtues that most of us long for as well as what we desire that people think of us. The reality is that these character virtues only come through the pain and difficulty of experiencing tough circumstances and tough times (Brooks, 2015). In other words, how an individual uses his or her pain is what makes him or her stronger in character as a result. Buechner (1991) recalls telling a particularly painful story of his past and some of what he learned from it to a group of conference attendees. Afterward, one of the financers of the conference came to him and said, "You have had a fair amount of pain in your life, like everybody else. You have been a good steward of it."

This is the reality we are speaking about in facing the difficult question of addressing the truth about safety in and unsafe world. We are speaking about not wasting the pain of lack of safety and untrustworthiness by perpetuating more emotional reactivity through blame, shame, control, and escape. Being a good "steward" of pain means that the client is able to do a bit of alchemy with his or her pain, turning what is one of the most unpleasant realities about life into the invisible issues of character and peace. It does not change the reality of living in an unsafe world, it just is a stance made to utilize the pain for good instead of ill.

As therapists, the question facing us is how we help clients utilize the pain and trauma in their lives to produce this invisible, but very real character. The therapist usually cannot open with this issue in the current situation of the client who is experiencing the trauma or pain without sounding trite and disrespectful to the current client story and pain. The lack of safety and the pain that exist with the client is too predominant and too overwhelming to sort out what is being developed that can be seen as a strength. Pain, after all, is painful. It consumes our attention and emotional space and calls for empathy and connection. Therefore, the therapist must help the client come to the determination to be a good steward of their pain by "going through the back door" through a scaffolding conversation that builds the client toward a willingness to consider that their current pain or trauma may contain hope to yield something different in their character. First, a therapist can help the client *recall the past where pain and trauma have actually resulted in growth and character.* Second, the therapist can help the client by *recalling situations in his or her family life that, while painful and bad at the time, yielded something redeeming and good.* Finally, the therapist can utilize the scaffolding to help the client *conjecture about growth and character development in the present situation and consolidate the commitment to stewardship of the pain.* In the following case example, a 58-year-old man was suffering from a situational depression after he was laid off from his management position unjustly. His subsequent rumination about the injustice of the situation and contemplation of legal reaction and even retaliation was resulting in isolation and problems with his spouse. After identifying his pain cycle, the therapist is working with the man in the eleventh session regarding the regulating truth of good coming from painful situations. Notice in this section of the case example how the therapist uses the scaffolding above in order to help the client come to a more secure position around an emotionally regulating truth.

Therapist:	You mentioned to me before that your father was in World War II. What was his story?
Man:	He was a tough old bird. He was born in 1925 so joined the army at the absolute worst time toward the end of 1943. So

	he was shipped over to Europe for D-Day and was caught up in the Battle of the Bulge.
Therapist:	That must have been tough.
Man:	Yeah, it was. He never really talked about anything much. He actually was in a group that was overrun by German troops during the Battle of the Bulge and was actually taken prisoner for about 45 minutes.
Therapist:	Forty-five minutes?
Man:	Yeah, he was in a group of three that was overrun and captured, but the one guy who was watching them was wounded by a stray bullet and the three of them escaped and made their way back toward the American lines.
Therapist:	Harrowing. I know you said your father never told you much about the situation there. What did he tell you?
Man:	(Pause). Well he told me that story when I was getting married. He told me the story and then said, "While I was being held there and realizing how many of my … in my platoon had been killed, I said to myself that if I ever got out of this mess, I was going to marry a good woman, work hard, and be faithful to her all my life." That was the marital advice he gave me.
Therapist:	How did it work out for him?
Man:	Pretty well. He was married to my mom for 47 years before he passed. Worked hard and was steady for his whole life. I really think keeping the promise was his way of honoring those who didn't make it back.
Therapist:	He used this horrible situation and never forgot it, but seemed to use it to be a steady faithful man.
Man:	I believe he did. You know, I was not that close to him because he just did not talk that much. But I did have a tremendous amount of respect for him and how he was that steady guy after being in a situation of so much trauma.
Therapist:	(Pause). Did you ever have a situation where you had a defining moment? Maybe not as dramatic as your Father, but still defining.
Man:	(Long pause). You know, there was a time when I was working in a little, badly run glass manufacturing company. It was really bad. It was my first real job out of college and I thought I was going to do well. I wasn't happy there at all, but it was a job. Then a recession hit and within a year of taking the job, I was laid off.

I thought as I was driving back to my apartment after I got my notice and I thought, I am going back to school to get my MBA so I will never be in this situation again. (Pause and smiling). I know that sounds ironic now given my current circumstance, but it was a defining moment.

Therapist: You were laid off from a job you didn't like anyway, and that is when you took the step to get your MBA so you wouldn't find yourself in that situation again. What direction did that take you?

Man: Oh, it was a real game changer. I learned things that prepared me well and it really set me up to get jobs in upper management. I even met my wife while I was at that college.

Therapist: So here was the bad thing that happened to you and like your father, you make a determination that you are going to do something very different. (Pause). And that decision changed many things for the good.

Man: That's really right. I didn't realize it at the time, but it really set me on a totally different trajectory with my life. That glass company is long since bankrupt.

Therapist: (Long pause). I know that all situations are not the same. You have experienced this really unjust layoff that has created all sorts of turmoil for you. (Pause). I'm not asking you to name it because I don't know if you really are able to know it at this point, but is there a defining moment in this present situation? Or if there is, what would your guess be that the defining moment will be?

Man: (Long pause). I will need to think on it. (Long pause). I see what you are meaning, but I will need to think on it.

The man came back to the next session and stated that he had been thinking about the situation since the last session and had discussed it with his wife. "I think the defining moment for me is will I be able to focus more on what I can do in my future than concentrate on what is past. Sort of like deciding what my next step is and trusting that I will find my way." The shift in perspective did not immediately alleviate all the questions for the man nor the pain of the injustice, but it did change his focus to concentrating more on the fact that there were still possibilities for him and called him back to his virtue of courage of living toward the future instead of focusing on the past.

All of us, therapists and clients alike, live in an unsafe world that poses difficult questions about how we can live without being overwhelmed by our reactivity in the forms of anxiety, over-control, blaming, and anger or escape. An unsafe world calls for all of us to emotionally regulate ourselves with rock solid truths and not simple platitudes. Empowerment to be able to recognize the cyclical processes, protect ourselves, and set appropriate boundaries in situations is something tangible that allows us to stay in life. Further, utilizing belonging assures us that we need not face the pain and trauma of life alone. Finally, recognizing that the powerful attributes of character and good can come from pain and trauma sets us on a journey of utilizing an unsafe world and untrustworthiness to build meaning and extending sound relationships into the most essential elements of virtue. As therapists, we owe this type of veracity to our clients when we are helping them emotionally regulate in an unsafe world.

6   Practice, Self-Control, and Mindfulness

If you have read the book carefully up to this point, you will realize that although Restoration Therapy is actually quite simple in content, it becomes deep and profound in the process of therapeutic practice. After all, there are only four major signposts along the way in Restoration Therapy. First, we help people understand and recognize their pain cycles. This is the joining stage of therapy where the therapist listens carefully and is empathetic to the story of the client. The therapist then starts helping the client see his or her points of emotional dysregulation in terms of identity and safety or the status of relational love and trustworthiness. As these essential feelings and primary emotions emerge in the context of the story, the therapist tracks what the client does or his or her *reactive coping* to the violation of love and trustworthiness which has prompted the disturbances of identity and safety. The therapist then draws this cycle in a cognitive map also including how relational partners themselves react to the client's reactivity. This is how we get to the pain cycle and, in normal types of cases, it takes between five and eight sessions. Second, we help the client understand and experience the truth or the emotionally regulating counterpart that disrupts his or her feelings of violated identity or sense of safety. As we have stated before, this is the most difficult aspect of therapy in Restoration Therapy because it is the strategic place where the client can recognize his or her truest and most peaceful identity and cope with the implications of safety in an unsafe world. The previous two chapters give detailed information about what we have learned thus far in helping the client consolidate these truths both emotionally and experientially and, in normal types of cases, we find that most often this work takes between five and eight sessions.

Third, we begin to work with the client to identify and understand the completed peace cycle. This is the cognitive map of emotional regulation for the client as the therapist takes the emotionally regulating truths identified in the second signpost or goal in therapy and helps the client identify what he or she is able to do in terms of actions that are driven by *agency* instead of being reactive and destructive when he or she is grounded in a particular truth. Simply put, emotionally regulating truths yield client actions that are both loving and trustworthy in relationships while the pain cycle or emotionally dysregulated feelings yield client actions that violate love and trustworthiness. In identifying these peace cycle actions and behaviors— nurturing others, valuing self, balancing relational give and take, and reliably connecting to others—the client is basically setting up a self-reciprocating model of confirmation of their emotionally regulating truth (Balswick, King, & Reimer, 2016). That is, as the client engages in emotionally self-regulating truths about him or herself and takes agency actions that are loving and trustworthy in the peace cycle, relational others usually react with healthy and agency actions themselves which reciprocate or validate the very emotional regulating truths the client started with in the peace cycle. Love and trustworthiness beget love and trustworthiness. This enables the client to then gain a powerful experiential component of intimacy in relationships as well as comfort within his or her own identity and safety. In therapy sessions, when a client first experiences the experiential movement from the emotional dysregulation of the pain cycle into the emotional regulation of the peace cycle, it is a powerful moment when he or she can hardly believe how much better he or she feels.

All therapists have had these types of powerful sessions where one would think that such a powerful experience for a client would provide enough insight and different feelings that he or she would forever be different. As Hargrave and Pfitzer (2011) point out, *insight* is a wonderfully motivating factor in therapy as a client understands something new and has first experiences of change. But is it sufficient for long-term change? The research seems to be fairly clear that it is not (Atkinson, et al., 2005; Siegel, 2007; Hanna, 2014). What is also needed is a framework of effective *practice* in order to mindfully habituate the experiential changes into the neuropsychology of the brain. The first three processes, signposts, or objectives in Restoration Therapy are mostly aimed at helping the client achieve *insight*. When we move to the fourth objective in Restoration Therapy, we are really moving to the process of *practice*. As such, Restoration Therapy gives an effective "one, two punch" in the process of making change by combining both the motivational benefits of insight and the consistent and mindfulness benefits of practice (Hargrave & Pfitzer, 2011).

Fourth, in Restoration Therapy we do the work of practicing through the mindfulness strategy of what we call the four steps. As mentioned before, these four steps are designed to teach the emotionally dysregulated client to move him or herself from being in the state of the pain cycle to being self-regulating in the peace cycle. The four steps are: 1) Say what you feel; 2) Say what you normally do; 3) Say the truth; and 4) Say what you will do differently (Hargrave & Pfitzer, 2011).

In the process of working with Restoration Therapy clinically, we have found several things to be essential in making the mindfulness process "stick" with clients and produce change. First, we have found that many clients make better use of the four steps of mindfulness when they engage in some type of bilateral slow-down in preparation. Second, in the practice of the four steps in the therapy session, it is best to combine stimulation to as many regions of the brain as possible including mental, tactile, kinesthetic, visual, auditory, and interpersonal stimulation. Third, repetition is not only a key element in getting the process of emotional regulation into the brain, but also in helping the client reorganize and reconsolidate new emotional neuronal connections in preference to old patterns that include old triggers. Fourth, novelty and surprise greatly enhance the process of practice with a client. Fifth, the intensity of therapeutic sessions focused on practice is a key element in reconsolidating new neuronal connections and brain changes. Sixth, the more levels of relational involvement in the practice of changed behavior and emotional regulation there are, the more likely it is that the experiential reality and neuronal change will take place personally, in family relationships, and in community involvement. We will discuss these six aspects of what we have learned therapeutically in detail in the rest of this chapter.

Slowing Down the Client with Bilateral Activity

There is a common proverb, "A journey of a thousand miles begins with one single step." Of course, the first step toward the goal is always the most important. But when we are speaking of an emotionally dysregulated brain where old identity wounds and safety questions have provoked full-on reactivity of fight and flight, the first step is most often the hardest for a client to take. Mindfulness is a wonderful thing. It lifts the awareness of the pre-frontal cortex and our cognitive abilities to be able to analyze, observe, recognize, and integrate the various aspects of our feelings into our awareness where we can effectively choose how to accept and deal with our brain (Hanna, 2014). It is as if our mindful self is able to step out of ourselves and analyze the feelings, thoughts, motivations, and behaviors without being duly influenced by those things. A mindful brain is an observing and curious brain as it notes and analyzes itself. But as LeDoux (1996) has forcefully pointed out, our cognition is not the primary driver of human behavior, rather it is our *emotional brain* which is much more powerful. In fact, between emotion and cognition, it is not close as the emotional brain dominates the behavioral landscape particularly when there is emotional dysregulation. It is not that our cognition or potential for mindful regulation is powerless, it is simply important to remember that cognition likely will need some serious help to impact emotional dysregulation. Imagine a driver, screaming down the freeway at 110 mph in the wrong direction. It is unimaginable for the driver to immediately turn around and go the other direction. The driver would first need to slow down dramatically, take an exit ramp off the freeway, make his or her way to the lanes going in the opposite direction, and slowly gain speed to enter the flow of normal traffic. Immediately stopping emotional dysregulation and physiological stimulation poses a similar situation. We first must help the client *slow down* the physiological process of fight or flight reactivity in order to help the prefrontal cortex of the brain gain enough power over the emotions to consider the four steps.

Although we have tried many ways of facilitating this emotional slow-down, by far the most successful and most efficient is a 1–3-minute activity involving a bilateral engagement. This can be very simple thing like having the client catch a bean-bag type ball with one hand that is tossed by the therapist and then tossing it back to the therapist using the other hand. The sequence usually involves 20–25 tosses and catches in succession between the therapist and the client. In another simple activity, the therapist hands a plain sheet of paper to the client and keeps one for him or herself. The therapist then demonstrates and gives directions to the client to fold the paper in half and then crease it hard with the tips of the fingers. Then the therapist asks the client to unfold the paper and demonstrates to him or her how to fold the paper along the crease in an opposite direction. This process of folding, creasing, unfolding, folding, creasing, unfolding is repeated six times with the same piece of paper and results in the paper showing eight equal sections. This process, although very simple, takes about four minutes.

In a slightly more involved activity, the therapist has the client stand up with him or her facing the therapist with feet apart about shoulder width. The therapist then has the client sway back and forth matching the slow pace of the therapist shifting weight between the left and right side. After about a minute, the therapist has the client sing a very simply or favorite song with him or her while still implementing the swaying motion. The songs clients choose vary, ranging from 'Twinkle, Twinkle Little Star' to favorite lullabies, to Elton John songs. The point is, however, the slowing down of the emotionally dysregulated self takes place by using the bilateral activity for 3–4 minutes. Why does it work? Most likely, the slow-down works because the focus of the client is changed dramatically and when the focus is modified, the client loses the emotional trigger to maintain the physiological reaction. Also, the bilateral nature of the stimulation may have a calming effect, particularly to the mid-brain area (Shapiro, 2017).

To illustrate this technique, the following example is from a session with a couple where a male spouse became particularly angry in the session after an accusation from his spouse of not doing his fair share of the work. Since this was well into the therapy and in the stage of practice of the four steps, the therapist first worked with the spouse in going through the four steps and emotionally regulating her feeling of injustice that fueled the accusation. When the therapist followed the process over to the man, he was extremely agitated.

Therapist:	Likewise, let me help you go through your four steps. When you heard the accusation of not doing your part, what did you feel?
Man:	(Very angry). I don't care! I don't want to do anything. I am simply done with this process.
Therapist:	You are so angry about the accusation that you don't want to have anything to do with the process?
Man:	I'm not going to do anything. It is hopeless. We just go back to the same story line over and over again no matter what the reality is!
Therapist:	(Louder than her normal voice). I hear you. You are really upset. (Pause and then in a more modulated and softer voice). I want you to take this piece of paper and I will tell you what to do with it. (Hands the man the paper which he takes with a heavy sigh). I want you to fold the paper in half just like I am doing. (Folds the paper in half and the man complies). Now, crease the paper hard with your finger-tips. (Creases the paper from the middle to side using alternating hands and the man does likewise). Now, unfold the paper out and refold the other way against the crease. (Unfolds the paper and folds it back the other way, man does likewise). Now crease the fold you just made. (Therapist continues to fold, crease, and unfold the paper with the man six times with similar directions to above. The man complies each time).
Therapist:	(Taking the paper from the man and setting it aside). Now, take a good comfortable deep breath and let it out. (Pause and drawing attention to the man's pain cycle). When you were accused of not doing your fair share, what were you feeling?
Man:	(Pause and much calmer). I felt like there was nothing I could do to ever measure up.

We have witnessed this change of focus and calming effect over and over in therapy whether it is folding paper, tossing a ball, swaying and singing, or even dribbling a ball with alternating hands. The activity slows the process down and the physiological stimulation decreases dramatically. This allows the client to exit the pain cycle freeway and execute a turnaround to use the four steps to gain momentum and speed on the peace cycle freeway heading in the other direction. Notice here that the therapist does not explain the activity before she executes it with the man. We have found overwhelmingly when clients are emotionally dysregulated and physiologically aroused, it is better to simply start *doing* the activity instead of explaining. If the therapist believes he or she must explain, make it brief and simple such as, "I want to do an activity with you to help your ability to focus." Notice also the therapist immediately picks up the therapeutic process of the four steps instead of processing the anger or even the activity. She is skilled in the process and already knows and understands why the man is upset and physiologically aroused. She makes the choice that the four steps will set the peace cycle into motion and thereby produce a better opportunity for complete emotional regulation. To process the activity or the anger here makes it much more likely the man will lose the benefit of his change of focus to facilitate change. When a therapist is utilizing these bilateral activities, we believe they should be executed and then the therapist should quickly return to the focus of the four step practice.

We should mention here that the bilateral activities we mention here are somewhat different from eye movement desensitization and reprocessing (EMDR) therapy (Shapiro, 2017), but some of the aims of the process are the same. Although how exactly EMDR works for individuals who have trauma is something of a mystery—as is often the case where we don't understand exactly how the brain works on topics ranging from the effects of psychopharmacology to neuroplasticity—it is clear from the research that EMDR does help people from a variety of situations and trauma backgrounds. For those therapists who have training in EMDR, we find that it compliments much of the work we do in Restoration Therapy and should be used both as we have outlined here, but also for other situations where the client can benefit. We believe in the quest to help clients to learn how to self-regulate themselves emotionally, EMDR can augment Restoration Therapy practices nicely as well as vice versa.

Involvement of Many Regions of the Brain

In speaking about imagery techniques in helping clients make experiential connections with the truth, we discussed and demonstrated many frameworks of the therapist using his or her voice and setting the mental imagery in a powerful way. We believe that these frameworks greatly assist the client in having an actual experience with the regulating emotion of truth instead of just being trapped by the confines of language. In the same way, we believe there is much to be said for employing or involving as many different regions of the brain as possible when it comes to practicing the pain cycle, the regulating truth, the peace cycle, and the four steps into habituation. The end goal of the practice stage of Restoration Therapy is to bring these elements and skills into the client's experience as much as possible so these skills are available to him or her when he or she is emotionally dysregulated. Therefore, it makes sense to utilize as many regions of the brain as possible when working toward this goal.

There are tried and true ways clinically that we use in Restoration Therapy in the practice process of the four steps. First, once the therapist starts to have a clearer idea of both the pain and peace cycle, he or she will often draw this cycle out. Some therapists like to do this on a dry erase board or large poster size sheets of paper to have out during any session with the client. Others like to have the client pain and peace cycles on card stock paper that can easily fit into the client's file. No matter where the visual cognitive maps of the pain and peace cycles are drawn, it is helpful to have them out in every subsequent session for two reasons: 1) They greatly assist the client and therapist both in interpreting events, feelings, and reactions that happened recently or in the current moment and tend to keep the therapy organized; and 2) The familiarity of having the pain and peace cycle out each session employs the client's ability to drive the material into deep memory (Hargrave & Pfitzer, 2011). The therapist need not draw the pain and peace cycles perfectly before they are placed in the context of the session to be used. The pain and peace cycles are "living maps" which are used as a starting point and then modified many times as the therapist and client co-construct a framework that is both meaningful and helpful to the visual acumen of the client. Many clients will take pictures of these cycles that the therapist draws for their work between sessions. Many restoration therapists send a copy of the cycles home with the client to place in a conspicuous place so he or she can visually make contact with the material when emotionally dysregulated. For couples, there is also a smartphone application (called *marriagestrong*, one word) where spouses can complete their cycles and then link them together. The main point is that these visual maps greatly enhance and engage both the visual and prefrontal cortex and eventually result in a memory tool.

Another tried and true technique restoration therapists use stimulates the auditory cortex areas of the brain. Particularly in the course of learning the four steps, the client is encouraged to say these four steps as they apply to the pain and peace cycles *out loud*. There are several reasons why this should be done out loud. First, the brain is a fast processer of information— really fast. Estimates of how fast the brain processes information are at least 9,000 times faster than the fastest microprocessor chip (Lewis, 2014). This is astounding and takes place in humans with no practice or training. But when this is combined with the reality that we have close to a billion neurons in our brains and each neuron has potentially a thousand connections to other neurons and each neuron is capable of firing messages many times per second, we can see than not only is the brain fast, but fast beyond our comprehension (Bollow, 2015).

This speed, however, does not always make for a good impact when we are processing important information or wanting to be mindful of our processes. If we are seeking to help a client remember and practice his or her pain or peace cycle, the sheer speed of thoughts and processes competes for the attention of the client. Many times a client will be into his or her pain cycle before he or she is really aware that it is happening. For example, if the brain were going through a deck of cards every second, the brain's chance of memory or emotional impact of any one card is quite low. This is why slowing down the brain, particularly through auditory processing, makes sense.

When a client says the four steps out loud, he or she must first conceive the word in the prefrontal cortex. The intention of saying something like, "I feel alone and unloved," must be processed and organized in the auditory cortex and Wernicke's and Boca's areas and then into our prefrontal cortex in the client awareness. Then, it is transferred to the motor cortex where the language is organized into movement and intention so the words can proceed from the client's mouth to say, "I feel alone and unloved." This information then is processed by the hearing of the client and auditory and sensory cortex where he or she hears what has just been said and then understood, hopefully at a deeper level, in the prefrontal cortex.

All of the work that happens in the brain very quickly, actually slows the processing down significantly by the novelty and changes the focus of the client to be able to better attend to what he or she said. This would indeed *not* be true if the client simply *thought* about what he or she felt. The message of feeling and the four steps in general are likely to get lost in the overwhelming milieu of thoughts, emotions, and competing processes. Having the client say these things out loud does not guarantee the four steps will have a great impact, but it does ensure that the processing of the information will slow down. Further, the stimulation of the auditory processing part of the brain ensures a deeper processing of the material and opens the door to more client change (Hargrave & Hargrave, 2015).

There are other ways, however, to bring stimulation to various parts of the brain combining tactile and kinesthetic activities. For instance, in the following case a man was discussing his pain of feeling unloved and alone and how it contributed to his shaming and inconsolability. The therapist uses two blankets he happens to have in his office because the air conditioning would often make his office quite cold. Notice here how he uses both the tactile and the kinesthetic stimulation of the man's brain in order to process the four steps.

Man:	(Pause). I just have difficulty. Hard to explain. It is like I get consumed or covered up by the pain of being alone and unloved and then it is like I can't move.
Therapist:	(Pause). So you know the pain cycle is there, but it covers you up and consumes you to the point where it is hard to consider something different.
Man:	That's right. I just get overwhelmed and it is hard to do anything else.
Therapist:	(Standing up). Stand up with me for a minute. (Standing and facing one another the therapist takes two blankets and hands one to the man). So when you feel unloved and alone, it consumes and covers up the real you. (Therapist takes the blanket and puts it over his own head). And when you get covered up like this—(Pause)—it is hard for you to consider doing anything else because the real you disappears. Put your blanket over your head like I have it on mine. (Man complies). (Long pause). What does it feel like to be under that cloud that consumes the real you?
Man:	It feels like the feelings of unloved and alone are overwhelming. (Long pause). I just can't see anything else.
Therapist:	Of course, it covers you over. (Pause). I feel it too. (Pause). And what do you do when you feel overwhelmed and covered up by being unloved and alone?
Man:	(Pause). I just disappear into myself. I start beating myself up with how hopeless and worthless I am. How nobody wants to be around me.
Therapist:	(Pause). Of course, that makes sense. Nobody takes the time to be around you because they can't see you. (Long pause). Now here is where the real effort comes in, because you can choose to stay covered up by those feelings for as long as you want. But if you choose to, you can start saying the truth about who you are. (Pause). Take your time. It is your decision.
Man:	(Long pause). It would be silly to stand here with a blanket over my head.
Therapist:	(Long pause). Yes and no. In one way, you do have a choice of taking off the blanket with your truth. But if the feelings of being unloved and alone are too powerful for you, you will

	have to choose to leave yourself overwhelmed and consumed by those feelings. It is your choice, and it is real.
Man:	(Long pause and then takes the blanket off his head). I am loved by many people. My children, my parents, and two friends and I can always call on those people and don't have to be alone. (Chuckles a bit and says to the therapist). You still have the blanket on your head.
Therapist:	(Pause). Of course I do. Say your truth again then tell me what you will do differently instead of beating yourself up with shame.
Man:	(Pause). I am loved by many including my kids, parents, and friends. They are with me and I am not alone. (Long pause). And what I will do differently instead of shaming myself, is I will make connections with those who care for me. (Client removes the blanket from the head of the therapist).
Therapist:	(Pause). Ah, that is better. I can see you and make contact with you. (Pause). Thanks for making contact with me.
Man:	(Smiling with a soft voice). Anytime.
Therapist:	(Sitting down). So you chose to say your truth and make connection. You are powerful enough to overcome these overwhelming feelings of being unloved and alone.
Man:	(Long pause). The reality is that I am. I guess when I saw these feelings as a physical blanket that made it impossible for you to see me or even see myself, it brings it home that I have let myself get covered up. (Pause). It was helpful to physically have that illustrated.

In this case, the therapist did not have a particular plan in his mind before having the client stand up or putting the blanket over his own head. He simply heard the client say he was "covered over" and it opened the idea of utilizing the blankets. From there, he simply trusted himself to use the four steps in the context of a multi-layered impact combining visual, auditory, tactile, kinesthetic, and interpersonal brain stimulation. The therapist trusted he would find his way in helping the client. We often say in training therapists, "Real courage is to stand up with a client in session without being clear what you are going to have the client do." This particular therapist was courageous and found his way with the client to produce a broader and deeper impact than if he would have simply done an auditory practice of the four steps alone.

In Restoration Therapy, therapists will often utilize these types of visual, tactile, and kinesthetic involvements to bring home particular points by utilizing stimulation to various parts of the brain. For instance, a therapist had a couple move the sofa in her office so it served as a "barrier" in the relationship. At other points of the therapy, she would have the couple "hide" from one another while still processing information to help them understand the difficulties when they withdrew from one another. Another therapist had a couple stand on a chair anytime they were taking a controlling or power position with the other to further bring to mind their power plays with one another. The types of visual, tactile, kinesthetic, and interpersonal work are only limited to the therapist's creativity in deploying information to various parts of the brain.

The Importance of Repetition

Emotional memory is quite powerful. Meaning is placed on these memories. Statements such as "I am stupid," "I am a failure," "No one cares for me," "My parents hated me" are all examples of these emotional summations that are placed with images which are extremely difficult to overcome (Ecker, Ticic, & Hulley, 2012). In fact, most of these emotional memories have been considered *indelible* or unchangeable, meaning that the individual could input competing thoughts to the brain but could not erase or lose the emotional memory (LeDoux, 1996). There has been, however, interesting research in more recent years to suggest that perhaps these types of memories are not as indelible as once thought and perhaps may even be erasable. The first findings along this line came in the way of electroconvulsive therapy (ECT) or pharmacology that would show, in certain instances, the loss of substantial neuronal connections. After such loss, most of the existing neuronal connections were not reconstructed or *reconsolidated* resulting in the loss of the emotional memory. This reconsolidation, as used here, means the process by which neurons make synaptic connections and then those connections are locked representing specific encoded memory. It has been inferred by many neuroscience researchers that deep and emotional work can indeed meet the criteria for reconsolidation of new encoded emotional memory (Ecker, Ticic, & Hulley, 2012). In other words, the deep emotional work such as experienced in imagery, interpersonal exchanges, and tactile and kinesthetic involvement can produce the reconsolidation of new emotional memory. Restoration Therapy certainly qualifies as the type of emotional work that can integrate new emotional memory into individuals and relationships. However, *it is the repetition or practice of these new emotional memories or neuronal connections that makes the processing stronger and more familiar to the brain.* It is in the use of the new behavior that the brain gains familiarity and preference. For instance, if you were to brush your teeth with the opposite hand than you normally do, you would likely observe and feel the clumsiness of the unfamiliar and new behavior. It would not be smooth and is likely be a little painful. However, if you continued to use the opposite hand brushing your teeth, you would notice a daily improvement and steadiness of the process as your brain adjusted to the new procedural memory. It is part of the wonderful gift of *neuroplasticity* where the brain is able to make and recognize important new synaptic and neuronal connections and utilize them effectively (Siegel, 2007).

These facts are very good news when we are aiming to integrate emotionally self-regulating truths concerning identity and sense of safety. It tells us that we are not just bound to the old emotional messages of the way we feel. We can become mindful of these emotional messages and be intentional and mindful about creating new and deep emotional memories about ourselves, our relationships, and our situations. Further, by practice and *repetition,* we can utilize the neuroplasticity of our brains to recognize and become familiar with these new emotions and behaviors that we choose to do rather than just react to. We can reconsolidate our connections in our brains to include a new preferred behavior. As Ecker, Ticic, and Hulley (2012, p. 20) state, "The prison of emotional memory, built over eons of evolution, comes with a key, and that key has now been found. Synapses can be unlocked. The limbic life sentence can be commuted." Can old and powerful emotional memories be erased? Perhaps. But it is clear that the grip of our emotional reactivity can be contained through deep emotional connection and work through therapy and mindfulness. It is also clear that our brain can clearly cooperate with us in reconsolidating new emotional memory that becomes our *preferred* model of processing identity and safety. It comes with intentionality, work, and most importantly repetition connections are mindfully remade in a place of truth and emotional regulation.

In the following case example, we see the work of the therapist using repetition to move the couple through the four steps and into a deeper experience of their peace cycles. The couple had been married for 19 years and had a conflictual type marriage where the husband was dominating and controlling and the wife withdrew in order to cope. Both came from addictive backgrounds where the husband's father was a low functioning alcoholic. The wife's mother was a heavy pot smoker and eventually became addicted to meth. Both husband and wife had struggled with addiction before they married but reported being sober through the course of their marriage. The couple had one son, 12 years of age. Their pain cycle is shown in Figure 6.1.

The couple were able to identify with the pain cycle below and made good progress in identifying emotionally regulating truths and alternate behaviors in the peace cycle. The couple worked with the therapist for several weeks in session on practicing the four steps to regulate their conflicts which had occurred during the week. The couple's peace cycle is found in

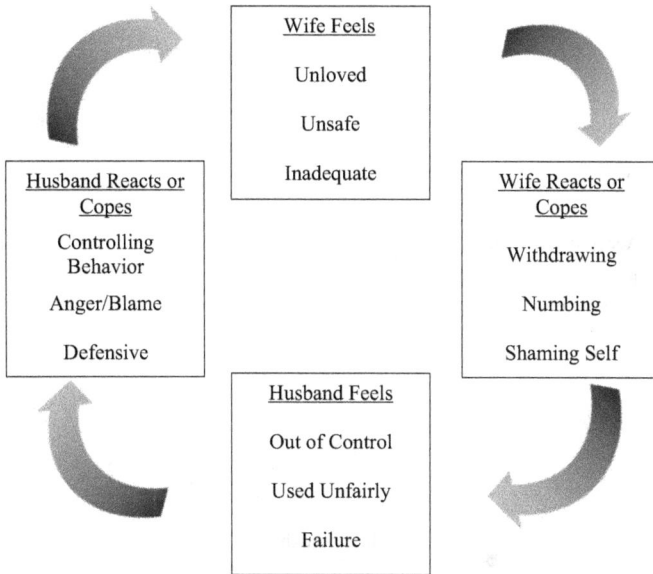

Figure 6.1 Husband's and Wife's Pain Cycle in Case Example

Figure 6.2. After consultation with a supervisor of the case, the therapist moved into heavy repetition in helping the couple practice and deepen the emotional impact of the regulating truths, especially in the last step of the four steps where the couple were asked to do what they would do differently with one another in session.

Therapist:	(Pause). Even though this was a small thing this week, it follows the same pattern of conflict that you both get into with one another. If I heard you correctly, you (wife) were cooking dinner and then you (husband) came in with what you thought was a better way to do it. You (wife) were really resentful of what he said but you just acted like you were ignoring him. You (husband) were then resentful that you were being ignored and you said, "I am so sick of your lack of response." At that point, you (wife) slammed down the cooking spoon you were holding and went to your room and shut the door. You (husband) then finished cooking the meal and ate by yourself. Did I hear it correctly? (Both husband and wife nod, but not looking at one another).
Woman:	I was just doing my part when he had to barge in.

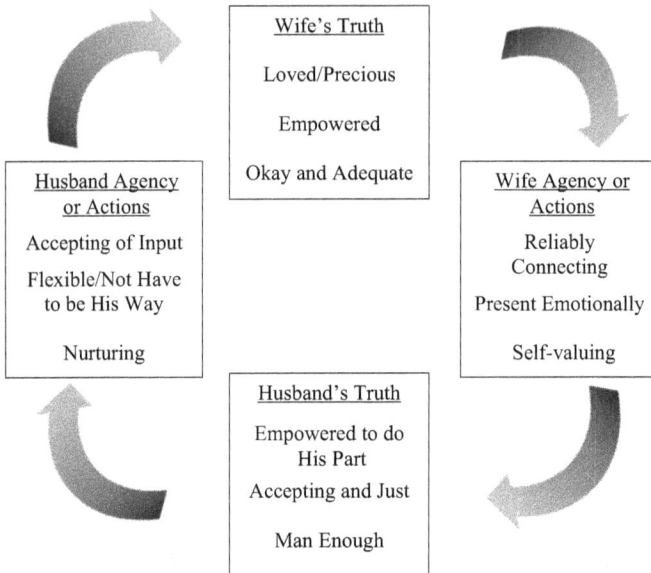

Figure 6.2 Husband's and Wife's Peace Cycle in Case Example

Man:	(Staring straight ahead). I was just making a suggestion.
Therapist:	(Long pause). And so the conflict is very much active here tonight. (To the wife and pointing at the pain cycle). When he came into the kitchen and gave you the suggestion, what were you feeling at that point?
Woman:	(Leans up to look at the cycle). Definitely feeling inadequate.
Therapist:	(Long pause). And when he said, "I am so sick of your lack of response," what were you feeling then?
Woman:	Unloved and unsafe.
Therapist:	(Pause). And so all the normal triggers were pushed. Unloved. Unsafe. Inadequate. (Pause and pointing at the pain cycle). So what did you do to cope with your pain?
Woman:	I withdrew by ignoring him and then I just left the room. When I was in the room I was telling myself I could do nothing right.
Therapist:	(Pause). You were feeling unloved, unsafe, and inadequate. What you did was withdraw and then you started shaming yourself. You still feel those same things now. So what is the truth? (Pointing at her peace cycle).
Woman:	The truth is that I am loved and precious. I am empowered to do my part and I am okay and enough.

Therapist:	(Pause). Say it again.
Woman:	(Pause). I am loved and precious. I am empowered to do my part in this relationship. I am okay and enough in what I do.
Therapist:	(Pause). Good. (Pause and looking at the man and pointing at the pain cycle). So after you made your suggestion to her and she ignored you, what were you feeling?
Man:	(Pause). I was feeling like I needed to tell her how to do it properly, then I felt like it was unfair that she just ignored me and left.
Therapist:	(Pause). And when you felt out of control and felt it was unfair, how did you cope with what you felt?
Man:	I made a controlling statement of telling her what to do and then I got angry and blaming.
Therapist:	(Pause). Just like you feel right now. (Pause and then pointing at the peace cycle). So what is the truth about you?
Man:	(Pause). I am empowered to do only my part. I am an accepting and just person.
Therapist:	(Pause and still pointing at the peace cycle). And when you get in touch with that truth about yourself, what would you have done differently?
Man:	(Long pause). It is tough. (Long pause). I am empowered to do my part and I am an accepting and fair person. (Long pause). If I were letting her do her part, I should have just been fine with what she was doing and tell her how much I appreciate her for fixing dinner. (Pause). Which was true, by the way (Looking at his wife). You are a fine cook and it would have been great.
Therapist:	(Pause). And you also said you would have appreciated her. You started saying the dinner was great, but can you directly speak to her in a nurturing way about appreciating her?
Man:	(Pause and then looks again at his wife). I do appreciate you. I don't tell you anywhere near enough all about the things that you do right. I don't tend to look for them.
Therapist:	(Pause). Tell her those things you appreciate now.
Man:	(Pause). I know you work as hard as I do and I know you do the bulk of the cooking at home. I appreciate you working also. It really makes a big difference in our family life. You are a good mother and hard worker.
Therapist:	(Pause). Good. (Pause). Now I'm going to ask you to say it again but this time, I want you to reach across and make some kind of physical contact with your wife. (He moves next to her and takes her hand).

Man:	(Long pause and with a soft voice). I do appreciate you. You are a very hard worker that makes so many important contributions to our family. You take care of our son and you take care of me in really caring ways. (Pause). And you are a great cook.
Therapist:	(Long pause and then looking at the wife). Remember those truths in your peace cycle. Loved and precious. Empowered to do your part. Okay and adequate. Say those things out loud.
Woman:	I am loved and precious. I am empowered to do my part. I do things adequately.
Therapist:	(Long pause). So if you were able to be in those truths, what would you have done differently when he came in and told you what to do?
Woman:	I am not sure.
Therapist:	(Pause). Remember, you are empowered to do your part.
Woman:	(Pause and then looking at her husband). I should have told him that I've got this and it will be okay. I am adequate to cook this meal.
Therapist:	(Pause). Say that again but looking directly at him.
Woman:	(Looks at her husband). I should have said to you, I've got this and I am adequate to cook this meal just fine.
Therapist:	(Pause). Very good. Now if you could stand up with me and stand here like you were cooking. He comes in (Motions to the husband to stand up) and tells you his suggestion. (Invites the husband to speak).
Man:	Your oil is not hot enough.
Therapist:	(Pause and then to the woman). What is your truth?
Woman:	I am empowered to do my part. I am loved and precious and adequate.
Therapist:	(Long pause). So make some physical contact with him and tell him what you would have done differently.
Woman:	(Takes his hand). I've got this and I am adequate to cook this meal.
Therapist:	(Pause and speaking to the husband). And your truth?
Man:	I am empowered to only do my part. I am accepting and fair and nurturing.
Therapist:	(Pause). So say what you would have said differently.
Man:	(Still holding hands). You are adequate and you are perfectly able to do things your own way. I appreciate you for the hard worker you are, fixing this dinner, and being a good wife and mother.

Therapist:	(Pause). So, I wonder if you would have been able to emotionally regulate yourselves then like you just did now, I wonder if you would have been eating dinner together that night? (Both spouses laugh).

Although the therapist here breaks some of the tension with the last question, it was nonetheless a serious question which the couple were able to discuss. The man said while holding his wife's hand, "You know, when I was sitting there eating dinner alone, I knew I was dead wrong. But then I was feeling like a failure because I blew it. But instead of doing what I knew, I became defensive and justifying of my statement to you." After processing for about five minutes, the therapist once again repeated the setting and had the couple do their four steps, emotionally regulate, and then connect and express appreciation for each other. Certainly the couple had additional practice to work on, but this session along with the repetition in the context of still feeling they were in the pain cycle made a deep impact on them in committing to further work on their own. By their report, they placed their pain and peace cycles on their refrigerator because they said that at least half of their arguments occurred in the kitchen.

Using Novelty and Surprise in the Work of Practice

Mindfulness is the practice of awareness while noticing things outside of the normal consciousness such as feelings, thoughts, and experiencing and while accepting the information, being able to make informed choices about new possibilities for change. As we have mentioned before, in order for mindfulness to be effective, particularly in the practice of change, it is absolutely essential to slow the brain down. This is a special challenge in the context of emotional dysregulation. Exactly when a person would benefit most from mindfulness is exactly the time when he or she is exposed to the semi-automatic responses of reactivity due to the challenges of identity and sense of safety. Therefore, it is essential to bring to bear all the elements possible in the work of slowing down the semi-automatic processing so that mindfulness, change, and practice become a real possibility.

Novelty and surprise are closely related in that both have an influence in arousing interest and motivate exploratory behavior. When we encounter something that is unique, different, or shocking, we tend to slow down and make more careful observations in order to understand. There is a difference between novelty and surprise, however, in that novelty refers to a different or unique quality of something that is normally experienced while surprise is the encounter of a new or unique quality that is unexpected or sudden. Both novelty and surprise capture the attention of the client and have the added benefit of usually involving various cortex areas of the brain (Barto, Mirolli, & Baldassarre, 2013).

Novelty and surprise are often only limited to the therapist's creativity in thinking in metaphor, description, story, and opportunity. We are consistently amazed by some of the novel and surprising things therapists develop during this practice stage of therapy. For instance, one therapist who is particularly artistic has a novel approach in that she has a couple draw or collage separately their pain and peace cycles. Sometimes these are quite simple and sometimes quite elaborate. After giving each an opportunity to process the drawing or collage, she has them integrate their work into their couple pain and peace cycle. The representations the couple draw then become as powerful as the drawn pain and peace cycles and serve to focus deeper interest and understanding in their practice of change.

Another modification of a novel approach is when a therapist utilizes some kind of child play figures such as LEGO or playmobile figures. Both of these types of figures come with ample hats, equipment, and accessories that give the figures different looks and themes in imagery play. Many therapists develop a box of these types of figures and accessories in order to work with both individuals and couples in a novel way to illustrate pain and peace cycles. For instance, the following is a case example from a couple. The couple had done substantial work in improving their relationship and were close to mastering the four steps in regulating themselves. However, both had been stagnating in their work for the past two sessions. As a result, the therapist was seeking a new motivating factor for them to finish their work. Notice how the therapist utilizes the play items to engage the couple in a new and novel way of thinking about both their pain and peace cycles.

Therapist:	I would like to do some new work around your pain and peace cycles. (Takes out a shoe box containing various figures and accessories).
Woman:	Oh, are we going to play today?
Man:	(Smiling). It has been a long time since I played.
Therapist:	Actually, we are going to play some, but playing with a point. (Taking out the couple's pain and peace cycles). I would like you to take a look at each word in your pain cycle—what you feel and how you cope. Then I would like you to pick out a figure and put on a hat and vest or something on the figure that represents how you feel when you are emotionally dysregulated. (The couple start digging through the box to find different items). (After about five minutes). Show me what you have and explain it to me.

Woman:	I chose this kind of Genghis Kahn character because I am actually fragile and feel controlled because I'm always in a situation of being in a fight. I have a big heavy helmet and beard because no one sees me or respects me.
Man:	I have this pirate character. I am not a captain, but just one of the hands with only one job because I feel incompetent. I have just a little knife and not a sword because I feel unsafe and fearful.
Therapist:	Nice work. Now I would like you to not change what you already have in your figure, but add objects in the hands or around it to illustrate what you do. (After about five minutes). Show me what you have.
Woman:	I put this scroll in my hand because I start controlling and ordering people around. I also have this bow in my other hand because I shoot these critical arrows at you when you don't do exactly as I say.
Man:	Mine is pretty simple. I have this cannon that has only one cannon ball. I snap quick with anger and then it is over. Then I have this chest that I go hide in to withdraw and shame myself.
Therapist:	(Pause). Now think about this last week when you got into your pain cycle. Explain to me what happened using your figures.
Woman:	(Couple initially discuss a situation with their daughter going to college). I was feeling really anxious about my daughter getting ready to apply for colleges and very threatened about where she will eventually go. I started reading her the scroll and telling her all the things she needed to do. (Therapist places a girl figure on the table with the woman's figure).
Therapist:	(To the man). And where were you in this picture?
Man:	I did my thing. I could see what was happening and felt like the control was driving my daughter away so I shot my cannon and said, "You have got to just back off."
Therapist:	(Pause). And then.
Woman:	I shot him with a couple of arrows. I said, "You never support me when we need to get things together around here," and "you are useless."
Therapist:	(Pause). And then.
Man:	I went and jumped in my chest—I just left the room and we didn't talk the rest of the night.
Therapist:	Okay. Now I want you to tell the story again but I want you to move your figures in the interaction just like it was

happening last week. When I say hold it, take your hands off
the figures because I will take a picture of your play scene.

Woman: (Pause). You're taking pictures?

Therapist: I will give them to you in a few minutes.

(With encouragement, the couple act out the scene once
again with the therapist taking 15 pictures).

(After about five minutes of the therapist assembling the
pictures, the couple is shown a stop-action movie of the
figures enacting the pain cycle with the description of the
couple).

Woman: Wow, that is powerful to see.

Man: It is surprisingly silly when you see us act it out with the figures. Why would we not just do the peace cycle to begin with?

The therapist then followed a similar format of having the couple create
figures from their peace cycle and having them act out the story involving
their daughter showing what they would have done differently. Step by step,
they dismantled their figures and replaced them with things that represented
their regulating truths and actions of agency. Then they narrated and acted
out the peace cycle utilizing the new figures. Again, the therapist created
a very short stop-action movie of the new pictures so the couple now
had a movie on both their pain cycle and their peace cycle. The therapist
encouraged them, "So sometime this week, you will have the opportunity to
get into your pain cycle. I want you to watch these two 25 second videos of
your pain and peace cycles and see if it makes a difference to you doing your
four steps." The couple came back the next session very much energized.
The wife said, "We had a very different week. We were just about to get
into it about our money and bills and we watched the two videos. We both
looked at one another and he did his four steps and then I did mine." The
husband reported, "It was like we were able to turn on a 'dime' after we had
watched it and it just made sense to by-pass that silliness of the pain." The
wife added, "In my mind's eye, I was seeing that video all week. I don't think
we have had a week where we practiced our four steps as much." The husband agreed. This simply represents a novel and surprising creativity that was
able to help this couple. The therapist really did not have many skills using
technology, but simply had an application that was easily used in the therapy
session to put the videos together. As a result, the couple were able to utilize
the novelty as a way of yielding a mindful approach to their practice work
on the four steps. This creativity is not "tricking" clients, but rather capturing
their attention and mindfulness using different tools.

The use of novelty and surprise may take a variety of forms. One therapist that we regularly consult with wrote a rap for a couple's pain and peace

cycle. In four lines each for the husband and wife, he summed up their pain and peace in rhythm and rhyme.

Husband: I often feel unloved and like I'm failin'
I start shame wailin' and get lost performin'
But by the mornin' I know I'm loved and enough
To nurture your heart and connect over sup'.

Wife: I know I'm the one feelin' alone and unsafe
I often take the bait and start to criticize
I ain't havin' those lies, 'cause I'm safe and belong
I let you be you and sing you my love song.

Not only did he perform the rap for the couple, he taught the rap to the couple. Imagine if you will this couple in their late fifties performing the rap together. Not only did the couple think the rap was surprising and novel, they thought it fitted them perfectly and was hilarious. They worked on the rap over and over in session and then were instructed to do the rap at the first sign they were going into the pain cycle and afterwards to do the four steps. By the therapist's report, the couple made the rap a "connecting joke" in which the tension of the moment in the pain cycle was broken. They were then able to do their four steps unencumbered and were much more successful in integrating practice into their marriage. What at first glance seems like a joke in the therapeutic process actually took on meaning to be a connecting joke to allow the couple to move into a much more emotionally regulated state. We have seen therapists have couples create a pain cycle/peace cycle poem together as well as create songs together. The point is that as long as the therapist can employ novelty and surprise in the practice stage of therapy, creativity and talents should be used. It takes courage to be able to execute this type of creativity in therapy, but as with having clients stand up in therapy, therapists are usually surprised themselves how constructive the involvement can be in the learning of the clients.

Intensity of Therapeutic Sessions

We started to become aware several years ago that restoration therapists were seeing the last phase or objective in the process as an opportunity to start wrapping up therapy. Of course, in many ways, this only seemed natural as individuals or couples had been in therapy for many sessions (on average about 14) accomplishing the work in the first three objectives. Individuals and couples during the practice stage of therapy already know the pain cycle well, emotionally self-regulating truths, and the peace cycle agency actions—the rest of therapy should be quite easy. But as we have discussed, this practice phase is essential in Restoration Therapy to help clients learn how to emotionally self-regulate and gain the habituated mindfulness practice needed to employ change. Hargrave and Hargrave (2015) made estimates about how many times the client needs to practice the process of the four steps in order to make the changes habituated. Their estimates were that if a client practices the four steps around 10 times in 12 days, the client will firmly have memorized both his or her pain and peace cycles. If the client practices the four steps 15 times in the course of 20 days, the client is usually able to look at the times they fell into their pain cycle and, in retrospect, clearly articulate what was going on in the pain cycle and what the alternative should have been in the peace cycle. But if the client practices the four steps 23–25 times within the course of one month, the client will usually be able to recognize his or her pain cycle *while it is happening in the here-and-now moment*, and emotionally regulate him or herself utilizing the peace cycle. These clients, in other words, when they bring *intense and purposeful practice* to the four steps, likely will be successful in moving themselves from the pain they were feeling and the subsequent destructive trajectory of the reactive coping to self-regulated peace cycle behavior resulting in the agency of loving and trustworthy actions (Hargrave & Hargrave, 2015). We still find veracity in these clinical estimates.

When, however, the client spreads out the practice of the four steps inconsistently and without intensity, he or she is quite slow in integrating behavior that is emotionally self-regulating. It is common for these non-practicing clients to carry on therapy for a year or more in this last phase of the process without integrating substantial progress toward change. As we have mentioned before, this type of client has *insight* but lacks *skills* in order to instigate change.

The Restoration Therapy Model has been used in a format called *intensive marital therapy.* In this intensive model couples usually go to a sequestered place where they, along with three or four other couples, meet in a group with two co-therapists over four days for about eight hours per day. Using this model of intensive marital therapy, the first day couples tell their narratives and process a pain cycle. On the second day couples work on identifying their emotionally regulating truths as well as completing their peace cycles. Because the work is done in a group format, each couple is not only exposed to their pain and peace cycles but also the pain and peace cycles of others. In the marital intensive format, the last two days are given to practice. The third day, couples are divided between therapists and they work on the issues that brought them to therapy focusing primarily on emotionally self-regulating from the pain cycle to the peace cycle. Most of the time, the couple is working with one other couple and one therapist. On the fourth day, the same couples and same therapists divide and work on problem solving conflictual issues that the couple has very different perspectives or opinions on while still working on self-regulating behavior in keeping with the peace cycle. Because of the expense and four consecutive days in a row being dedicated to the process, it is most often that three quarters of the couples who attend these marital intensives place themselves in the *highly distressed* category. Yet, with this intense type of therapy, results are quite astounding. Eighty three percent of the couples at the end of a two year follow-up remain married with the couples showing statistically significant better scores in terms of marital satisfaction, trustworthiness, and depression (Sonnekalb, 2012). Intensive therapy done over a short period of time combining the practice of many hours is effective as a marital therapy. But this is not all. As couples continue to practice using the skill of Restoration Therapy and the four steps over the course of two years, there is significant differences in the marital satisfaction, levels of depression, and trustworthiness over those couples who do not practice or practice very little (Alquist, 2018).

It seems justified to reason based on the findings of the marital intensive model to combine this practice of intensity with clients who come to weekly therapy. In other words, instead of "winding down" therapy during the practice phase of Restoration Therapy, the therapist is likely doing the client a favor by tweaking up the intensity of therapy for a short period of time. This does not mean necessarily the therapy continues to for more sessions than planned, but rather that these sessions are planned in an intense fashion. For instance, the normal estimate of time for this practice phase is around five or six sessions in normal cases. Instead of having those sessions spread out over six weeks in traditional therapy, perhaps the therapist works with the client for two sessions per week for three weeks or even a double session on one day and another session during the week for two consecutive weeks. The primary intent with this intensity is to help the client work on as much reconsolidation of the new behavior in the brain as possible and feasible in a short amount of time. We believe this level of intensity brought to the client at the very end of therapy congeals the reformatting of the brain to include not only the memorization of the pain and peace cycles, but also gives the client the ability to clearly see the effects of pain in retrospect and make a peace cycle choice in the midst of emotional dysregulation. Clinical observations tend to bear out this belief in the effectiveness of intensity. We will continue to collect clinical outcome measures utilizing intensity in the practice phase of therapy, but there is an undeniable fact at work in therapy: The more clients practice the skill set of emotional regulation in moving from the pain cycle to the peace cycle via the four steps, the more constructive behavioral change is possible.

Relational/Interpersonal Practice

Restoration Therapy is first and foremost a systemic therapy. It is such because we work at a level of pattern of both first and second-order change. We carefully listen to the stories of the client narrative, work to identify deep emotional pain, and potential healing messages in the emotionally regulating truth. But Restoration Therapy is also systemic because it is *experiential* in nature. Nothing makes the practice stage of therapy come alive more than applying the element of the fourth step—say what you will do differently— and then to actually do differently with another human. The reality of this experience does many good things for the individual as the loving and trustworthy action that flows from the emotionally regulating truth acts as a behavioral reinforcement of the truth itself. When one individual nurtures another or practices self-value, it reinforces the experience that he or she is loving and worthy of being loved. Further, the engagement enhances the relationship with others so the individual knows that he or she truly belongs. Likewise, when an individual practices the process of sharing the balance of give and take with another and reliably connects, it reinforces the truth about the individual that he or she can use his or her empowerment for the process of intimacy instead of cutoff or manipulation. In the process of practicing interpersonal love and trustworthiness, an individual confirms truth in him or herself and makes it much more likely that he or she will feel the truth at a deeper level. It is not only self-regulating but also self-reciprocating behavior (Hargrave & Pfitzer, 2011).

We often say that people are both hurt by relationships and that they are healed by relationships (Hargrave & Zasowski, 2016). There is no doubt that relationships can be particularly damaging in terms of early attachments shaping identity and safety, injuries, and lack of love and trustworthiness from peers, mentors, teachers, and coaches, and finally, the tragedies and trauma of living in an unsafe world. Still, there is only one pathway to eventual healing and it proceeds from relationships. Scott Peck (1987) who was the author of one of the best selling self-help books of all time, *The Road Less Traveled*, once said in an interview that Alcoholics Anonymous was the most profound therapeutic movement of the twentieth century. Why? He said because it promoted healing by the interaction of relationships from one person with the next. It is worth noting that the need for relational interaction has survived through every transition of world history (Small, 2011). Even in situations where we think it is natural for aging people to move more toward social isolation, it has been shown that their risk of disability decreases as their social activity increases (James, Boyle, Buchman, & Bennett, 2011). Relationships are good for the brain and interactions used to heal attachment wounds create sound neuronal change that leads to more stable, balanced, and resilient behavior (Hanna, 2014).

Of course, there are a variety of relationships the therapist can help work with a client experientially. In the therapy room, this often includes spouses and family members. We know, however, of many therapists who integrate work of relationships with friends, colleagues, or co-workers, and, at times, even neighbors. Any relationship that holds the possibility for the client to experientially practice emotional regulation is a valid relationship to work out healing and change. One of the areas in which we feel this is most true is within the context of the therapeutic relationship between therapist and client. It is not uncommon for individuals to get emotionally dysregulated by the therapist. We often witness this not only in the therapy we do, but also in the therapy that we supervise and consult. One example is reflected in the following case. A couple were in the practice stage of therapy and making substantial progress. In one of the sessions, however, the wife made the statement, "I seem to be the problemed one here and it seems like I am always the focus of therapy." The therapist felt strongly this accusation from the wife was unfair as he was very aware of working with both the husband and wife on their own individual pain cycles as well as their own emotional regulation. The therapist responded, "I hear what you are saying, but I am not sure what I can do to be more balanced in this process." This session was being observed for the purposes of supervision and the therapist was notified to take a break for consultation. The pain cycle of the therapist is shown in Figure 6.3.

When the supervisor asked what the therapist was feeling, the therapist quickly identified that he was feeling rejected and not measuring up and he reacted to the wife's comment by being defensive and slightly blaming the woman. He quickly regulated himself emotionally and was asked to go back in the session with the two-fold purpose of: 1) Revealing to the woman that his last statement was based in his own pain; and 2) Following the woman's statement back into the pain.

Therapist: I consulted with my supervisor and it was very helpful to me. I realized that your statement threw me into my own pain cycle. My last statement of saying that I didn't know what more I could do more balanced really was just a statement of defensiveness.

    You have a perfect right to have questions about the process and I have myself regulated now and want to hear you again.

Woman: (Pause). First, thank you for saying that. (Pause). I was saying that I feel like I am the problemed one in the relationship and that I am the focus of therapy.

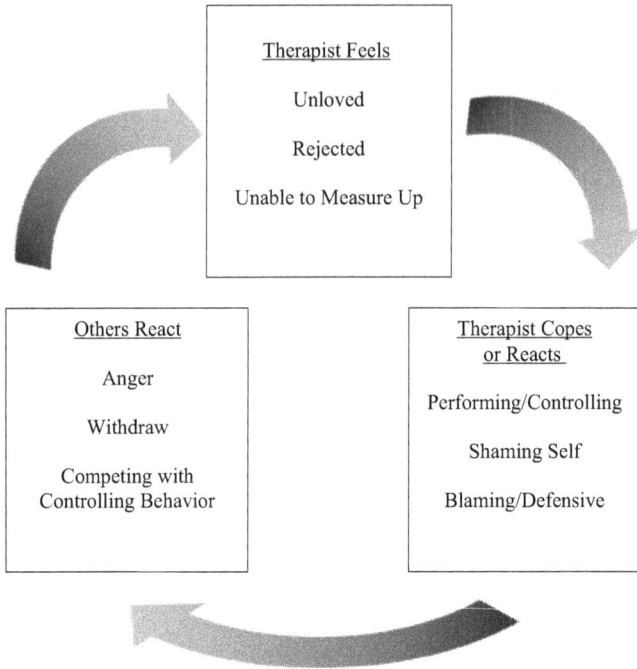

Figure 6.3 Pain Cycle of Therapist

Therapist:	(Pause.) You feel you are the problem and the real focus of therapy.
Woman:	(Nods affirmatively). I just feel like my background is so much more complicated and hurtful. (Pause). I deal with all of these deep emotional pains and with him (Pointing to the husband) it is all so cut and dried. I'm usually the one causing him pain.

Here the therapist makes a reparative statement to the therapeutic relationship by revealing the defensive statement came out of his own pain cycle and not because of her. The woman acknowledges the repair and is now able to resume the posture of her own emotional dysregulation. She relates that in comparison to her husband's pain cycle, her pain cycle carries much more injury from the past and she feels responsible for the bulk of her husband's pain. The woman's pain cycle is shown in Figure 6.4.

Therapist:	I see. (Pause). You feel that in comparison to your husband, your background and pain is much more complicated and that you are the one that causes his pain.

	(Pause). As I think about that a little, I can see how my statement did something to you. What did you feel when I made that statement before break?
Woman:	I thought, well here we go again. I shouldn't have said anything. I am the problem again.
Therapist:	(Pause). That makes so much sense. So when you focus on your pain cycle, my statement led you to feel …
Woman:	(Long pause). I feel unacceptable and inadequate.
Therapist:	(Long pause). Again, that makes so much sense. (Pause). So let's go back to your statement. I'm the problemed one. I am the focus of therapy. (Pause). Can you give me some context so I understand the statement?
Woman:	(Pause). I think I've been carrying it around with me all week. He really is doing his work, but I really struggle emotionally to get myself to the peace cycle. He does it like it is no problem. (Long pause). It just feels sometime like he is carrying around a hundred pound weight and I'm carrying a thousand.

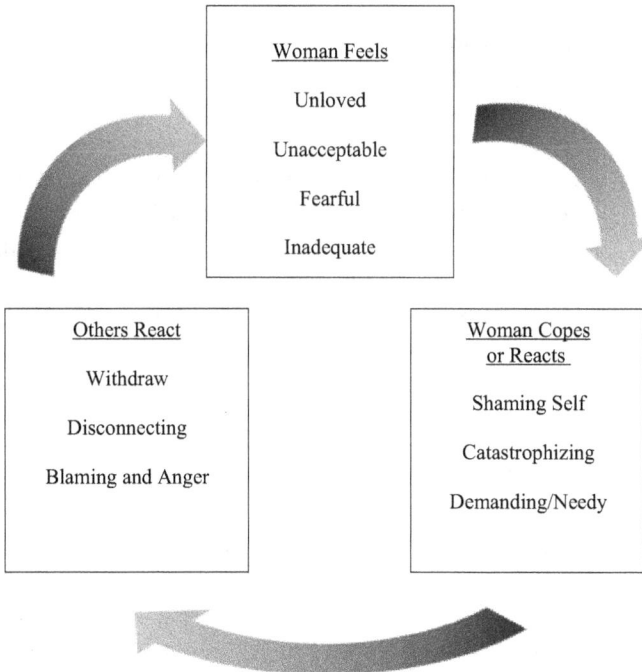

Figure 6.4 Pain Cycle of the Woman in Case Example

Therapist:	(Long pause). Let me make sure I get it right this time. You have been carrying this around all week. Even though he is doing his work, he doesn't have to deal with as much emotionally as you deal with. You really have a struggle keeping yourself doing your work.
Woman:	(Long pause). Yes. When you say that back to me, I think I know where the statement came from. He was talking about the conflict we had in the car going home from here last week and how he used his four steps to get back on track. (Pause). You said something and both of you chuckled.
Therapist:	(Pause). You are exactly right. I said, "It is always the car," and then we laughed. (Pause). I get it. What were you feeling at that point? (Referencing the pain cycle).
Woman:	I was feeling unacceptable and inadequate. Maybe somewhat fearful that you were making fun of me and siding with him.
Therapist:	I can see how that statement brought on those types of feelings. So when you made your statement, I am the problemed one. I am the focus of therapy. What were you doing in your coping?
Woman:	(Pause). I was shaming myself and really feeling sorry for myself—thinking I was "less than" my husband. (Long pause). Then I made a needy statement hoping to get some affirmation.
Therapist:	(Pause). And what you got from me, because I got into my pain cycle, was a defensive and sort of blaming. What did you see your husband do?
Woman:	(Long pause). I felt like you (speaking to the husband) withdrew and disconnected some. (Husband nods).
Therapist:	(Long pause). And when you felt him withdraw and disconnect, what did you feel?
Woman:	(Long pause). Unloved, unacceptable, and inadequate—just right back into the cycle.
Therapist:	(Pause). So now try on your last two steps with your husband. What is your truth and what would you have done differently?
Woman:	(Looking at her husband). I know I am loved and accepted by you and many others. I am not perfect, but perfectly adequate and do not have to be fearful of what you think, the therapist thinks—or what even what I think sometimes. I am who I am. Loved, accepted, and perfectly adequate.
Therapist:	(Long pause). And what would you have done differently?

Woman:	(Pause). I should have said something like, "I appreciate you doing the work on your part of the pain." I need to keep on my side of the fence and keep doing my work on my pain.
Man:	(Pause). I do have as much work to do as you and I do appreciate you. We're both getting better and better at this thing.
Woman:	(Long pause). I know. I just need to remember to keep partnering with you instead of getting trapped into comparisons.

Nothing can take the place of in the moment, interpersonal practice when the emotionally dysregulated feelings of the client are present. This also includes the interpersonal relationship between the client and the therapist. The initial statement from the woman brought up feelings of inadequacy in the therapist and in turn prompted his defensiveness. Instead of continuing to justify his defensiveness, the therapist gets back on track by taking responsibility for his pain cycle reactivity and although he does not spend much time or specifics on himself, he is able to use his part of the interaction to understand the woman's pain cycle reactivity. Once the relationship is back on track and the therapist is able to help the woman clarify her first two of the four steps—what she feels and what she normally does— the therapist has her finish her four steps in the context of the relationship with her husband. Most importantly, the session dealt with the practice right in the room. We often train therapists by saying a maxim we love: Be faithful to do the work in front of you. In this case, if the therapist would have continued to ignore his part in the interaction and justified it, it is doubtful the woman would have ever gotten to the heart of her pain cycle. Instead, within the course of a few minutes of the therapy, the woman was able to face and deal with her own pain and the couple were back on track. At the end of the session the woman said to the therapist, "You know, I had been carrying around that inadequate and unacceptable feeling with myself all week, but here it finally became clear to me what I was doing. I really am getting better at this thing."

Self-Control, Emotional Regulation, and Virtue

Self-control and emotional regulation are linked together in a way that cannot be easily separated. Emotional regulation by definition is a control process whereby people take an undesirable and unpleasant feeling and exert control over the cognitive and emotional process (Koole & Aldao, 2016). As we have pointed out here, it is normal to have disturbances in what we refer to as *primary emotions* because these are the emotions that relate to the basic forms of identity formed in attachment and relational safety formed through interactions with others (Hargrave & Pfitzer, 2011). These early attachments and relationships are not made and executed perfectly because people are imperfect by nature, so the primary emotions as they relate to love and trustworthiness are often dysregulated. But then these emotions cause the brain to react in a stressful and reactive manner, usually focused in the mid-brain. Once this occurs, reactive emotions such as blame, anger, self-loathing, shame, over-controlling, defensiveness, perfectionism, withdraw, numbing, and impulsiveness ensue *semi-automatically.* Psychologists often speak about primary emotions (some lists include 5, 7, and 8 primary emotions) which usually include anger, disgust, fear, happiness, sadness, and surprise (Ekman, Friesen, & Ellsworth, 1982). The reasoning that these emotions are primary usually stems from the observation that many of them also exist with animals and it links in nicely with the evolutionary basis for emotion. But the most substantial reason they are referred to as primary is because there are universal *experiences* and *facial expressions* that accompany with these emotional states. Although we would not take issue with the fact that there is a universality about these emotions, we would maintain that most of these emotions are indeed *reactive in nature* and not primary emotions. In other words, emotions that are primary relate to identity and relational safety whereas secondary emotions relate to reactive emotions (Hargrave & Pfitzer, 2011). Therefore, when we speak about emotional regulation, we are aiming at the *primary emotions* because those are the emotional disturbances that provide the fuel for the *reactive or secondary* emotions. If one can regulate the primary emotions, by definition the reactive emotions are also regulated. The same is not true that just regulating reactive or secondary emotions also regulates the primary emotions. It is like the difference as far as a systemic therapist is concerned between first-order and second-order change. First-order change simply changes behavior like re-arranging furniture in a house with termites. Second-order change goes after the real problem that is deep and emotional and primary. This is the crux of the emotion that begs for self-control.

Most importantly, it is clear that emotional regulation of these primary emotions can be learned through training and practice. When it comes to controlling or down-regulating unpleasant or negative emotions, people with training perform better in measures of self-control as compared to others with no such training and also report using the skill much more in their everyday lives (Christou-Champi, Farrow, & Webb, 2015; Baumeister, Gailliot, DeWall, & Oaten, 2006). As it turns out, self-control is a very big influence on the course of how people live and operate in life. When looking at the most important influences on issues like college students' grades, research has shown that self-control was the *only* measure among dozens of personality traits that had predictive power on grade-point average. This reality of self-control also holds true when SAT or students' IQ scores are included (Wolfe & Johnson, 1995; Duckworth & Seligman, 2005). More applicable here, individuals who are better at self-control are better regarded by peers, are good at forming and maintaining secure relationships with others, and are more empathetic with others. They are also more stable psychologically with less anxiety, depression, and drinking problems and get less angry and aggressive (Baumeister & Tierney, 2011).

Self-control has many benefits in and of itself. It is key in achieving emotional regulation. The research clearly shows that it is a skill that can be trained and learned. As Baumeister, Heatherton, and Tice (1994) point out, lack of self-regulation may well be the major psychological pathology of society. They point to lack of self-control as contributing to the demise and unhappiness in a variety of relationships. Why, then, is there any question about the need for self-control? First and foremost, self-control does not come naturally. Most of what we know in terms of our personal preferences, habits, and emotional dysregulation either comes to us in our early development or is developed naturally out of our reactivity. Change, by its very nature takes *attention, ability*, and *intentionality* (Bandura, 1997). Simply stated, it takes a great deal of effort to produce self-control through practice and this is not necessarily something people enjoy doing. Second, self-control is not very popular in Western society. There are times were this oscillates back and forth in terms of preference, but currently Western cultures seem to adopt a mindset that emotion represents our truest and most important expression of ourselves (Hargrave, 2011). In other words, if I as a human being do not express or act on something I feel, then I have lost touch or have not been true to myself. Of course, although emotions are extraordinarily powerful in the brain (LeDoux, 1996) they certainly do not represent our truest or most important self any more than our cognitions or motivations. We are, in fact, whole human beings with whole human brains that are complex and wonderful. One part cannot and should not represent the whole of our identities.

Self-control is actually part of the larger picture of something we call *virtue*. It is interesting how virtue has fallen out of vogue in current society—perhaps in response to the clear preference toward emotion discussed above. Virtue is commonly defined as a conformity to a standard of morality, right, or good. Notice here the words "conformity," "morality," and "right." Not very popular words in a post-modern and constructivist age where we define "good" not by any standard of truth, but rather by a standard of our own construction. This is why virtue is seemingly so passé. But as Brooks (2015) points out, virtue is actually a worthy road that does us as humans good and certainly does our relationships good. Virtue is the key to sound and wise character. When we define characteristics such as being loving, faithful, and hopeful, we find that in actuality, no person believes these attributes are bad. The same is true of virtues such as courage, generosity, peacefulness, compassion, gentleness, and patience. It is only when we get to virtues such as goodness, honesty, and self-control where people balk a bit; but even then, most humans overwhelmingly agree that these virtues are desirable. Why? Because the behaviors that flow from these virtues are good for the person who practices them as they are self-reciprocating by nature (Balswick, King, & Reimer, 2016) and good for relationships in general. How do we learn these virtues? We learn them through the experience of life and the intentional practice of the behavior that flows from our identities and senses of safety. It is not easy work to accomplish, but it is valuable work nonetheless. We are reminded of Erikson's (1985) psychosocial stages of development. In each stage of the developmental challenges, he stated an "adaptive strength" or virtue that developed in the individual when the stage was negotiated. These virtues of hope, will, purpose, competence, fidelity, love, care, and wisdom correspond with the eight stages of life respectively. The virtues or adaptive strengths he identified have to be learned through the hard processes of life. Likewise, we find that most of the enduring virtues or characteristics that we value most—the so-called "eulogy" virtues we mentioned in the last chapter (Brooks, 2015)—are the ones that we learn intentionally and mostly through experiences that are hard, challenging, uncomfortable, or trying. We recall one of our friends discussing his time in the Marines in basic training. He said, "I hated every minute of basic, but I would not take anything in trade for the experience. It was so hard, but in the end, it taught me that there was nothing I could not accomplish if I was not concerned with who got the credit."

The great writer and poet Angelo (1993) once said, "Courage is the most important of all of the virtues, because without courage you can't practice any other virtue consistently. You can practice any virtue erratically, but nothing consistently without courage." We agree, but would also add the virtue of self-control. Self-control and courage allow us to take on life and produce goodness, care, love, and trustworthiness through the hard processes of practice and learning. No virtue comes from emotional dysregulation. It is through emotionally regulated truths and peace that we yield the harvest of virtue.

Part 3

Considerations in Restoration Therapy

7 Using Restoration Therapy with Special Populations and Situations

An exciting outcome of having an expanding community of clinicians using the Restoration Therapy Model in their clinical practice is the way that the core framework of the model has been effectively applied to a number of different clinical populations. In this chapter, we will discuss some of those special populations and provide suggestions on how the Restoration Therapy Model can be used to bring about change and healing in these diverse clinical situations. First, we want to highlight some key conditions that we believe must exist in order for therapists to practice Restoration Therapy effectively and for there to be positive therapeutic outcomes.

The first condition is that the client must be able recall and tell a coherent narrative about his or her experiences of pain both in the past and the present. Identifying pain is a fundamental first step in the model and it is on this point that the remainder of the work builds. Related to this first condition of recalling experiences of pain, is the second condition required—the capacity for insight. Not only do clients need to have the ability to recall experiences of emotional pain from their past and their present, but they need to be able to derive meaning from those experiences and then connect those experiences to their current challenges. And finally, once clients know their four steps, it is imperative that they practice using the tool so that the therapeutic gains that have been established will be sustained over a longer period of time. The motivation to persist with the four steps and mindfulness in change as well as the belief in the benefits of practice efficacy are essential in sustaining long-term, second-order change.

Restoring Resiliency: Working with Children

Based on these conditions, there has been significant discussion about whether or not the Restoration Therapy Model can be used with clients with limited capacities due to their developmental age. We are finding that with some modifications to the interventions, some children under the age of 13 can benefit significantly from the model and that its efficacy can be sustained. What we have seen ourselves and have heard from clinicians working with children is that clients as young as eight years old have been able to grasp the model in a somewhat simplified form and apply it to their lives.

Most of this work with children, however, must proceed with caution as the cognitive development and the ability to think abstractly is a necessary element in the identification of emotionally regulating truths. There is another significant issue concerning emotionally regulating truths: Although we believe in the responsibility of *adult* self-regulation of emotional pain, we do not believe this holds true for children, particularly pre-adolescent children. We believe that children learn eventual emotional regulation through the attachment relationship with a caregiving adult and attachment figure (Ainsworth & Bowlby, 1991). The child, in other words, learns eventual self-regulation through the practice of *co-regulation* of the attachment figure. Children not only have a different level of cognitive development from adults, they also have a different *ethical responsibility* from adults (Boszormenyi-Nagy & Krasner, 1986). Children are entitled to the love, nurture, care, trustworthiness, and emotional learning given to them from appropriate caregivers. Equally, the child carries no responsibility to serve as a stabilizing and emotionally regulating force in a caregiver or attachment figure's life. To require a child to take care of him or herself emotionally or take care of caregivers emotionally is absolutely and bluntly *parentification* and carries devastating developmental effects for the child and destructive results in the intergenerational family (Hargrave & Pfitzer, 2003; Goldenthal, 1996). As such, the restoration therapist must be cautious in utilizing the model with children.

However, we do recognize that a large part of the Restoration Therapy Model is quite concrete in nature. We often refer to therapy with children as being preventive work because we are equipping them with the language and tools to be attuned to their affective experience and to recognize the cognitive-affective-behavioral patterns that they are living out in their peer and familial relationships. In fact, with children, these patterns are less likely to be as entrenched in children because they tend to be more pliable than adults. Furthermore, we find that children are often more readily able to summon feeling words and coping behaviors, which we would attribute to the fact that they tend to be less guarded and self-conscious about matters regarding their feelings. Thus, using Restoration Therapy with children provides an encouraging opportunity to help trace new patterns that promote healthy intrapersonal and interpersonal relationships.

What tends to be the barrier for children in therapy is the lack of emotional language or minimal experience of having emotional expressivity modeled to them by the adults in their lives. Restoration Therapy provides an opportunity for these children and their caregiving adults to grow in this regard. When using Restoration Therapy with children, it is important to remain flexible and open to the process, remembering that children's developmental understanding of feelings and emotions will initially be related to secondary emotions, not primary emotions. The distinction between primary and secondary emotions is challenging enough for adults to understand and can be even more so for children, but we have seen that sometimes children are able to grasp the distinction and gain real insight about their pain. Because primary emotions refer to the core, fundamental levels of identity and safety, allowing children to identify the secondary emotions initially can be a helpful first step. Developmentally, children are not yet negotiating the task of identity formation (Erikson, 1963), and yet the violations to their identities that they experience are already taking effect. Our task is to assist children to attach helpful language to what they are experiencing as we begin to identify how pain works in a cyclical pattern.

When working to develop a child client's pain cycle, we do so in a step-wise fashion. We first solicit feelings that almost always are secondary emotions and then we use those feeling words and expressions as a step stool to reach for primary emotions. Two tools that have been particularly effective have been the use of metaphors and Kuypers' (2011) work on zones of regulation.

The use of metaphor can be powerful in therapy and is highly effective when working with children. Whether through play or storytelling, metaphors allow the client to initially engage the therapeutic work from a distance, making parallel associations and utilizing the imagination in a way that is impactful as seen in Figure 7.1. Children as well as adolescents tend to move into the imaginary realm with ease due to the fact that imaginary play and symbolic thinking are normative for cognitive development during school-age years (Kail & Cavanaugh, 2015). In cases where this is limited, we find that oftentimes the child has experienced significant trauma or is living in an environment that prohibits the freedom to play and exercise his or her imagination due to poverty of resources. But for the most part, children are well-suited to the use of metaphors and imagination to begin accessing and developing a language for their emotions.

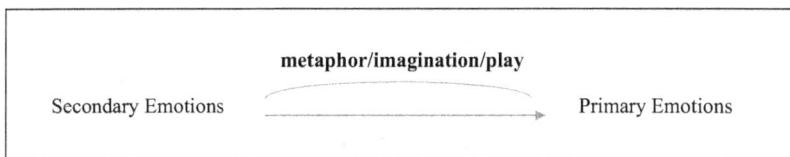

metaphor/imagination/play

Secondary Emotions ————————————→ Primary Emotions

Figure 7.1 Parallel Associations of Emotions and Metaphor/Imagination/Play

Along the lines of using metaphors and symbols, the use of characters from stories, movies, or shows with whom children strongly identify can be particularly useful. Characters can be used in a variety of ways. They might reveal an aspect of the client's story or serve as a role-model for discovering his or her identity and using that discovery to overcome pain. For example, in the Disney film, *Tangled*, Rapunzel searches for what turns out to be her true identity as a daughter of the king and queen and this eventually allows her to more fully develop into the person she is meant to be. Although the type of identity that Rapunzel discovers is in regard to her status as a princess as opposed to a peasant who is held captive up in a tower, and not about her primary emotions, we are able to see that the revelation of her status identity allows her to more fully realize her identity as someone who is loved, desired, not alone, and belongs. Using this story and Rapunzel's character, which a child might readily relate to, can serve as an entry point to the deeper primary emotions. We use this example, in particular, because it is one that has been used by clients and resulted in poignant insight and change. Symbols and play objects can also be used effectively as metaphors with children as they are able to make connections between secondary and primary emotions. Thoughtful questioning as well as reflective observation often enables the child to explore these connections effectively and meaningfully.

Another powerful tool we have seen to be effective in our work with children is found in the concept of *zones of regulation* (Kuypers, 2011). Kuypers is an occupational therapist who created the zones framework as a cognitive-behavioral management intervention that helps increase a child's awareness of his or her feelings as well as what Kuyper refers to as their state of alertness in different situations. The framework was developed in the clinical context of working with children on the autism spectrum as well as those diagnosed with attention deficit hyperactive disorder. It is a framework that has been implemented in schools, but has also been a helpful tool in the therapeutic context in raising awareness of feelings with children. It's a color-based framework where each color represents a category of feelings as well as a signal to the child about how to respond once he or she recognizes what he or she is feeling. For example, the red zone indicates intense feelings such as anger and rage and a heightened state of alertness. The red zone also signals to the child to stop what he or she is doing and employ strategies to move out of the dysregulated red zone and to move toward regulation in the green zone, where the child feels calm. Although we do not use the zones framework to the extent that it was designed to be used, we have used it as a facilitative tool rather than a central intervention. It has been a helpful tool to recognize those initial secondary emotional states and to be able to reflect on how the child client was feeling during a situation he or she is sharing or how he or she is currently feeling in the room. Once the child client is able to identify the secondary emotion, we follow up with questions that are intended to lead us toward primary emotions as seen in the following case example with a child.

Therapist:	Tell me more about when you were in the red zone this past week.
Child:	I was in the red zone yesterday when my little brother played with my Lego set without asking and I got mad at him. My parents blamed me for making my brother upset but they didn't say anything to him about playing with my Lego set without permission and that made me even more mad!
Therapist:	What were you feeling then?
Child:	I felt angry and frustrated.
Therapist:	Who were you angry and frustrated with?
Child:	I don't know. Maybe my brother or maybe my parents. I don't know. Maybe both.
Therapist:	Why were you feeling angry and frustrated?
Child:	Well, for one, my little brother shouldn't play with my stuff without asking and he knows it. He was probably trying to get on my nerves on purpose so that I would get in trouble. But definitely my parents. It's not fair that they got me in trouble but not my brother. He gets away with everything and it's just not fair.
Therapist:	So when you're in the red zone and you're feeling angry and frustrated, what messages are you hearing about yourself?
Child:	You mean messages from who?
Therapist:	Well, yeah, so when you're feeling angry and frustrated because although your brother did something he wasn't supposed to do, you're the only one who got in trouble. I guess I'm wondering if underneath those feelings of anger and frustration if you're believing something about yourself and that the way that situation turned out says something about you. Does that make sense?
Child:	Well, yeah. I mean I guess I feel like my brother gets away with way more than I ever do and sometimes I even get blamed for his mistakes. It's like they treat him better than me as if they love him more than they love me. I know that's not true, but it feels that way. It's like ever since he was born I became less important to my parents and that I can never be as good to them as he is.

Once children are able to begin understanding and constructing the language for their primary emotions, we begin drawing out their pain cycle. With this client the primary emotion he identified was *Not Important*.

| *Therapist:* | So, it seems to me that when you feel like you're "not important" you get angry and frustrated. (Drawing out the pain cycle in red). How does that look to you? |
| *Child:* | (Looking at the pain cycle, the client quietly nods and gives nonverbal indication that the pain cycle represents his experience). |

The pain cycle is simply a concrete and visual representation of the child's cognitive map of pain and tends to have resonance with children as the visual image, in its simplicity and clarity, facilitates a meaningful and deeper understanding of his or pain. Drawing out the pain cycle in red helps reinforce the fact that when the child is in his or her pain cycle, he or she is dysregulated and in a zone that is destructive to him or herself and to relationships. It is important to note here with particularly younger children, we often use play figures such as Lego or playmobile figures that can be modified to represent a child's red zone feelings without necessarily drawing a pain cycle per se. When we eventually get to the point where we are identifying truths and starting to develop the peace cycle, we use the color green in parallel with the green zone which represents a regulated, calm state. The four steps are written out in green as well as an additional signal to the child client that the purpose of using the steps is to regulate his or her emotions out of the red zone and into the green zone. The intentionality with differentiated colors and the connection we make between primary and secondary emotions help reinforce the child client's understanding of the connections between thoughts, feelings, and behaviors.

Restoring Sustained Change: Working with the Family System

Conventional wisdom says that when we work with children, we work with families and that when we work with the relational system in the room, we are much more effective. Family therapy can be comprised of a variety of constellations of family members and the clinical attunement to the appropriateness of who should be present in the room based on developmental age vis-à-vis the nature of the presenting problem is imperative. Once all considerations and contra-indicators to family work have been vetted and it has been determined that having multiple family members in the room is clinically optimal, Restoration Therapy can facilitate the structure and organization of the therapeutic process, making managing the layers of content and multiple perspectives in the room less overwhelming. And, more importantly, working with the family allows the therapist to work directly with the system in which the presenting problem is embedded, making the goal of bringing about sustainable change more achievable.

A powerful aspect of doing Restoration Therapy with families is that the family is given the opportunity to bear witness to the process of each member sharing vulnerably about their pain and recognizing how their pain contributes to their relationship difficulties. Each time a story about pain is told, there is a risk of relational injury or betrayal. Oftentimes violations of identity and safety first occurred within the family and if the violator is in the room, it takes tremendous courage for those stories to be told by the one who was violated. Here, the therapist's multi-directed partiality (Boszormenyi-Nagy & Krasner, 1986) is critical to preserving emotional safety in the room. Listening impartially to each person's story and bringing recognition to the violations that occurred between family members in the room requires the ability to listen, hold, and re-direct simultaneously. Each adult member constructs his or her own pain and peace cycles, with children often being able to observe the process of emotional regulation with the adults and then learn the modified process of emotional regulation themselves. Eventually, multiple pain and peace cycles might be joined to reveal the interactive, interpersonal nature of pain. Doing so facilitates greater ease in maintaining a distinction between each person's cycle. But more importantly, initially keeping each person's cycle separate demonstrates the reality that each member has his or her own pain that he or she needs to understand and be attuned to. Thus, the therapist may need to have multiple white boards in the room in order to draw out each individual cycle.

Joining members' cycles is an important step in helping clients understand the impact their actions, and ultimately their emotions, have on others when they live out their pain. When drawing out the interactive pain cycle, the therapist must be cautious not to convey a dynamic of co-dependence or co-regulation, but rather to exemplify the basic family systems concept of reciprocity, recursion, and shared responsibility (Becvar & Becvar, 1996). Here, the assumption is that each person has influence on the other and that patterns emerge in relationship interactions. There is an interplay of power and responsibility and we keep in mind that in some relationships, for example the parent-child dyad, reciprocity is not mutual and perfectly equal in the same way that mutuality is expected in peer relationships. In fact, we find it helpful to maintain a structural perspective (Minuchin & Fishman, 1981) regarding the subsystems within the family system and, therefore, are mindful of the boundaries between the parental and sibling subsystems. However, the idea that each person has an impact on the other is true in all relationships.

The following is a case vignette of a mother, and her 15-year-old adolescent daughter, who recently started getting into trouble at school and at home. The daughter was the third of four children and is living at home with her mother and younger brother, who is 12. The daughter's older siblings are away at college and her parents separated four months previously. The daughter is responsive to the therapist but is visibly irritated with her mother as she makes minimal eye contact with her, maintains a clear physical distance, rolls her eyes when she speaks, as well as being highly critical when she talks about her.

Daughter:	My mom is ridiculous and I'm so embarrassed when she comes to my school. None of my friends' parents come to campus and embarrass their kids like my mom does.
Mother:	Well, not everyone has a child who is acting out, making poor decisions, and can't be trusted!
Daughter:	Can't be trusted? You should talk. You're the one who messed things up with dad!
Mother:	Oh, that's an awful thing to say and you know it's not true …
Therapist:	I'm going to interrupt, here. I can see and hear a lot of feelings in the room and I can understand, there's a lot going on right now. (To the daughter). I'm hearing you say that your mom can't be trusted. As you're saying that, I'm wondering what you're feeling.
Daughter:	I'm feeling irritated and angry at her. Our family has totally fallen apart and she just wants things to be fine so she's acting as though nothing happened! It's so irritating.
Therapist:	That makes a lot of sense to me. What you're saying is that there seems to be a big difference between what's going on in your family's life and how your mom is behaving. How should your mom be acting?
Daughter:	Well, I get it that she has a lot of responsibilities at work and at home with my brother and me and I guess I'm glad she's not totally depressed and checked out like I probably would be if it were me. But it's still frustrating that we don't really talk about what happened and she just wants everyone to be happy all the time. That's impossible!
Therapist:	And when you say, "what happened", what are you referring to?
Daughter:	My parents' divorce and everything that's happened to our family as a result.
Mother:	We aren't officially divorced yet.
Daughter:	Same difference. Separated, divorced. At the end of the day, it all feels the same.
Therapist:	I imagine you have a lot of thoughts and feelings about your parents' separation, but I also heard you mention something about how there isn't much communication about what's

going on and how you feel like you're supposed to act happy all the time. When you feel like you're supposed to act happy all the time, what's the message that you're getting from that?

Daughter: I'm not supposed to have feelings about what's going on.

Therapist: You do have feelings though?

Daughter: Heck yeah, of course! My family is split up and nothing is normal anymore.

Therapist: So, when you have feelings about what's going on and yet your experience is that you're not supposed to feel those things, or at least talk about them, what does this tell you about yourself?

Daughter: It tells me I'm alone. I feel alone and I feel like I'm supposed to keep to myself about my feelings. It's like divide and conquer. My family is divided up into many pieces and we're all supposed to keep to ourselves, now. We can't be in this together.

Therapist: You feel alone?

Daughter: Yup. And it stinks.

Therapist: And when you feel alone, what do you do?

Daughter: I don't know. I guess I just keep to myself. I just want everyone to leave me alone.

Starting with the daughter's pain was intentional. The meta-message is that the parent is to be available to listen to and hold the child's pain. In this case, it turned out to be very beneficial since part of the daughter's pain was due to the fact that she felt she was not allowed to express negative emotions about her parents' separation and this became an opportunity to express herself. We consider it important for parents to be present with and aware of their children's pain and to have the tolerance and compassion to care for them. There are times when it can be beneficial for parents to model the openness and vulnerability that is required to meaningfully identify their pain and to affirm the value of understanding pain. However, this has to be carefully discerned based on factors such as the developmental age of the child, the presenting issue, any safety concerns for the child, cultural values regarding parental hierarchy, and the appropriateness of the content that the parent discloses. Regarding parental disclosure, it might be helpful to have a preliminary conversation with the parent about the process and to explain that the primary purpose of having the parents' pain cycles shared with the children is to gain insight about how difficult patterns of interaction develop when each member reacts out of pain. If a parent has experienced deep trauma that would not be appropriate for the child to hear and, in fact, could cause vicarious traumatization to the child, then the therapist can arrange for individual sessions with the parent and provide some guidance on what would be appropriate to disclose in the family sessions. In this particular case, it was appropriate for the daughter to know her mom's pain cycle. Although the mother had significant stories about family dysfunction in her family growing up, she did not report any significant trauma event that would be inappropriate for the daughter to hear. Furthermore, the daughter is 15 years of age and her maturity and capacity for insight made it possible for her to listen to and meaningfully engage in the discussion about her mother's pain.

Therapist:	Earlier your daughter shared about feeling restricted in talking about the issue of your separation with your husband, and the impact it is having on her ability to process everything that is going on. How does her description fit with your experience?
Mother:	I wasn't too surprised to hear her share what she did. I'm not telling the kids they aren't allowed to talk about it, but I know that I simply don't have enough time in the day to get through our normal routine, let alone sit and talk about our feelings. It's like I'm a juggler and I have to keep my eyes on the moving balls. The moment I look away, the balls will fall.
Therapist:	Sounds like you're in survival mode.
Mother:	Yeah, I guess you can say that. But it's been like that for a long time. Well before my husband moved out, I was the person who had to keep the balls moving. It's just that now the kids have only me so for the first time they're seeing everything I have to do to keep us going.
Therapist:	So, not only are you in survival mode, but you solely bear the huge responsibility to keep the family moving forward.
Mother:	Yes, but like I said, that has always been the case. Even when their dad was in the home, it was up to me to keep us going. I'm the workhorse *and* the driver at the same time. It's a hard and lonely place to be, but someone's gotta do it!
Therapist:	What's your earliest memory of taking on the task of being the workhorse and driver?
Mother:	When I was 11, my parents divorced and my younger sister and I stayed with my mom. At the time I didn't realize what exactly was going on, but years later I came to understand that my mom was severely depressed. Sometimes she wouldn't get out of bed for days. When that happened, which was often, I had to take care of myself and my little sister. No one else filled in the gaps so I did it.

Therapist:	Wow, that was very courageous of you. Although you did it out of necessity, caring for yourself and your sister still took courage. And it seems that you haven't stopped since.
Mother:	Ha! Yes, you can say that. I've been the workhorse and driver for most of my life.
Therapist:	No time for feelings.
Mother:	No way! My mother felt things too deeply and it robbed my sister and me of a mother. And what good does it do us to sit and talk about how we're feeling when we need to move on?!
Therapist:	I applaud you for your courage and perseverance as you've had to navigate through some really painful times in your life. But I'm wondering if you could just take a few moments to reflect on what you feel when you're working so hard.
	Others aren't stepping up and you need to fill in the gaps. So, what you do is you suck it up and work hard. This is what the world sees, a hard working, driven person. That external layer is what we'll call the "workhorse and driver." But there's more beyond that exterior. There are feelings, emotions, and other aspects of your experience, but we can't see it because all we can see is what you do. If we were to peel back the exterior layer, what feelings and emotions would we see?
Mother:	(Pause). I'm tired, I'm exhausted. I'm alone in all of this. I'm stressed because it all falls on me and no one is stepping in to help me. I'm mad about that. I feel taken for granted. (Tears begin to well up in Mother's eyes).

From here, the therapist isolates some of the significant emotions of *being alone* and *taken for granted* and goes back into the mother's earliest memories of feeling these things. For the first time, the mother reveals a tenderness and a vulnerability that her daughter has not seen before. As the daughter bears witness to her mother's expressions of pain and heartache, she appears to soften toward her mother. The softening is a sign of empathy and compassion that the therapist should not discourage. It is also important to watch for and address a response of feeling guilty for giving her mother a hard time or feeling responsible for taking care of her mother. These would be understandable responses, but the key lesson is to understand her mother's pain and where her reactivity comes from, not to feel obligated to take responsibility for her mother. After completing construction of each individual pain cycle with the mother and daughter, as seen in Figure 7.2, and when they both understand their pain cycles and recognize when they are cycling in their pain, the therapist begins to help them understand how difficulty arises in their relationship when they are both operating from their pain. An

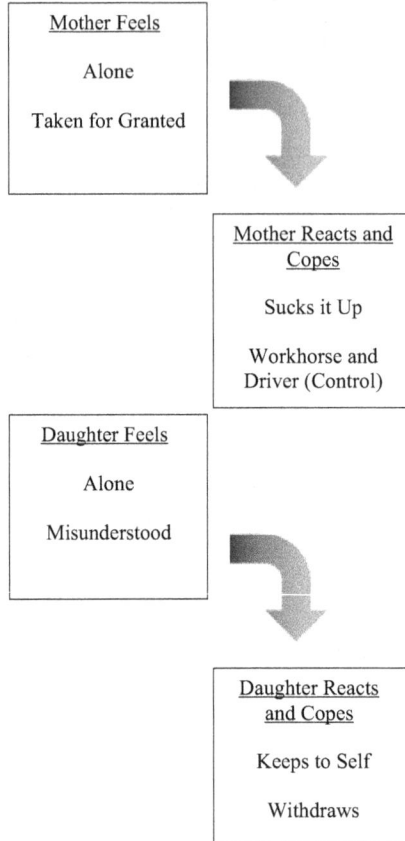

Figure 7.2 Pain and Coping Cycle from Mother and Daughter in Case Example

effective way to make this transition is to use a story the clients have already shared in prior sessions. Thus, the therapist recalls the interaction brought up in an earlier session and pointing to the interactive pain cycle, as seen in Figure 7.3, describes how pain drove the interaction as it unfolded between the mother and daughter.

Therapist:	I'm thinking about a situation we talked about a couple of weeks ago where (Looking at Mother) you received a phone call from the school about your daughter leaving the school without permission.
Mother:	Oh yeah, that was a bad one.
Therapist:	Well, if I recall, you received the phone call while you were at work and you were already having a pretty stressful day. In

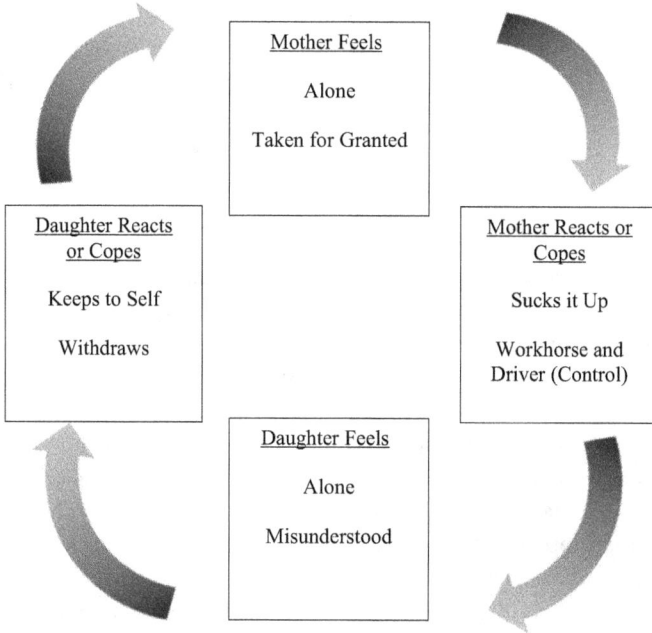

```
                    Mother Feels

                        Alone

                  Taken for Granted


Daughter Reacts                              Mother Reacts or
   or Copes                                       Copes

Keeps to Self                                  Sucks it Up

 Withdraws                                    Workhorse and
                                              Driver (Control)


                    Daughter Feels

                        Alone

                    Misunderstood
```

Figure 7.3 Interactive Pain Cycle of Mother and Daughter in Case Example

that moment, you thought, oh boy, here we go again with my daughter! But almost immediately after, you talked about feeling *alone* because in your mind, there is no one else who can help out with this situation. So, as you were feeling alone you decided you needed to *suck it up* and just deal with it.

When you got home you confronted your daughter. (Looking at the daughter). You said that you were already feeling pretty down because you also had a pretty bad day at school. When your mom confronted you, you felt like she wasn't interested in hearing your side of the story. There was a reason why you left campus without permission, but your mom wasn't really interested in hearing about that. You felt *alone* and *misunderstood* but instead of trying to fight your way through it, you withdrew and *kept to yourself.*

As you *kept to yourself* and pulled away from your mom, mom, you felt *taken for granted.* If I remember correctly, you said that you felt like regardless of how hard you work to take care of your children and help them make the right choices in their lives, they just don't seem to care. And so, as you're feeling *taken for granted*, instead of acknowledging how painful that is to you, you decide to tighten the reins and take *control* of the situation by taking away her phone and grounding her for a month. And as you remember, your daughter responded by withdrawing even further.

This step of joining pain cycles to illustrate the interpersonal impact of pain, is the same one that therapists take when working with couples. It begins with exploring and understanding each individual's pain and then gaining insight about how this plays out in relationships. We recommend that whenever possible, use the clients' real-life scenarios to walk through the interactive pain cycles. They already have emotional associations with the experience and thus will likely be able to engage at an affective level.

When working with multiple members of the family system in the room, identifying truths and developing peace cycles provides an opportunity for family members to be truth speakers to one another. Although it is not always the case that partners, parents, and siblings are truth speakers, therapists should remain open to the possibility and seize the unique opportunity of having the truth speaker present in the room to speak truths. When working with parents and children, therapists should pay special attention to the position the child is placed in to speak truth into the parent's life. For example, it would be more appropriate for older adolescent and adult children to be truth speakers than it would for young, elementary school-aged children. Children can be encouraged to speak positively about their parents and to be empowered to be encouragers, even to adults. However, they should not feel the responsibility of being truth speakers in the way that parents are expected to be for their children. In the case of this mother and daughter, the daughter might find it empowering to speak truth into her mother's life, but we would suggest that this would occur only after the mother has listened to her daughter and spoken truth into her life. It is important that the daughter does not feel she owes her mother when she has yet to feel heard and understood by her.

Therapist:	These past couple of months we've been talking a lot about the difficulties that have been going on at home with your family and more specifically, with your daughter. I imagine your relationship hasn't always been difficult. Do you remember a time when your relationship with her had less conflict?
Mother:	Oh sure. Even just a couple of years ago it seemed like our relationship was so much smoother than it is these days. We would talk and hang out while preparing dinner or baking a

	cake for one of her siblings. I think it's fair to say that we both enjoyed spending time together.
Therapist:	What do you remember enjoying about your daughter?
Mother:	She's creative and has a great sense of humor. She's quick-witted and she has it in her to be really kind. She has never been the kid who likes to be the center of attention, but she isn't shy either. She has a quiet confidence that I really admire. She's been like that since she was a kid.
Therapist:	Those are some really amazing ways to describe your daughter. It is apparent to me that you truly love your daughter and really know her qualities. How do you make sense of the fact that you and your daughter are having a lot of conflict these days?
Mother:	I don't know. I guess she became a teenager and perhaps she was also affected by a lot of the fighting that her dad and I did in the house. We separated six months ago and although there is no more fighting between her dad and me, I think it's been a real adjustment to have just me as the only parent in the house.
Therapist:	(Speaking to the daughter). How would you answer that question?

From here, the daughter is encouraged to share with her mother the pain she has experienced over the past year. A softening occurs between the mother and daughter during this conversation, a softening that began when the mother took some time to reflect on the positive attributes she observes in her daughter. As they continue, it seems that they are experiencing a positive exchange in their relationship and this leads to a conversation about their truths.

Restoring Core Truths in Clients with Personality Disorders

Working with clients who present with personality disorders (PDs) can be challenging because the work is often slow and deep, requiring stamina and patience on the part of both the client and the therapist. Furthermore, clients with PDs can be strenuous in the way they engage their therapist, posing challenges to the therapist at a personal level which can be arduous to manage. According to the DSM, clients with PDs are affected by maladaptive cognitive, affective, and behavioral patterns that are pervasive and rigid, but clients are often unaware that this is problematic and instead find fault with others for their interpersonal difficulties. Currently, psychotherapy is considered to be the treatment of choice for clients with PD and the fact that clients do not always perceive or understand the part they play in their own difficulties can make the therapeutic work that much more perplexing.

Clients with PDs are perceived as complex and challenging to engage in treatment as well as retain once treatment has begun (Wampler et al., 2018; Martino, Menchetti, Pozzi, & Berardi, 2012; McMurran, Huband, & Overton, 2010) and thus an important part of the therapeutic work is to intentionally address the issue of retention. One way to do this is to be transparent and explicit about the roadmap we're using with clients. We find that clients appreciate the opportunity to see the map, so to speak, and get an idea of where we are and where we are going. We have co-determined the destination or goal for therapy, but oftentimes the road map for how to get there is tucked away in our minds as the experts in the room. Although we continue to be the experts in the room, inviting our clients to see the map promotes their investment in the therapeutic process and engenders a sense of confidence in the client that we can, in fact, arrive at the destination. For the therapist, the explanation of the road map serves as a reminder that one of the greatest benefits of a theory is that it helps organize each session as well as the macro-perspective of the therapeutic work (Hargrave & Pfitzer, 2011). Describing the therapy model and establishing expectations for how the work will unfold affords clients agency and investment, but also adds an element of predictability to the work. This can be particularly beneficial when working with clients with PDs who, in some cases, are inclined to present with more unpredictability and chaos than other clients.

The Restoration Therapy Model has a clear and discernable road map for the therapeutic process. The four stages delineated earlier in the book can be described in a way that clients can grasp and we have found that this has been particularly helpful for clients with PDs. A client who we worked with was diagnosed with borderline personality disorder (BPD) and had been in therapy for years to address a multi-faceted diagnosis that included BPD as well as major depression and a few other mental health and medical conditions. This client, a female, came in for couples counseling with her husband, who had read a number of books about BPD and had extensive knowledge about the diagnosis. In spite of his book knowledge about BPD, however, his range of emotional and interpersonal responses to his wife was remarkably limited and this was one of the major sources of strain in their relationship—the woman feeling as though her husband did not love or care for her. Over the years, the husband became increasingly more measured with his emotional expressivity in an effort to minimize the chances of upsetting his wife. He felt he needed as much predictability and transparency about the therapeutic process as possible in order to feel safe in therapy. Thus, throughout the long and slow-moving work, referring back to the road map was particularly helpful for him in order to build trust with the therapist and remain anchored in the therapeutic work when he was experiencing the chaos and unpredictability of his wife's disorder. Eventually, the husband was able to share his deepest thoughts and feelings with his wife and this level of transparency turned out to be helpful for her in remaining engaged in the work, though there continued to be significant ups and downs regarding her satisfaction with her husband's involvement in therapy.

We conceptualize pain for clients with PDs as the fuel that feeds their erroneous thoughts, emotions, and behaviors regarding themselves and others that result in interpersonal and intrapersonal discord. Although this conceptualization is not so different from how we consider the function of pain with any other client, the cognitive and affective processes among clients with PDs are deeply embedded in their temperament and core beliefs about the world so that disentangling the pain from these core schemas is particularly challenging. We find, therefore, that Restoration Therapy with PD clients takes much longer than with clients who do not have such a disorder. As trainers and supervisors we often say with regard to working with personality disorders, "The way out to health and peace is the same for everyone." In other words, the road map of Restoration Therapy is the same road map no matter the disorder. We acknowledge, however, that the execution of this road map in the four objectives of Restoration Therapy is much slower, perhaps involving as much as triple the normal number of sessions for an average client. As restoration therapists, we extend the time dramatically in understanding the pain and violations of identity and safety. We are careful to tie the stories of the pain back to the reality and responsibility of behavioral actions that are violations of the love and trustworthiness of others. This is a slow process that also dramatically increases the amount of sessions. Finally, we as restoration therapists have to exercise extreme patience in these types of cases, understanding the pain of identity and safety disturbances are more dramatic and deeper with this population and responsibility, insight, and change all occur at a much slower pace.

Restoring Agency and Communion: Working with Clients Affected by Chronic Illness

"I feel as though I've lost control of my body." This is a common refrain from clients who are dealing with acute or chronic illness or a disability. The experience of disconnect and, oftentimes, betrayal from their bodies that results in a global perception of losing control is prevalent and one of the primary precursors to depression and anxiety that develops, secondary to illness. Furthermore, when illness precludes people from being able to continue the tasks and responsibilities in their families or of their vocation and activities of interest, the loss can cut deep into their identity, leaving them feeling as though the loss is irrecoverable. For example, when working with adolescents who have sustained a sports-related concussion it is important to recognize that for many of these adolescents their primary social network is organized around their team and a core aspect of their identity is based on their performance as athletes. These clients, who we refer to as high-achieving student athletes, can struggle and become distressed when they are required to take a temporary or long-term break from their sport, as well as other routine activities, in order to allow their brains to recover from the concussion. The rest may be temporary and the client may eventually resume play, but nevertheless they are removed from one of their most significant social systems and are prohibited from engaging in many of the usual activities that provide structure and satisfaction to their daily lives both at home and at school. This isolation coupled with the uncertainty of the recovery period can lead to psychological distress resulting in depression, anxiety, and a global perception of diminished control. This iatrogenic effect—the unintended consequence of the treatment causing sickness—is common with concussion patients and the secondary diagnosis that is pervasive among concussion patients is post-concussion syndrome (PCS) which describes the phenomenon where there is evidence that the brain is healed, but the symptoms persist (Broshek, De Marco, & Freeman, 2015). When PCS clients are referred for psychotherapy, an important task during the early stages of the therapy is to help them acknowledge and grieve the loss of their social connections with their teammates and the loss of their identities as athletes.

Conditions such as PCS where an acute illness or injury transitions into a chronic situation pose opportunities for clients to deal with emotional pain that results from their medical condition as well as the emotional pain that may have existed prior to the initial medical event. In fact, we consider the physical pain to be a "pathway to emotional pain" because we have seen that the experience of being ill or having diminished physical capacity forces people to confront their limitations. This reality can be difficult to come to terms with particularly when it occurs unexpectedly. As humans, we are always making sense of our experiences. When experiences line up with what we already know and believe about the world, we aren't as cognizant of how we're making sense of those experiences. However, when there is dissonance between our assumptions about life and the world and our lived experiences, we become distressed and in order to resolve the distress we try and make sense of the experience by attributing meaning to what has occurred. Illness is an example of an experience that usually does not line up with our expectations about life and the world. When clients are confronted with illness they try to make sense of it and they will draw meaning that either constrains or facilitates their ability to deal with the illness effectively (Wright & Bell, 2009). When we identify the beliefs, particularly those about identity and safety in regard to the illness, that constrain clients and prevent them from moving toward healing, we can address those beliefs and help restore those that facilitate growth and healing. Some of those constraining beliefs are the pain that existed within the client prior to the illness and some are those that emerged within the illness experience. This pain clients experience from the loss of control can be experienced as a violation of safety and identity. The safety violation may be due to the unpredictable nature of illness. The unpredictability can refer to the sudden onset of symptoms or the ongoing experience of unexplained symptoms that eventually lead to a diagnosis. Whether the diagnosis comes at the beginning of the illness experience or much later, the feeling of disconnect and loss of control over the body is common and, perhaps, the detachment or externalization becomes a way of coping with the disconcerting reality that clients cannot always be in control of their physical health.

We hear this in the language clients use to describe their relationship to their bodies—"*I can no longer trust my body,*" or "*I feel betrayed by my body.*" It is as though the body has become an external entity that has violated them and herein lies the complication about violations of safety and trustworthiness that occurs with illness: By externalizing their physical being, clients have fragmented themselves into violator and violated. Who would knowingly cause the kind of disruption and suffering upon themselves that illness or disability cause? Illness or disability has happened *to* them and even in instances where there is an obvious external cause such as a contagious virus or an injury caused by another person, the blame for the vulnerability and the betrayal is still placed on the person's own body, in this case, a fragmented part of the self.

Before discussing how we work with clients who are dealing with violations of safety, it is important to understand that clients with illness oftentimes also experience violations of identity. This is particularly the case when the client's ability to carry on in their vocational or leisure tasks is compromised by the illness or the treatment for their illness. In many ways, we are defined by our abilities and what we can do. Consider the fact that when we meet someone for the first time one of the initial questions we ask is, "What do you do?" Intuitively, we begin to organize our perception about others based on what they do, how they devote their time and energies, and what their interests or vocation may be. And we define ourselves in these same ways. Our identities are expressed through what we do, both in our work and in our leisure, and by the roles we carry in our workplace and in our families. What we do matters and it is painful when we lose control over that often taken-for-granted aspect of our being. When confronted with chronic illness, we must navigate the changes in what we can *do*, as well as negotiate a new reality of who we *are*. This can be particularly challenging when the illness is not visible to the outside world. Rolland (1994) presents a psychosocial typology of illness and identifies the visibility of the illness as a factor that affects the client's illness experience. On the one hand, visible indicators such as hair loss on a client undergoing chemotherapy or the use of a wheelchair for a client with multiple sclerosis signal to the outside world that the client is physically not well and can too quickly and narrowly define the person's identity as simply "sick." And yet, on the other hand, when the symptoms of illness are invisible, the compassion, empathy, and shared connection around vulnerability can be difficult to obtain from the outside world and the acknowledgment of the illness experience can be as elusive as the symptoms of illness. It can be too easy to hide the illness experience and become isolated in it when the symptoms are invisible, but at least the client has some degree of control over how others engage their illness experience whereas those whose symptoms are visible have less control in this regard. Here, the visibility, or lack thereof, of illness can serve as a significant deter- minant of how much control the client has over the impact of illness on their identity as a sick person and the inherent and varying sense of value and worth that comes with that identity.

We have identified some common ways that we see clients with chronic illness experience violations of safety and identity. Certainly, emotional pain is complicated and is often fraught with a mix of pain that is fresh from the illness narrative and pain that has existed in the inner reaches of the person's psyche for years. In the early phase of therapy with clients affected by illness, a major part of our work is to understand their illness-related emotional pain and to listen for pre-illness pain that is being triggered by the medical situ- ation. Illness forces clients to confront the limitations of their physical exist- ence and can engender fear and anxiety about their future as well as arouse them to question their life decisions. And furthermore, as stated above, it is not uncommon that the illness narrative serves as a pathway to delve more deeply into emotional pain that existed prior to the illness. Clients will likely cope in this time of uncertainty the same way they cope with their pain in other circumstances.

While accounting for the particular complexities of each client and their illness narratives that are embedded in larger narratives of pain that may or may not be related to the illness, we consider broadly what it means to restore identity and safety to clients affected by illness. Restoring identity has two parts. First, we help recover parts of the person's identity in terms of their identification as a person who is more than a patient—you are a spouse who desires physical connection and intimacy; you are a technician who possesses the skills and expertise of your trade; you are a friend who goes out and enjoys a good meal with friends. But second, and more significantly, we work with clients to restore their identities in terms of their primary emotions: Their value, their worth, and the belief that they can be known in spite of *and* with their illness. As we listen to and validate their experiences of being alone and unknown in their new identities as an ill person, we listen for the truths that transcend illness and the evidence of those truths that may have emerged in the midst of their illness narratives. Because of the experience of losing control of one's identity to the illness and the common phenomenon of feeling as though one's identity has been engulfed by one's experience with illness, we situate the illness in proper perspective by "putting the illness in its place." We acknowledge the significant impact of illness on the client's life while working to restore the fullness of their identity that is not defined solely by illness. This is particularly important for clients with chronic illness who are in it for the long haul and are constantly negotiating what it means to live in a "new normal" with their chronic illness. Loved ones who have been by their side throughout their experience. The knowledge and expertise of their vocation that cannot be taken from them, even if they are not able to actualize those gifts at this time. Reminders that their value and worth is not limited to what they are able to do, but to enliven the truth that they have worth and have gifts to offer even if it might look different in their new normal.

Restoring safety focuses on addressing the issue of control by promoting agency and communion—a principal goal of therapy among family therapists who work primarily with clients affected by illness. Having a diminished sense of control over their health can lead clients to feeling as though their loss of control is global. Therefore, an important part of the work is, again, putting the illness in its proper place as we recognize the unpredictable nature of illness and its impact on the clients' and caregivers' sense of control and perception of safety. When clients are able to put the illness in its proper place, they are exercising agency as they effectively choose where the illness belongs in their lives. Here, the work of restoring safety occurs in concert with restoring identity.

In addition to promoting agency, we promote communion and begin by helping the client de-fragmentize their body. The client makes this move with intentionality and control as they choose to restore coherence and congruence in their embodied identity, rejecting the disease while accepting and reconnecting with their bodies. We cannot change the course of the disease by making symptoms more predictable, but we can help our clients understand and believe that in the midst of the uncertainty of their health, they can control how they manage their experience from a psychological, relational, and spiritual perspective.

Restoring Intergenerational Ties: Working with Bicultural Children of Immigrant Parents

As a second generation Korean American, I (Miyoung) think a lot about both the beauty and the challenges of growing up in an immigrant family. Although the community where I lived was diverse in ethnicity and race, I was only one of a few Korean Americans in my school. At a young age, I was made quickly aware of how different I was and began to wrestle with the desire to look like, be like, and have a family like my peers at school. I don't recall having shame about my culture as much as I remember wanting to be like everyone else so that I could fit in and belong. At the same time, my family attended a Korean church that was built by members of my parents' generation who had lived through the Korean war as children and emigrated from Korea in the 1960s and 1970s. Like many immigrants of their generation from other countries in the world, they had come to America in search of a safe, secure, and promising life for themselves and for their children. Some refer to this group of first generation immigrants as the "frozen" generation because the cultural values and traditions that they brought from their homeland remained static in the new country. Even as their peers in Korea changed with the increasing Western influence during the late 1900s, the immigrants' cultural values from the homeland endured the pressures of assimilation and the melting pot in America. My parents often told my brother and me that Korea was a nation of people who have always had to fight to preserve their identity amidst the threat of colonization from China in the West and Japan in the East. Therefore, though they had great hopes that their children would be successful by making the most of the benefits of living in America, they had equally strong expectations that we would maintain strong Korean identities, and one of the places where this value was strongly reinforced was the Korean church. The Korean church was my family's cultural hub. This is where we joined with other multi-generational Korean families and shared in our Korean solidarity through language, food, art, music, and social relationships. Thus, at school I had experiences of trying to belong to the majority culture and at church I had experiences of belonging to my ethnic minority culture. These different contexts required each of us to have the ability to shift in our identities in order to navigate the different social norms and expectations in each context.

The inherent challenge of these two sets of expectations for both the first and second generations—be successful in this country while remaining true to the traditional culture of a country in which you don't live—is that the question of identity related to loyalty, belonging, and acceptance can be an ongoing dilemma. For the first generation (those born and raised in their home country and migrated to the US as adults), it is a matter of contending with the reality of transnationalism, living with their hearts in two coun-tries (Falicov, 2005) and in many ways, no longer belonging fully to either country. For the second generation (those born in the US to first generation parents), the tension they face is the fact that they often only know one culture from experience but are expected to value and prioritize a second culture, their parents' country-of-origin, about which they know very little from experience. Their experiences of being bicultural present the same challenge that their parents face, they don't fully belong to either country or fit in with either culture. And thus, part of the work with our clients who are navigating this tension is to help identify what restoring identity means when there is less clarity about who they are and to whom they belong.

This aspect of identity that is related to culture has a direct link to our primary emotions. How we are seen, perceived, and known based on our cultural identity, particularly our ethnicity and our race, can bear heavily on how we experience the world in which we live. The identity notion of belonging can be especially challenged when it matters that we don't belong to the majority group. And the way that belonging connects to our sense of value and worth can be deep, as seen in Figure 7.4.

What complicates this issue of belonging is when the individual does not fully belong anywhere. For example, as a bicultural Korean American, I (Miyoung) am a US citizen and share the rights of all US citizens, but as a person of color, I am often aware of the fact that in the larger framework of our society I do not belong to the majority group. I hear innocent strangers and new acquaintances comment on my impressive fluency in English or the fact that I don't speak with a foreign accent, a constant reminder that because of my race, I am a perpetual foreigner, constantly dealing with others' assumptions about whether or not I belong in this country. At the same time, when I visit Korea, I do not quite belong there either. Although I look Korean and have sufficient language skills to navigate on my own, without doubt I am a foreigner as reflected in my mannerisms and my lack of flu-ency in the Korean language. As much as I feel a sense of connection and

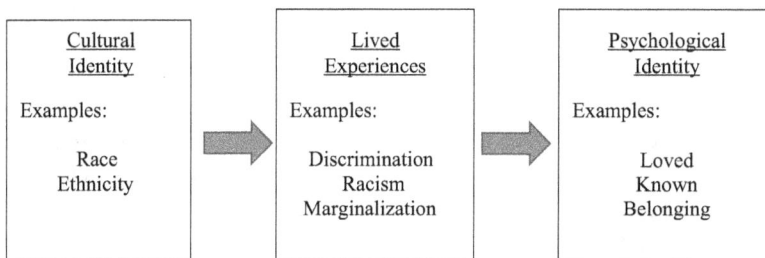

Figure 7.4 Connections Between Culture, Experience, and Identity

familiarity when I'm in Korea, I am aware that I do not belong there and that Korea is not my country either. So, when we talk about belonging, we are referring to the psychological connection and attachment to a place or group, not the legal or technical meaning of belonging as it relates to citizenship.

"I don't fully belong here and I don't fully belong there. So where do I belong?" This is a question I have asked myself many times and have heard some of my clients ask in therapy. They aren't coming in with this identity question as their presenting issue, but as they unpack the pain of their disappointments and failed expectations, this issue of belonging emerges as a prominent theme in their lives. And what tends to happen is that as they struggle with existing in the in between, they struggle to belong to themselves; to know themselves. This notion of knowing oneself can challenge the very core of traditional cultures that place the family and/or the wider community at the center of the individual's identity. The individual is the reflection and expression of the larger group and therefore the self is very much tied to the identity of the group. This perspective is not necessarily problematic in and of itself, but when it intersects with a cultural norm that states that the health of the individual is measured by their ability to distinguish themselves apart from the group, an intrapersonal and interpersonal tension can develop. Bicultural individuals will tend to hold both perspectives, as opposed to choosing one, and according to the context they are in, they may shift their perspective. This is an adaptive response to a difficult situation, and is common among bicultural individuals. Shifting and adapting to context is a part of resiliency and is oftentimes essential for survival, but it can also make it challenging to develop a core identity that transcends context. I have struggled to know and then to hold on to my truths from context to context so that as the social context shifts, my truths can hold me steady amidst the chaos. Because my experience in different contexts of my life varied in terms of being known and believing that I had worth amidst the uncertainty of belonging, it took a long time for me to identify truths about my identity.

In my work with bicultural clients, particularly Asian American clients, I have to be careful not to make assumptions about their bicultural identification based on my own experience. At the same time, it is the awareness of my own experience that has helped me be more attuned to and curious about these issues of identity that can be easily overlooked among ethnic and racial minority clients who are living out this tension as second generation children struggling to relate to their first generation immigrant parents. The Restoration Therapy Model is particularly helpful in working with these clients because the issue of identity is a core part of the model. What is important to keep in mind is understanding the connection between cultural and psychological identity while also maintaining a distinction between the two. Much like the way we described our work with clients affected by chronic illness where physical pain serves as a pathway to understanding psychological pain, exploring the client's narrative around their cultural identity can be an important part of understanding their psychological identity. We would go a step further to state that stories of pain about their cultural identity will likely illuminate the pain they experience about their psychological identity. Moreover, it is important to consider the truths that can emerge from their cultural identities as well. Although clients might feel conflicted about their cultural identities, likely there are aspects of their culture that are positive and to which they feel connected.

Case Example

A 47-year-old Japanese American male came for therapy to deal with unresolved grief about his father's death, seven years prior. Friends and family members noticed he was still having episodes of being in a "funk," much like he was having immediately after his father died, so after several people recommended that he see a therapist, he finally decided to seek help. This was the man's first experience in therapy and he was initially slow to open up. What seemed to be a turning point in his comfort with the therapeutic process was when he shared his family's narrative during the construction of a genogram. He was a third generation Japanese American and is the older of two brothers. His paternal grandparents immigrated from Japan during the early 1900s and settled in Washington state, where his father was born in 1938. In 1942, his father's family was sent to an internment camp where they remained for three years. When they returned to their hometown in 1945, his father was seven years old and though his father's recollection about the details was dim, he remembered that his family experienced significant stress as the grandparents struggled to secure work and his father found it challenging to adjust to school. The client shared that when his father was alive, he didn't share much about his childhood, but that he did often indicate that the hardships of his family's life were meant to be redeemed by the successes of his own family's life. The message he received from these statements was that it was up to his generation to redeem the pain and suffering of his parents' generation. He described this task as an honorable duty as opposed to a burden, but nevertheless he acknowledged the weight of this responsibility and this opened up the conversation about his own pain related to this task.

The man was married and had two high school-aged children. His wife also was Japanese American and owned her own practice as a chiropractor. The man worked as a paralegal. He attended law school and had hopes of opening up his own law office or joining a major firm, but was unsuccessful at passing the bar exam and after three attempts, he decided to stop trying.

Until his father died, he felt like he lived a "normal" life without any significant issues. But when his dad died within a few months of being diagnosed with late stage stomach cancer, he described his life as being turned upside down and then stuck in that position of suspense and uncertainty. He expressed surprise at this reaction.

Man: I'm surprised that my dad's death has hit me so hard. His absence doesn't change anything in my family's day-to-day life so I don't know why I feel like I'm hanging upside down. And it's been seven years so I don't get why I'm still stuck.

As he explored this idea of being stuck, he began to express the regret he feels about his relationship with his father.

Man: There are so many things that I was still hoping to do with my father. My father isn't a man of many words, but he enjoyed time with his family. For many years we talked about my parents and my family taking a trip somewhere for vacation, but with the kids in school and busy with friends and camps during the summer, it never worked out. I also wanted to save up money so that I could take my parents on trips and treat them well. The least I can do is take them on trips and let them enjoy the successes of their children. If only I was more successful.

Therapist: More successful?

Man: Yeah, I didn't quite measure up to my or my parents' expectations, at least not with my career. I feel like I was such a disappointment to them.

Therapist: What makes you feel like you were a disappointment to them?

Man: Well, they never explicitly said they were disappointed, but they would talk about their wishes and hopes for their kids and about how we were their hope for a better future. And of course, I want to make my parents happy and proud of my brother and me, but I don't feel like I ever fulfilled their wishes and gave them what they deserved.

The man described his own sense of accomplishment as being intertwined with his parents' happiness—something that seemed to be less about their relationship than it was about the cultural value and expectation of the individual's responsibility to the family. This intergenerational obligation is normative in many traditional Asian cultures and stems from the notion that balance and harmony is to be sought within all relational systems. Harmony in both horizontal (peer) and vertical (intergenerational) relationships is valued, shifting the emphasis from the individual to the relational space between individuals. This expectation for individuals to be concerned about family honor and relational harmony is common among Asian American families but can lead to dissonance for the second generation members who did not grow up in a society that is organized by this traditional cultural value. The internal dissonance can lead to interpersonal dissonance and conflict. In the man's case, he did not explicitly express dissonance, but after his father's death, he began to acknowledge the ambivalence he had about his parents' expectations and yet his deeper sense of obligation to honor them with a "successful" life.

Therapist: What do you believe your parents hoped for?
Man: Well, they wanted me to be happy and they believed that the best way for me to be happy was to have good relationships in my family, live with financial stability, and to be successful in all of my pursuits.

Here, the therapist begins to slow down the process and unpack each significant point that seems to create a situation in which the man feels stuck.

Therapist: That makes a lot of sense. It seems like what your parents wanted for you is not so different from what many parents want for their children. But I'm wondering if there was something different about how you experienced these expectations.
Man: Well, yeah, of course they wanted me to be happy and all of these things are obvious ways for a person to be happy. But sometimes it felt like if I had very little room to struggle or be uncertain about my future. Anytime I expressed any ambivalence, they got very concerned, like it was a huge problem. They often talked about the hardships they experienced and their desire to spare me of those same types of hardships. But I would hardly compare my hardships to theirs and it seemed like having hardship meant something different for them.
Therapist: What were the hardships?
Man: I guess being Japanese in America has its share of baggage. For example, my dad lived in an internment camp for three years when he was a kid. Our family doesn't talk about it, but it clearly had an impact on my dad's family and ours. Even the fact that we don't talk about it in spite of the fact that we know it happened, has impact. It leaves me wondering what on earth happened?! Then after camp, they had a hard time re-settling into American life.

Therapist:	To know about hardship but not be able to talk about it, this must be very difficult. I'm hearing you say that you've been impacted by both what your dad's family went through and the inability to talk about it.
Man:	Yeah. I don't think I realized it at the time, but years later after I had gone away to college and begun my own professional career, I began to think about my dad's hardships as a Japanese American and I wondered if some of my own experiences were similar. Although I never lived in an internment camp, there were plenty of times that I'm pretty sure I was discriminated against because I'm Asian. But I never felt that I could talk to my parents about this. If I struggled the way they struggled then my life wouldn't be any better than theirs and their sacrifices would have been in vain.
Therapist:	Did you struggle in your life?
Man:	Well yeah. Like I said, I know I was discriminated against because of my race.
Therapist:	When was the first time you remember being treated differently because you are Asian American?

Two significant points of insight have been expressed. First, the man describes the discrimination he has experienced as an Asian American and, second, he describes the constraint he felt about expressing any struggle to his parents. It is not uncommon for ethnic and racial minority clients to have limited opportunity to articulate their pain related to experiences of racism and xenophobia. Up to this point, the man has alluded to this connection, but being able to explicitly name the painful experience is an important step in acknowledging his pain. He describes the experience of being teased as a young kid by being referred to as "karate kid" or "sushi boy." He explains that his friends were just having fun, but he nevertheless felt embarrassed about being seen as a stereotypical Asian. Most of his friends at school were non-Asians and although he felt accepted by them, he was acutely aware of their differences and felt that his differences made him inferior. As he grew up, he continued to struggle with feelings of inadequacy.

Therapist:	Can you tell me about the first time you remember feeling inadequate?
Man:	I'm not sure if I can remember the first time, but a time that stands out is when I was in high school. I was running for a student government position, secretary or treasurer, I believe. I was pretty sure I was going to win because I had a lot of friends and I knew they were going to support me. One day my opponent showed up with candy bars and really

cool magnets that everyone could stick on their lockers. His parents invested in his campaign and could afford to purchase hundreds of magnets with his photo on it. My parents didn't even know I was running for student government! It wasn't really something they valued or understood so I just did it on my own. I usually did things like this on my own, but this time it really mattered that my parents weren't involved. I knew there was nothing I could do to better my chances to win so I just gave up.

Therapist: You "gave up?"

Man: Yeah, I pulled out of the race. It wasn't that big of a deal anyways. It's not like I was running for president!

This was the first indication of the man's pain cycle. The focus of the next few sessions was on constructing his pain cycle and what emerged most prominently was the pattern of "giving up" when he feels "inadequate." This pattern was applicable when he told stories about being a student and pursuing his career. When he was passed over for promotions or failed the bar exam, he felt inadequate and in a state of defeat, he gave up. He recognized these as being both acts of relinquishing and self-preserving. A related pattern that came up as particularly relevant to his relationship with his parents was "withdrawing" when he felt "misunderstood." He recounted stories about his parents not understanding his desires to fit in at school and his struggles to feel normal. But he didn't want to disrespect them or disagree with them so he would withdraw and keep his feelings to himself. He stated that growing up, he recognized that this probably wasn't the healthiest way to deal with his feelings, but he didn't know how to respond differently.

Both of the man's primary coping responses are flight responses. When confronted with difficult emotions, he is inclined to disengage and pull away from the relationship. When the therapist points this out, the man begins to talk about how he often felt voiceless in his life and didn't always believe he could effect change. As he shares experiences of feeling inadequate and ineffective, he begins to associate these experiences with observations he had about his parents "quietly taking abuse from others." This also becomes an opportunity for the man to develop empathy for his parents as he feels they share common experiences of discrimination.

Man: I felt like my parents were discriminated against all the time, but they did nothing about it. It really frustrated me to see my parents just let others treat them unfairly. But now here I am, doing nothing about the many situations where I'm treated unfairly. I guess I realize how hard it must've been to stand up against it all.

For the first time, the man was animated and expressive as he acknowledged two very important points: He was treated negatively due to his cultural identity as an Asian American; and, His experiences of discrimination were not so different from his parents. Both points related to his pain, but the second one also opened up the opportunity for the man to work through the pain he had regarding his relationship with his parents, particularly his dad. He began to make the connections between the pressure he felt to redeem his parents' suffering, the angst he felt about being a disappointment to his parents, the shared experiences of discrimination, and feeling like he had to hold in his emotions for all these years. Overall, the man became more open and responsive to the process of exploring his pain. In particular, it seemed as though he was understanding for the first time the complexity of his own connection to his parents' hardship and what it meant for him to be responsible for redeeming their hardship when he was steeped in pain about his own.

In the therapeutic process, it seemed important to first provide the man with the opportunity to acknowledge and understand his pain that stemmed from experiences of racism and discrimination as well as the pain he had from his relationship with his parents. As he continued to explore his pain, he added a new part to his cycle that related directly to his relationship with his parents. When he felt he couldn't express his feelings to his parents or talk with them about his struggles, he felt alone and, consequently, coped by "stuffing" his emotions. A partial pain cycle for the man is shown in Figure 7.5.

Again, his coping response was a flight response which aligns with the traditional Asian cultural value to maintain harmony and the virtue of respect for elders through filial piety. Thus, what is regarded as a culturally-sanctioned and valued response was identified as a coping response to pain. This point is a complex one because of the conflicting implications of the same response. According to one cultural value, these flight responses of conceding, withdrawing, and controlling emotions can be perceived as honorable responses for the good of the group. And yet, according to another cultural value, these same responses can be perceived as detrimental to the individual. At this juncture of the work, it was important to hold both cultural values with multi-directional partiality (Hargrave & Pfitzer, 2003), just as a therapist would with multiple clients in the room. Because the cultural values represented people in the man's life, it was important that the values weren't pitted against one another. Rather, the task of holding the complexity of seemingly dichotomous sets of values was modeled by the therapist, allowing the man the freedom to fully explore both parts of his cultural identity without having to choose one over the other. This struggle to choose is at the heart of bicultural, second generation persons. Although they might

```
┌─────────────────────┐
│   Man Feels         │
│                     │
│   Inadequate        │
│                     │
│   Misunderstood     │
│                     │
│                     │
└─────────────────────┘

                ┌─────────────────────┐
                │  Man Copes and      │
                │     Reacts          │
                │                     │
                │   Gives Up          │
                │                     │
                │   Withdraws         │
                │                     │
                └─────────────────────┘
```

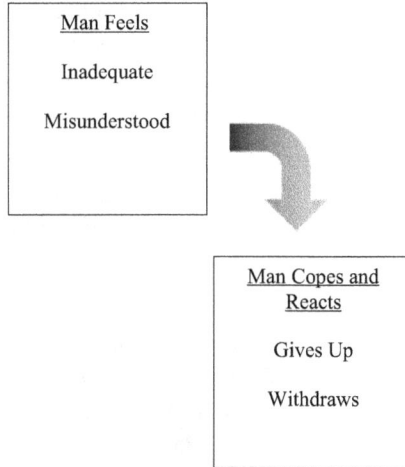

Figure 7.5 Pain Cycle of the Japanese American Man in Case Example

feel more at home with the surrounding culture, they feel obligated to their parents' culture. Thus, the challenge of being bicultural is being able to hold both parts, without having to choose one over the other.

After acknowledging and understanding his pain, the focus of therapy shifted to developing empathy for the man's parents so that he might be able to put his own pain in appropriate relational context. Furthermore, empathy could allow him the emotional freedom to forgive his parents for their role in his pain and to imagine a different kind of relationship with his mother. This part of the work is also a part of Restoration Therapy (Hargrave & Zasowski, 2016) where understanding the other person's violations as acts of their own pain creates an opportunity for understanding, empathizing, and re-humanizing the violator. Understanding is not the same as excusing the violations or disregarding their impact, but it releases the victim of responsibility for the violations, putting the pain in its proper place, and restores a sense of agency and choice to re-engage with the violator. In the man's case, understanding his parents' struggles and the isolation he imagined they felt throughout their lives as immigrants helped him frame his pain of feeling alone in a new way. For the first time, he considered his story and his parents' to be a shared narrative and feeling alone, although it was still part of his pain cycle, no longer had the same grip on him as it used to and from here his capacity to identify truths opened up. And just as it was important to hold the complexity of seemingly conflicting value systems, it was important to help the man identify truths that were embedded in both aspects of his cultural identity as a Japanese American. Holding these complexities and inviting normalcy and beauty in his bicultural identity had a positive impact when the man knew that he had a choice to hold both in tension instead of having to choose one over the other. This new reality gave him the freedom to identify and live into his truths. It also created new possibilities for him to navigate the intergenerational dynamics with his mother and other elders in his family and community.

Restoring the Power of Social Connection: Working with Groups

From the very beginning of the Restoration Therapy Model, a group setting has been utilized for a variety of applications. There are three primary reasons that Restoration Therapy is particularly applicable to groups. First, the model itself is well contained and simple in terms of explanations, objectives, and material. As a result, Restoration Therapy can be effectively *taught* as well as being *experienced*. Second, as with most group work, interaction between members actually promotes and clarifies the ideas of the pain cycle, the truth, the peace cycle, and the practice of the four steps. When one sees another person work with the concepts in Restoration Therapy, he or she is able to make a more personal application of the material. Furthermore, as a group interacts, members tend to clarify perspectives on the material which in turn helps others grasp the ideas quicker. Finally, the experiential nature of Restoration Therapy allows group members to try out and process their experiences in the context of real and dynamic relationships. When it comes to understanding and "trying on" new behaviors or actions, the group setting offers an excellent opportunity for members to practice the agency actions that flow from members' peace cycles.

Marriage Intensives

One of the more exciting applications of Restoration Therapy has been in marriage intensives. Marriage intensives are usually a four day framework where 4–5 couples go to a sequestered environment to work on their marriages. As mentioned in Chapter 6, many of these couples are in highly distressed marriages and have made little to no progress in traditional therapy. During the four days, the couples work in a group with two highly seasoned therapists. During the first day, each individual in the group tells his or her own narrative about experiences shaping his or her identity and sense of safety. Further, each individual identifies his or her own reactivity and coping behaviors. By the end of the day, the therapists process and are able to complete an interactive pain cycle for each couple. On day two, individuals come to grips with the futility of remaining in the pain cycle and learn how to approach the emotionally regulating truths for their own specific pain cycle. This is profound and difficult work in individual therapy, but we find that in the group setting where members start learning from one another and encouraging each other, the process has a dramatic impact and is surprisingly efficient. By the end of the second day, the therapists are able to draw and complete a peace cycle for each of the couples.

On day three of the intensive work, the therapists split the group between the two of them with each attending to either two or three couples. During the course of the day, the therapist works with each couple moving the members through the emotionally regulating process of the pain and peace cycle as well as engaging in experiential practice of doing the agency behaviors with and to the spouse. Usually, each couple works through three different scenarios with the therapist observing and making suggestions. Most importantly, each couple witnesses the work of other couples in regulating pain cycles into experientially connecting and affirming agency actions. Finally, on the fourth day, the group of couples once again works together in further practicing issues where the couple have been unsuccessful in resolution of issues and consolidating a plan for work after the intensive is completed.

As previously cited, the results of these group marital intensives are quite encouraging. Eighty three percent of the couples are still married at a two year follow-up. There are significant improvements in marital/relational satisfaction, level of depression, and level of trustworthiness over pre-intensive testing. Most encouraging, couples who continue to practice the skills of emotional regulation learned at the intensive show the highest levels of improvement in the measures taken. Framo (1992) was among the first to apply the group format in marital therapy and, we must admit, we were a bit intimidated to try to work with more than one couple in the room. After 12 years of doing intensive marital therapy, we can overwhelmingly report that Framo was correct in working with more than one couple in therapy. Because it is clear, transferable, and simple to apply, the Restoration Therapy Model, in particular, makes the intensive model more effective.

Psychoeducational Groups

Restoration Therapy does lend itself to a didactic model when combined with small group activities. One of the first applications of Restoration Therapy in a psychoeducational approach was using a curriculum called *Relatestrong* and *Marriagestrong*. In both programs, married and non-married individuals, respectively, take part in a 6–9-week program of approximately 90 minutes where they relate their stories in a small group, learn their pain and peace cycles, and practice emotional regulation through the four steps. This material has also been modified to a church curriculum called *5 Days to a New Marriage* for couples and *5 Days to a New Self* for individuals (Hargrave & Stoever, 2010; Hargrave & Hargrave, 2015).

Restoration Therapy has also been utilized as a psychoeducational process to improve parenting. In these groups, the focus is on helping parents recognize how the relationship with children prompts emotional dysregulation. Parents identify their own pain cycles and learn how to emotionally regulate themselves with chosen truths that are worked out in the group context. When the parents then work on their peace cycles, they are encouraged to explore as a group good parenting techniques that enable agency in forming loving and trustworthy relationships with their children. The point is parents learn how to keep themselves from destructive behaviors by utilizing the Restoration Therapy strategies of emotional regulation. They become versions of their "best selves" in perhaps the most important place of practice, raising the next generation.

A modification of the marital and parenting material has also been made to parents of special needs children. These families are often placed in situations of extraordinary stress as they deal with potentially high needs situations every minute of every day. Not only is the situation ripe to breed moments of emotional dysregulation, it also contributes to social isolation. In a sensitive application of the model, four parents with special needs children meet every other week via the internet in order to discuss restoration principles, emotional regulation, their marriages, and their parenting.

The work and applications of Restoration Therapy are certainly varied at this point, but in many ways the work has just begun. There are many more applications to specific disorders, situations, and settings that are simply waiting for a therapist who has the interest and necessary creativity to apply the model. This chapter has listed a few of the applications that have been utilized over the first 10–12 years of Restoration Therapy. There is little doubt that over the coming decade there will be many more to report.

8   Questions and Answers Regarding Restoration Therapy

Over the last ten years as we have trained students and licensed therapists in the Restoration Therapy Model, inquiries about the conceptual foundations and clinical applications of the model have emerged, providing great opportunities for us to dig and dialogue with one another about the nuances and distinct aspects of the Restoration Therapy Model. Thus, we decided to extend the conversation to our readers by sharing a handful of those questions and our accompanying responses related to three categories: pain, peace, and Restoration Therapy concepts and interventions. Readers will find that some of this chapter is a reiteration of clinical concepts and issues that were addressed in varying degrees in other chapters of this book. However, we see this as an opportunity to revisit some of the concepts that often come up as questions in our training contexts and share, perhaps, more nuanced perspectives on these topics. Our hope is that this chapter will clarify your understanding of the model while also stimulating more questions of your own!

Questions Regarding Pain

How Do I Get My Clients to Access Pain Beyond Secondary Emotions (Coping Behaviors) like Anger?

Often, when clients are asked how they are feeling, they will answer with a secondary emotion such as anger or anxiety, instead of a primary emotion. One of the best ways we can steer our clients toward primary emotion is to chase the pain with more specific questions. Remember, as restoration therapists, we are always looking to understand the client's story and feelings in terms of his or her identity and safety. Questions like, "What did that comment say about you?" or "How did that situation inform you about the relationship?" are much more likely to yield more information about how the client feels about his or her identity and safety.

However, there will be times when clients respond with answers that we would consider secondary emotions, or coping behaviors. In this case, we would encourage the therapist to continue to chase the pain and look for opportunities to identify feelings around identity and safety. For example, if a client claims that a hurtful statement from someone else made them feel angry, it can be helpful for the therapist to simply say, "Tell me about the anger." Often the client will elaborate and provide more clues as to how he or she was feeling about him or herself or their situation. Other times, clients will report what they would do when they are in pain as this is often easier to identify. This provides the therapist with an opportunity to work backwards and ask what feelings drive the behavior.

How Many Feelings and Coping Behaviors are Usually Included in Someone's Pain and Peace Cycles?

Human beings experience a wide array of emotions throughout their lives. However, most often, we feel the same 2–4 emotions each time we experience a painful situation. Two people can experience the same situation, but may feel totally different feelings based on their own stories and previous wounds. Pain cycles should represent the two to four feelings a client feels when they experience pain, and the 2–4 coping behaviors they employ when they are in pain.

In turn, a client's peace cycle will likely have 2–4 truths that directly address the feelings, and 2–4 actions he or she would like to do instead of their coping behaviors. Keeping the pain and peace cycles as simple and accurate as possible will make them much easier to refer to and work with as the treatment progresses.

The Pain Cycle Begins with the Primary Emotions, but When Identifying Pain, Is It Okay to Begin with the Coping Behaviors as Opposed to the Primary Emotions?

Yes, it is fine to begin with coping behaviors and, in fact, it is often where we actually begin. Coping behaviors are symptoms of pain, they are what we can "see." Behaviors serve as the harbingers of pain and help lead us to identifying and understanding primary emotions. Therefore, when a client says, "When my wife tells me it's my fault that we were late to her cousin's wedding, it makes me so angry I just want to scream!" we follow up with the question, "Beneath that anger, what message did you receive when your wife told you it was your fault?" or "When you scream, what are you feeling?" In both responses, we're focusing on what is happening at the subterranean level, below the coping behaviors of anger and screaming. By phrasing it that way, we're also acknowledging the client's coping response and most likely what he or she perceives to be his or her feelings. But we're also putting those behaviors in their right place by verbally situating them in relationship to the primary emotions.

What Does It Mean to Chase the Pain?

Chasing the pain is a technique used to clarify, process, and deepen the therapist's and the client's understanding of the client's pain. Developing the pain cycle can sometimes be an iterative process as clients gain more clarity or more confusion as therapy progresses, resulting in a modified pain cycle where feeling words are added, removed, or changed to more precisely and more fully capture the client's primary emotions. We are not in pursuit of the perfect pain cycle, but rather the right one. Sometimes clients need help in identifying words to express their feelings, but as much as possible we want to use their words as they are more likely to have resonance with them. And developing a solid pain cycle leads to creating meaningful peace cycles. If the client cannot relate to his or her pain cycle then he or she will struggle to create a peace cycle that will bear meaningful change.

How Do I Know When It's Time to Chase the Pain?

Chasing the pain can be done at any point throughout the therapeutic process when it is apparent that the client needs a little more time and assistance with identifying and/or understanding his or her pain. For example, after the pain cycle has been constructed the client might find that he or she is continuing to cycle through pain without gaining insight about it or making connections between pain and his or her daily experiences. In sessions, it feels like the movie *Groundhog Day* where clients arrive session after session with the same frustrations and difficulties about their relationship interactions or life circumstances and they are not connecting their pain cycle to those experiences. This is when it is important for the therapist to pay attention to what might be occurring at both the content and the process levels. Is there a limitation to the client's capacity for insight that would make the Restoration Therapy Model less challenging to use with the client? Did the pain cycle get constructed prematurely? Is there a difficulty in the client-therapist relationship or perhaps the client doesn't feel comfortable with the therapeutic process? Is the clinical issue related to a more complex situation (i.e. trauma, personality disorders), requiring more time to organize the client? These are examples of process issues that will require some modifications to the therapeutic process. Matters of content and process are interrelated and when we're chasing the pain we're paying attention to both, particularly content. Do we have the right primary emotions on the pain cycle? Is there more to the pain narrative that needs to be explored? Are there pain narratives that we have yet to address? Attending to these kinds of questions will drive the process of chasing the pain.

In Working with a Couple, What is the Role of Each Individual in Identifying Their Partner's Pain Cycle?

Tempting as it might be, it is not the role of either individual to contribute to or correct their partner's pain cycle. Each person must articulate his or her own pain and peace cycles in order for the process to be effective. However, if the therapist sees one partner attempting to contribute to or correct the other partner's pain cycle, this will likely give the therapist important information and provide an opportunity to use the live interaction in the room to identify feelings and coping behaviors and possibly utilize other interventions described in this book.

Is It Appropriate for a Client to Teach Their Partner about the Restoration Therapy Model and, Specifically, the Pain and Peace Cycles, if the Partner isn't Coming to Therapy?

This question is very similar to the one we just responded to above, but we thought there's enough difference between them to justify including this question and because this is one that comes up often we have included it. The thing is this, we can't control what clients do during the remaining 6 days and 23 hours of the week they are not with us in session. When clients begin to have positive results and feel the benefits of the therapy, they will more likely tell others about it. Furthermore, the people in our clients' lives will likely notice a change. Therefore, it is not uncommon that clients will begin to explore what they're learning in therapy with the people in their lives. When our individual clients tell us stories about teaching their partners about the pain cycle, it is a good sign that they understand what's happening in therapy. We might even affirm them by telling them what we're observing. At the same time, it is important to remind our clients that it is not their responsibility to "fix" others, but rather to focus on being attuned to themselves, understanding their own pain, and regulating their own emotions. By doing so, we further remind them, they are doing their part in changing the relationship interaction and what their partner does with that change is up to him or her. Our clients can only control what they do themselves. We use this as an opportunity to ask our client if he or she would like to invite his or her partner to come in for couples therapy.

Questions Regarding Peace

How Do I Know My Client is Ready to Move from Focusing on the Pain Cycle to Identifying Truths?

Of course, we never stop working with the pain cycle. During the very first session we're listening for pain and once we've started constructing the client's pain cycle it becomes ever-present in the room, both in conversation and in the form of some type of visual aid. After building rapport and establishing a therapeutic alliance, understanding pain is the first primary building block in the therapeutic work. Both the therapist and the client need to understand the client's pain in order to gain insight about behavior patterns and to achieve progress toward change. And there comes a point in the therapeutic work when it is time to begin identifying truths in order to develop the client's peace cycle. Identifying truths is the second major building block in therapy. Determining the right time to begin shifting is not an exact science, but there are a couple of indicators that can signal a readiness to begin that shift.

One indication is when clients begin coming to sessions reporting times throughout the week when they recognized their pain cycles and can share specific stories from the week about being in their pain. The simple question, "Tell me about a time this week when you were in your pain?" can elicit these stories, but sometimes clients will volunteer stories without the therapist's prompting. It is particularly telling when clients share without inducements. Furthermore, it is interesting to see at this early point in the work, how regulating the awareness of their pain can be. Although they are not yet walking through their four steps, they are essentially rehearsing the first two steps and this newfound awareness of their pain can begin to have positive impact during this early stage of therapy. We can infer from this awareness that they are becoming familiar enough with their pain cycles and that they can "see" them without our prompting. After clients begin recognizing their pain outside of the therapy room, we typically observe over the next few sessions that they are recognizing their pain with increasing regularity and frequency. This is also evidence that they are developing a consciousness about their pain. This is very important because they cannot change what they do not know and so until they know their pain, they will not be in a position to choose truth instead of pain when they eventually know their peace cycles.

Another indication that clients are ready to begin shifting toward identifying truths is when they understand that pain will always be a part of their lives. This understanding is not a prerequisite to moving toward truths, but it provides some indication that clients have a complex understanding about pain. More often, this conversation about how pain will always exist occurs after they learn the peace cycle and are disappointed by the ongoing experiences of pain. We have found that this reality can be difficult for clients to accept because of the common expectation of being fixed, which is equated with being pain-free. But occasionally clients are able to understand the complexity of pain early on in therapy and this understanding can facilitate a greater openness to truths.

What Helps a Therapist Decide What Interventions to Employ in order to Help a Client Claim the Truth?

Choosing which intervention to use in order to help the client experience and embody truth can be challenging as there is never a guarantee that a particular intervention will be effective in achieving your goal. Be encouraged that if an intervention does not yield a desired result, there is always an opportunity for another intervention.

However, in telling their story, the client will often provide clues as to which interventions might be effective. For example, if a client has children or is close to the children in his or her life, it might be helpful to begin visualizing that child as the first target in a re-parenting intervention. Or, the client may have vividly described a poignant moment in his or her childhood during a previous session that the therapist can easily return to in order to set up a re-parenting exercise with the client as a child as the first target. Other times, a client will share an accomplishment or a moment he or she is proud of, like running a marathon. This can be very helpful in setting up a stronger, wiser self-intervention.

How Can I Use the Concept of Agency Explicitly in Therapy?

Agency is an important concept in the Restoration Therapy Model because of the crucial role it plays in facilitating sustained change both at the behavioral and neurological levels. For example, clients have to make the choice to practice the four steps persistently and consistently in order to experience their benefits. Practice strengthens and reinforces messages about truth and helps establish and embed new neuropathways in the brain. However, practice requires a decision to interrupt the old patterns and reinforce the new.

Another example of when agency is important in Restoration Therapy is when clients are identifying truths that they are struggling to internalize and believe. Pain tends to be easy to identify and believe, but truths can be much more elusive. Clients might know their truths at a cognitive level, but struggle to accept them at an affective and emotional level. When this occurs, we might try a number of different strategies to help our clients accept their truths. But eventually, those truths will take hold once the client intentionally chooses to accept them.

But to be clear, agency is not simply a matter of making choices. Making choices is an act of power and when this act is void of benefit or regard to self or others, it is instead considered reactive exploitation. Perhaps we can say that first-order agency occurs when we choose a behavior before full cognitive and emotional commitment has been established, but nevertheless the action is for the good. Second-order agency is when actions and decisions stem from a fully integrated and regulated emotional and cognitive understanding of the action and why it serves a positive end. In fact, agency is the use of power for good (Hargrave & Pfitzer, 2011), and is tied to hope. Hope is … the perceived capability to derive pathways to desired goals, and motivate oneself via agency thinking to use those pathways (Snyder, 2002). Much of what we do as therapists relies upon the client's hope, as well as ours, for change, healing, and growth. In a sense, promoting agency is the way we encourage our clients' hope to take flight and, therefore, framing agency as an enactment of their hope can be empowering for clients.

There are a couple of ways we have found the concept of agency effectively discussed and applied. First, during the major hinge points throughout therapy, such as the time between developing the peace cycle and teaching the four steps, overtly explaining agency and the benefits of positive choice can be helpful. Explicitly discussing agency in the session such as including the word on the visual aid can also be helpful. We have seen therapists place the word in the space between the pain and peace cycles, suggesting that at every juncture where pain is confronted, clients have the agency to choose to live out of their pain or their truths as in Figure 8.1.

Questions Regarding Concepts and Interventions

What Techniques and Interventions from Other Therapy Models Can Be Used with Restoration Therapy?

No need to reinvent the wheel on some things. There are many wonderful interventions and techniques from other therapy models that have been proven effective and work well with Restoration Therapy. The following are examples of just a handful of interventions and techniques that we have found to be particularly effective with the Restoration Therapy Model.

Psychoeducation

Revealing the therapy road map and teaching clients about the model can be beneficial to the therapeutic process. This is an effective way to gain client

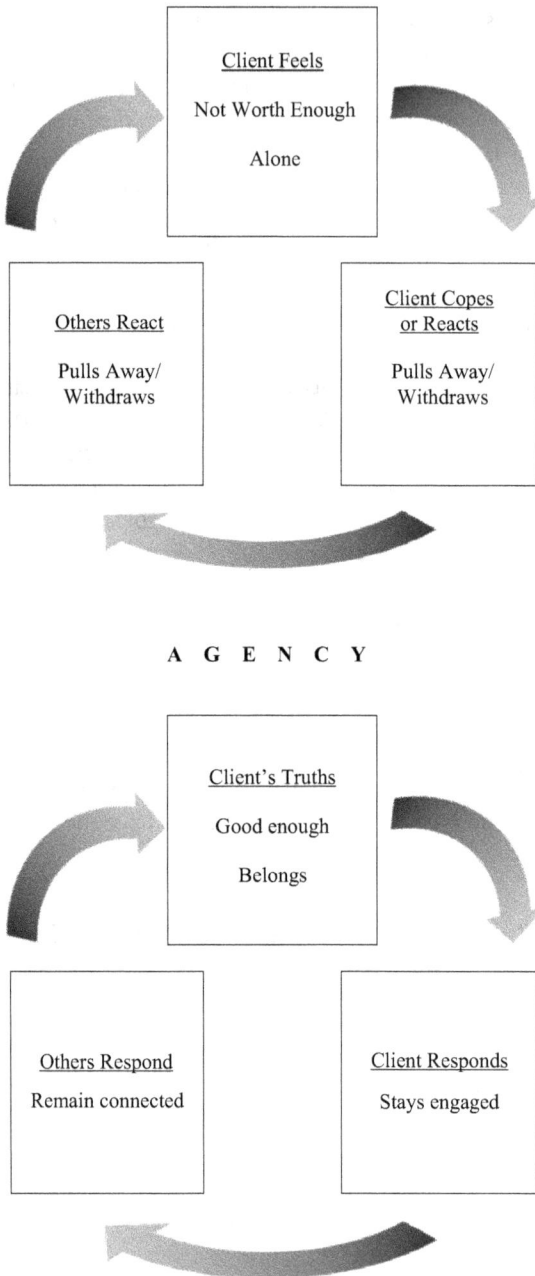

```
Client Feels
Not Worth Enough
Alone
```

```
Others React
Pulls Away/
Withdraws
```

```
Client Copes
or Reacts
Pulls Away/
Withdraws
```

A G E N C Y

```
Client's Truths
Good enough
Belongs
```

```
Others Respond
Remain connected
```

```
Client Responds
Stays engaged
```

Figure 8.1 Using the Word "Agency" as a Transition on the Visual Aid

buy-in, particularly when the process is difficult. Furthermore, it is a way to help clients see where the therapy is going and to have patience with the process. For example, clients can be discouraged by the process of learning their pain cycles and discovering the pervasive nature of their pain. The therapist can encourage the client to forge ahead by sharing that there is an antidote to the pain cycle, which is the peace cycle where the hope and new possibilities of their truths can be realized. Or when teaching clients about the four steps, therapists can reinforce the importance of practicing by explaining the phenomenon of change that occurs at the neurobiological level. The psychoeducation approach can help affirm, reinforce, normalize, and clarify the Restoration Therapy Model while motivating clients to be patient, engaged, expectant, and encouraged.

Embodied Interventions: Structuring, Sculpting, and Bilateral Stimulation

Use the room. Get up and move around. Disrupt the usual modus operandi of the sessions in order to provoke movement and change or to deepen the therapeutic process. The Restoration Therapy Model is conceptually and pragmatically integrative as the therapist engages clients cognitively, emotionally, and physically. The physical level of engagement is what we're focusing on here. We believe there to be tremendous value in involving all aspects of the client's experience and in promoting congruence between their thoughts, feelings, and physical presence. Furthermore, we are continuing to learn and understand so much about how the body holds trauma and pain (van der Kolk, 2014). Thus, incorporating ways for clients to connect their emotional and physical experiences can have an immense impact.

Utilizing embodied interventions requires the therapist to have an ability to recognize and a willingness to engage in the therapeutic process outside of the therapy chair. It requires an openness to thinking outside the box, if you will, and being creative. We do not mean being creative like an art therapist (though that could be nice as well), but rather being willing to use the physical space alongside the words and nonverbal expressions as a means to promote insight and inspire change.

The basic structural therapy intervention (Minuchin & Fishman, 1981) of structuring or restructuring the physical space and seating arrangement in the room can be useful when trying to focus or enrich an interaction in the room. This may mean restructuring the seating arrangement by maneuvering chairs to allow couples to better "see" each other as they share their narratives of pain or communicate as truth speakers to one another. Or perhaps intentionally placing one client who has difficulty tolerating another client's pain in a seat in the room where they will pose less of a distraction, but can still bear witness to the client's exploration of pain. This move communicates to the client who is sharing that their story is important and warrants attention and that there is value in having the other client remain in the room to witness their act of sharing. This intervention also communicates to the client who was moved that although they are not invited to provide input at this time, it is important for them to remain in the room, listen, and witness their loved one courageously share their story.

Another way to use the room and encourage an embodied experience is by using the experiential technique of sculpting. For example, sculpting can be used to help generate the client's feelings and ideas about his or her truths by inviting him or her to provide embodied representations of what he or she currently feels about him or herself and what he or she would ideally feel and believe about him or herself. The clients sit in their poses for an extended minute and the primary emotions they have been describing thus far with words can take on deeper meaning as they enact those feelings with their bodies. When working with couples, we have found that whether the client is sculpting or observing, the images that are constructed often become primary reference points for the duration of therapy. For example, when working with a particular couple, the woman whose primary pain word was "alone", sculpted herself sitting alone on the floor, holding her knees up to her chest with her face buried in her arms. She placed her husband in the hallway, just outside the door. When she sculpted "known", she brought her husband back into the room and had the two of them facing each other, gazing into each other's eyes. After they worked out the awkwardness and discomfort of looking into each other's eyes, the woman's eyes welled up with tears. In that moment, the sculpture provided a tangible and powerful metaphor of hope for her to feel seen and known by another person. Up to that point, she could not imagine being seen or known by anyone else because of how deeply alone she felt. The sculpture provided a starting point for her to talk about her truths and to remember people in her life who see her and give her reason to believe she is known.

And finally, the third embodied intervention is bilateral stimulation. This technique is a core treatment component of EMDR (eye movement desensitization and reprocessing) and is effective on the basis that talking about anxiety-provoking and painful experiences can be done with less distress when the brain is stimulated alternately from side to side. The rhythmic bilateral stimulation can be visual, such as watching an object move from side to side, auditory, hearing sounds that oscillate from side to side, or tactile, such as tossing a ball back and forth between hands or tapping on the knees from side to side. In Restoration Therapy, this technique can be especially helpful when the client struggles to share stories about his or her pain. The therapist might find that the client keeps getting stuck and unable to proceed or seems blocked and unable to open up.

Eliciting the Imagination: The Two Screen Method, Imagery, and the Empty Chair

Much like the embodied interventions, eliciting the imagination is another way take a departure from the usual therapeutic process by inviting the client to use his or her imagination to create new possibilities. An intervention that has been particularly effective in identifying truths as well as reinforcing the notion of agency with emotional regulation, is the two screen method developed by Symington (2015). He developed this imagery method as a way of employing the tools of mindfulness and cognitive re-direction as well as altruistic actions to increase the client's ability to manage negative thoughts and anxiety and re-direct them to positive action. The idea is to visualize two screens that represent positive and negative thoughts and use mindfulness tools to keep the positive screen in the foreground and the negative screen to the side. A way that we have applied the two screen method to Restoration Therapy is to have the screens represent pain and peace, and then working to keep the peace screen in the foreground. This technique has been effective in helping clients develop a visual tool to identify their truths and to meaningfully interact with their pain and peace cycles. The fact that the negative screen does not disappear, but is placed to the side is consistent with the Restoration Therapy principle that pain is never eliminated but healing occurs when clients are able to choose to live out their truths instead of their pain.

The use of imagery is useful in Restoration Therapy, particularly when identifying truths through re-parenting. The most critical part of an imagery exercise is setting it up. This requires slowing down the pace and tone of the session and relying upon the therapist's vocal qualities and physical posture to help establish a conducive environment. When using imagery with re-parenting, it is important to allot enough time in the session for this intervention. In fact, it would be prudent to plan on devoting the entire session to it in order to have time to go through the exercise at a slow pace and to leave time to process it afterwards. When using imagery for re-parenting, it is important to do all that is possible to ensure its efficacy the first time. The impact of the exercise diminishes with each subsequent attempt and we would advise that a therapist has no more than three attempts with a client.

And finally, the use of the empty chair. This gestalt technique can be used in a variety of ways. The client can imagine him or herself at the end of therapy, presumably in a healthy and restored state, and invoke that imagined self talking to his or her current self in the empty chair as a means of eliciting truths through a re-parenting technique. The therapist can encourage the client to ask, "What message does your future self have for your current self?" The empty chair can also be used to represent an individual during the working up and working down intervention if there are not enough people in the room to role play the parts of all three generations.

Is It Ever Appropriate to Use Conjecture When It Comes to Helping a Client Identify Feelings, Coping Behaviors, Truth, and Actions?

Often clients will have difficulty producing the words that accurately describe the feelings they carry inside. In these cases, it can be helpful for a therapist to help the client name a feeling. However, the therapist must be careful to use conjecture and not simply guess. For example, if a client is using phrases like, "I just feel so stuck," or "There is nothing I can do to make my circumstances better or different," the therapist might say something like, "When I hear you say things like this, it makes me wonder if you are feeling powerless." Here, the therapist has enough information to inquire about a specific feeling. Notice that the therapist does not tell the client what they are feeling, giving the client the chance to try it on and see if it fits.

This is very different from guessing. If a client were to say that a particular relationship, statement, or circumstance made them feel "bad," the temptation might be for a therapist to guess, saying things like, "Does is feel like you're not good enough? Does it feel like you are unsafe?" The therapist in this case has no leads from the client, which is unhelpful and, potentially, harmful to the process.

What Are Some Ways of Helping the Client Follow Through on Their Fourth Step While in Session?

During the practice phase of therapy, clients will have ample opportunities to practice their four steps as they work toward emotional regulation in various areas of their lives. One of the most helpful things a therapist can do in this phase is to help a client follow through with their fourth step (the new action) *in session*. For example, if a client's fourth step is to reach out and connect with others, it might be appropriate to have the client pick up his or her phone and send one or two texts to friends, asking to set up a time to meet the following week.

If a therapist is seeing a couple, it can be very powerful when the clients are able to follow through on their fourth step in the room. For example, if one partner's fourth step is to be gentle, the therapist might ask the client how he or she would like to be gentle toward their partner right then. Here, the therapist has the opportunity to not only use words, but also body language to help the client connect with their partner in a gentle way. In essence, any opportunity the therapist can use to make the fourth step live in the here-and-now is an opportunity worth taking!

Can the Restoration Therapy Model Be Used with Culturally Non-Western Clients?

Yes, we have found the Restoration Therapy Model to be effective with clients across varying cultural and racial backgrounds. In both clinical and psychoeducation group settings, the Restoration Therapy Model and its underlying concepts have had resonance with clients and participants who identify themselves as being Latino/a American, Asian American, Black, or African American, among other cultural groups. We have also found the model to be effective when working with first generation immigrant clients as well as mixed-race and bicultural clients. The reason the Restoration Therapy Model is effective with clients across cultural settings is because the goal of Restoration Therapy is to restore identity and safety, two fundamental aspects and needs of being human. Depending on the client's cultural background, the expressions of identity and safety may have cultural nuances and may require some contextualizing, but we believe that all therapists should pay attention to the ways in which they are remaining sensitive to and aware of their clients' (as well as their own) cultural narratives regardless of which theoretical framework they use in therapy. As restoration therapists, we work collaboratively with clients to use the language and expressions that have deep resonance with their cultural values and mores. In doing so, we're creating space for their cultural narratives to be shared and to listen for experiences of pain and peace within those stories.

How Important Is It that I Know My Own Pain and Peace Cycles as a Therapist?

There are two reasons why it is a good idea for therapists to know their own pain and peace cycles. First, although it would not be appropriate for therapists to discuss their pain and peace cycles with clients, being aware of their pain triggers and using the four steps in order to manage their reactivity in session is important. Just as the Restoration Therapy Model helps organize clients when they are in their pain, it can serve the same purpose for therapists who spend hours listening to, processing, and holding clients' pain and are vulnerable to their own pain.

Another reason why it is beneficial for therapists to know and use the Restoration Therapy Model for themselves is because it can enhance their efficacy in their work with clients. Having personal experience with the model can give therapists a familiarity with the nuances and potential challenges within the process and perhaps make them more apt to tune into their client's process of identifying their pain and peace cycles and moving through the model in general. Therapists usually find it helpful to have traveled the road themselves and have a degree of familiarity with the process when they are helping clients navigate the therapeutic terrain.

References

Ainsworth, M. D. S., Blehar, M. C., Walters, E., & Wall, S. (1978). *Patterns of attachment.* Hillsdale, NJ: Erlbaum.

Ainsworth, M. D. S., & Bowlby, J. (1991). An ethological approach to personality development. *American Psychologist, 46,* 331–341.

Alquist, L. (2018). *Consolidating change in the brain: Effectiveness of brief intensive restoration therapy and the power of practice.* Unpublished dissertation.

Angelo, M. (1993). Plenary speech given at the 17th annual family therapy networker symposium. Washington, DC.

Atkins, A. (2013). *Tag archives: How many words in the average person's vocabulary?* https://atkinsbookshelf.wordpress.com/tag/how-many-words-in-the-average-persons-vocabulary/

Atkinson, B. J., Atkinson, L., Kutz, P., Lata, J., Lata, K. W., Szekely, J., & Weiss, P. (2005). Rewiring neural states in couples therapy: Advances from affective neuroscience. *Journal of Systemic Therapies, 24,* 3–16.

Balswick, J. O., King, P., & Reimer, K. (2016). *The reciprocating self: Human development in theological perspective (2nd Ed.).* Downers Grove, IL: InterVarsity Press.

Bandura, A. (1997). *Self-efficacy: The exercise of control.* New York: Freeman.

Bartholomew, K., & Shaver, P. (1998). Methods of assessing adult attachment: Do they converge? In J. A. Simpson & W. S. Rholes (Eds.), *Attachment Theory and Close Relationships,* pp. 25–45. New York: Guilford.

Barto, A., Mirolli, M., & Baldassarre, G. (2013). Novelty or surprise? *Frontiers in Psychology, 4,* 907. www.ncbi.nlm.nih.gov/pmc/articles/PMC3858647/

Baumeister, R. F., Gailliot, M., DeWall, C. N., & Oaten, M. (2006). Self-regulation and personality: How interventions increase regulatory success, and how depletion moderates the effects of traits on behavior. *Journal of Personality, 74(6),* 1773–1801.

Baumeister, R. F., Heatherton, R. F., & Tice, D. M. (1994). *Losing control: How and why people fail at self-regulation.* San Diego, CA: Academic Press.

Baumeister, R. F., & Tierney, J. (2011). *Willpower: Rediscovering the greatest human strength.* New York: Penguin.

Becvar, D. S., & Becvar, R. J. (1996). *Family therapy: A systemic integration (3rd Ed.).* Boston, MA: Allyn and Bacon.

Buechner, F. (1991). *The stewardship of pain.* www.30goodminutes.org/index.php/archives/23-member-archives/229-frederick-buechner-program-3416

Bollow, J. (2015). *How fast is your brain?* http://thephenomenalexperience.com/content/how-fast-is-your-brain

Boszormenyi-Nagy, I., & Krasner, B. (1986). *Between give and take: A clinical guide to contextual therapy.* New York: Brunner/Mazel.

Bowlby, J. (1988). *A secure base: Parent-child attachment and healthy human development.* New York: Basic Books.

Brooks, D. (2015). *The road to character.* New York: Random House.

Broshek, D. K., De Marco, A. P., & Freeman, J. R. (2015). A review of post-concussion syndrome and psychological factors associated with concussion. *Brain Injury, 29*(2), 228–237. http://dx.doi.org.fuller.idm.oclc.org/10.3109/02699052/2014/974674

Buber, M. (1958). *I and thou.* New York: Charles Scribner and Sons.

Burrows, G. D., Stanley, R. O., & Bloom, P. B. (2009). *International handbook of clinical hypnosis.* London: Wiley-Blackwell.

Christou-Champi, S., Farrow, T. F. D., & Webb, T. L. (2015). Automatic control of negative emotions: Evidence that structured practice increases the efficiency of emotion regulation. *Cognition and Emotion, 29*(2), 319–331.

Doherty, W. J. (1996). *Soul searching: Why psychotherapy must promote moral responsibility.* New York: Basic Books.

Duckworth, A. L., & Seligman, M. E. P. (2005). Self-discipline out-does IQ in predicting academic performance of adolescents. *Psychological Science, 16,* 939–944.

Ecker, B., Ticic, R., & Hulley, L. (2012). *Unlocking the emotional brain: Eliminating symptoms at their roots using memory consolidation.* New York: Routledge.

Ekman, P., Friesen, W. V., & Ellsworth, P. (1982). What emotion categories or dimensions can observers judge from facial behavior? In P. Ekman (Ed.), *Emotion in the Human Face*, pp. 39–55. New York: Cambridge University Press.

Erikson, E. H. (1963). *Childhood and society (2nd Ed.).* New York: Norton.

Erikson, E. H. (1985). *The life cycle completed: A review.* New York: Norton.

Falicov, C. J. (2005). Emotional transnationalism and family identities. *Family Process, 44,* 399–406.

Framo, J. (1992). *Family of origin therapy: An intergenerational approach.* New York: Brunner/Mazel.

Frankl, V. E. (1984). *Man's search for meaning: An introduction to logotherapy (3rd Ed.).* New York: Touchstone.

Goldenthal, P. (1996). *Doing contextual therapy: An integrated model for working with individuals, couples, and families.* New York: Norton & Company.

Gottman, M., & Silver, N. (2012). *What makes love last?* New York: Simon & Schuster.

Haley, J. (1993). *Uncommon therapy: The psychiatric techniques of Milton H. Erickson, M.D.* San Francisco, CA: Jossey-Bass.

Hanna, S. M. (2014). *The transparent brain in couple and family therapy: Mindful integrations with neuroscience.* New York, NY: Routledge.

Hanson, R. (2014). *Overcoming the negativity bias.* www.rickhanson.net/overcoming-negativity-bias/

Hargrave, T. D. (1994). *Families and forgiveness: Healing wounds in the intergenerational family.* New York: Brunner/Mazel.

Hargrave, T. D. (2000). *The essential humility of marriage: Honoring the third identity in couple therapy.* Phoenix, AZ: Zeig, Tucker & Theisen.

Hargrave, T. D. (2001). *Forgiving the devil: Coming to terms with damaged relationships.* Phoenix, AZ: Zeig, Tucker and Theisen.

Hargrave, T. D. (2010). Restoration therapy: A couple therapy case study. *Journal of Psychology and Christianity, 29*(3), 272–277.

Hargrave, T. D. (2011). Saving oneself: Forgiving the poisonous parents as an act of kindness to oneself and future generations. In S. Dunham, S. Dermer, & J.

Carlson (Eds.), *Poisonous Parenting: Toxic Relationships Between Parents and Their Adult Children*, pp. 199–216. New York: Routledge.

Hargrave, T. D., & Hargrave, S. A. (2015). *5 days to a new self*. Amarillo, TX: The Hideaway Foundation.

Hargrave, T. D., & Pfitzer, F. (2003). *The new contextual therapy: Guiding the power of give and take*. New York: Routledge.

Hargrave, T. D., & Pfitzer, F. (2011). *Restoration therapy: Understanding and guiding healing in marriage and family therapy*. New York: Routledge.

Hargrave, T., & Stoever, S. (2010). *Five days to a new marriage*. Amarillo, TX: Hideaway Foundation.

Hargrave, T. D., & Zasowski, N. (2016). *Families and forgiveness: Healing wounds in the intergenerational family (2nd Ed.)*. New York: Routledge.

Jacobson, N. S., & Christensen, A. (1998). *Acceptance and change in couple therapy: A therapist's guide to transforming relationships*. New York: Norton.

James, B. D., Boyle, P. A., Buchman, A. S., & Bennett, D. A. (2011). Relation of later life social activity with incident disability among community-dwelling older adults. *The Journals of Gerontology Series A: Biological Sciences and Medical Sciences, 66A*(4), 467–473.

Johnson, S. M. (2004). *The practice of emotionally focused marital therapy: Creating connection (2nd Ed.)*. New York: Brunner/Routledge.

Johnson, S. (2018). *Created for connection*. www.youtube.com/watch?v=EVhcbUqxKYI

Jung, C. G., & Long, C. E. (Translator) (2018). *Collected papers on analytical psychology: Included glossary of Jungian terms*. Seattle, WA: CreateSpace Independent Publishing Platform.

Kail, R. V., & Cavanaugh, J. C. (2015). *Human development: A life-span view (7th Ed.)*. Boston, MA: Cengage Learning.

Kieffer, C. (1977). New depths in intimacy. In R. W. Libby & R. N. Whitehurst (Eds.), *Marriage and Alternatives: Exploring Intimate Relationships*, pp. 267–293. Glenview, IL: Scott, Foresman.

Koole, S. L., & Aldao, A. (2016). The self-regulation of emotions: Theoretical and empirical advances. In K. D. Vohs & R. R. Baumeister (Eds.), *Handbook of Self-regulation: Research, Theory, and Applications (3rd Ed.)*, pp. 24–41. New York: Guilford.

Kuypers, L. (2011). *Zones of regulation*. Santa Clara, CA: Think Social Publishing.

LeDoux, J. E. (1996). *The emotional brain: The mysterious underpinnings of emotional life*. New York: Touchstone.

Levi, P. (1986). *Survival in Auschwitz: The Nazi assault on humanity*. New York: Touchstone.

Lewis, T. (2014). *Human brain microchip is 9000 times faster than a PC*. www.livescience.com/45304-human-brain- microchip-9000-times-faster-than-pc.html

Martino, F., Menchetti, M., Pozzi, E., & Berardi, D. (2012). Predictors of dropout among personality disorders in a specialist outpatients psychosocial treatment: A preliminary study. *Psychiatry and Clinical Neurosciences, 66*, 180–186. http://dx.doi.org/10.1111/j.1440-1819.2012.02329.x

McGoldrick, M., Gerson, R., & Petry, S. (2008). *Genograms: Assessment and intervention (3rd Ed.)*. New York: Norton.

McMurran, M., Huband, N., & Overton, E. (2010). Non-completion of personality disorder treatments: A systematic review of correlates, consequences, and interventions. *Clinical Psychology Review, 30*, 277–287. http://dx.doi.org/10.1016/j.cpr.2009.12.002

Merriam-Webster. www.merriam-webster.com/dictionary

Minuchin, S., & Fishman, C. (1981). *Family therapy techniques*. Cambridge, MA: Harvard University Press.

Nietzsche, W. (1977). *The portable Nietzsche: Edited and translated by Walter Kaufmann*. New York: Penguin Books.

Peck, S. (1987). Personal interview with Scott Peck. Fort Worth, TX.

Perls, F., Hefferline, R. F., & Goodman, P. (1951). *Gestalt therapy: Excitement and growth in the human personality*. New York: Gestalt Journal Press.

Rogers, C. (1961). *On becoming a person*. Boston, MA: Houghton Mifflin.

Rolland, J. (1994). *Families, illness and disabilities: An integrated approach*. New York: Basic.

Shapiro, F. (2017). *Eye movement desensitization and reprocessing: Basic principles, protocols and procedures (3rd Ed.)*. New York: Guilford.

Siegel, D. J. (2007). *The mindful brain: Reflection and attunement in the cultivation of well-being*. New York: Norton.

Singer, D. G., & Revenson, T. A. (1996). *A Piaget primer: How a child thinks (2nd Ed.)*. New York: Plume.

Small, M. F. (2011). The anthropology of marriage and family. *American Association of Marriage and Family Therapy annual conference: The science of relationships*. Alexandria, VA: American Association of Marriage and Family Therapy.

Sonnekalb, A. P. (2012). *Effectiveness of the restoration model: An intensive marital therapy*. Unpublished dissertation.

Symington, S. (2015). *Two-Screen Method® for anxious worry, addictive urges & bad moods*. www.youtube.com/watch?v=H3FEMbMXv6Q

Snyder, C. R. (2002). Hope theory: Rainbows in the mind. *Psychological Inquiry, 13*(4), 249–275.

Tedeschi R. G., & Calhoun, L. G. (1996). The Posttraumatic Growth Inventory: Measuring the positive legacy of trauma. *Journal of Traumatic Stress, 9*, 455–471.

Tedeschi, R., & Calhoun, L. (2004). Posttraumatic growth: Conceptual foundations and empirical evidence. *Psychological Inquiry, 15*, 1–18.

van der Kolk, B. (2014). *The body keeps score: Brain, mind, and body in the healing of trauma*. New York: Penguin Books.

Walsh, F. (2009). Integrating spirituality in family therapy: Wellsprings for health, healing and resilience. In F. Walsh (Ed.), *Spiritual Resources in Family Therapy (2nd Ed.)*, pp. 31–65. New York: Guilford.

Wampler, M., Pola, C., Verhaest, Y., Vandeneede, B., Demyttenaere, K., Vermote, R., & Lowyck, B. (2018). Predictors of dropout from a psychodynamic hospitalization-based treatment for personality disorders. *Psychoanalytic Psychology, 35*(2), 217–223. http://dx.doi.org/10.1037/pap0000160

White, M. (1997). *Narrative of therapist's lives*. Adelaide, Australia: Dulwich Centre Publications.

White, M., & Epston, D. (1990). *Narrative means to therapeutic ends*. New York: Norton.

Wolfe, R. N., & Johnson, S. D. (1995). Personality as a predictor of college performance. *Educational and Psychological Measurement, 55*, 177–185.

Wright, L. M., & Bell, J. M. (2009). *Beliefs and illness: A model for healing*. Calgary, Alberta: 4th Floor Press.

Yoon Hammer, M., & Hargrave, T. D. (2016). Cognitive maps and couples. In J. Carlson & S. Dermer (Eds.). *The SAGE Encyclopedia of Marriage, Family, and Couples Counseling*. Thousand Oaks, CA: SAGE Publications, Inc.

Index

For Product Safety Concerns and Information please contact our EU
representative GPSR@taylorandfrancis.com
Taylor & Francis Verlag GmbH, Kaufingerstraße 24, 80331 München, Germany

www.ingramcontent.com/pod-product-compliance
Lightning Source LLC
Chambersburg PA
CBHW070357270326
41926CB00014B/2589

9 781138 541092